Mastering Java Collections

From Basics to Expert Proficiency

Contents

Introduction

The Java Collections Framework (JCF) is a fundamental aspect of the Java programming language, providing developers with a robust and versatile toolkit for managing and manipulating groups of objects. Introduced in JDK 1.2, the framework has undergone numerous enhancements, establishing itself as an essential component for effective and efficient Java programming.

At its core, the Java Collections Framework provides a unified architecture for representing and manipulating collections, thereby eliminating the need for ad-hoc data structures and associated algorithms. This standardization ensures that common collection-related tasks, such as searching, sorting, and manipulating data, can be performed with minimal complexity and maximum efficiency.

One of the key advantages of the JCF is its ability to abstract the underlying data structures via a set of interfaces. These interfaces enable developers to focus on the functionality and behavior of their collections rather than their implementation details. Consequently, the framework fosters code that is not only reusable but also easily understandable and maintainable.

The Java Collections Framework encompasses several core interfaces, including Collection, List, Set, Queue, and Map, each catering to different collection types and use cases. For instance, List implementations, like ArrayList and LinkedList, provide ordered collections that allow duplicates, whereas Set implementations, such as HashSet and TreeSet, offer collections that ensure uniqueness. The Queue and Deque interfaces support ordered processing, while the Map interface manages key-value pair associations, with implementations like HashMap and TreeMap catering to different performance characteristics and ordering requirements.

Generics are a pivotal aspect of the Java Collections Framework, allowing developers to specify the type of objects that a collection can hold, thus enhancing type safety and reducing runtime errors. By leveraging generics, collections become more expressive and less error-prone, with the added benefit of eliminating the need for extensive type casting.

In addition to the standard collection interfaces and their implementations, the framework includes utility classes such as Collections and Arrays. These classes provide static methods for creating, manipulating, and searching collections, further streamlining common tasks and enhancing developer productivity. Whether sorting a list, shuffling elements, or performing binary searches, these utility methods offer efficient and optimized solutions.

With the advent of Java 8, the collections framework experienced significant improvements with the introduction of lambda expressions and the Stream API. These features facilitate functional-style operations on collections, enabling developers to write concise and expressive code for complex data processing tasks. Operations such as filtering, mapping, and reducing can now be performed with ease, leveraging the power of parallelism to enhance performance.

As Java continues to evolve, so too does its collections framework. Subsequent releases have introduced new collection types and concurrent implementations, catering to a broader range of applications and addressing the challenges posed by modern multicore processors. Concurrent collections like ConcurrentHashMap and CopyOnWriteArrayList provide thread-safe alternatives without compromising performance, making them indispensable for high-concurrency environments.

This book delves into the depths of the Java Collections Framework, offering an exhaustive exploration of its core interfaces, implementations, and utility methods. Each chapter is designed to provide a clear and detailed understanding of the framework's components, accompanied by examples and best practices. The goal is to equip readers with the knowledge and skills necessary to harness the full potential of the Java Collections Framework, fostering the development of efficient, maintainable, and robust Java applications.

Chapter 1

Introduction to Java Collections Framework

The Java Collections Framework is a comprehensive architecture for representing and manipulating collections of objects in Java. This chapter covers the basics of the framework, detailing its advantages, key interfaces, and hierarchy. It explains the distinctions between collection interfaces and classes, introduces common operations, and discusses the role of generics. Additionally, it provides an overview of legacy collections and highlights improvements made in recent Java versions.

1.1 What is the Java Collections Framework?

The Java Collections Framework (JCF) is a unified architecture designed to store and manipulate groups of objects. Introduced in Java 2 (JDK 1.2), the framework provides a set of interfaces and classes that operate on collections, allowing for the manipulation of data as a unified entity. This framework streamlines the structuring of collections, providing a coherent and efficient means to manage data.

At the core of the Java Collections Framework are several essential interfaces, including Collection, Set, List, Queue, and Map. These interfaces define the contract for collections, specifying the operations that can be performed on them.

Interfaces:

- Collection<T> - The root interface in the collection hierarchy. It represents a group of objects known as elements. The Collection interface is extended by other collection interfaces, such as Set and List.
- Set<T> - A collection that does not allow duplicate elements. This interface models mathematical sets.
- List<T> - An ordered collection (also known as a sequence). Lists can contain duplicate elements.
- Queue<T> - A collection used to hold multiple elements prior to processing. Typically, but not necessarily, elements are processed in a first-in, first-out (FIFO) order.
- Map<K,V> - An object that maps keys to values. A Map cannot contain duplicate keys; each key can map to at most one value.

Classes: A variety of concrete classes implement these interfaces, providing different functionalities and performance characteristics. Key classes include:

- ArrayList<E> - Implements the List interface with a resizable array.
- HashSet<E> - Implements the Set interface, backed by a hash table.
- LinkedList<E> - Implements both the List and Deque interfaces, providing a doubly-linked list.
- PriorityQueue<E> - Implements a priority queue.
- HashMap<K,V> - Implements the Map interface with a hash table.

To illustrate the structure of the Java Collections Framework, consider the following program, which demonstrates the use of an ArrayList to store and retrieve integers.

```
import java.util.ArrayList;
import java.util.List;

public class CollectionDemo {
    public static void main(String[] args) {
        // Create a list with integer elements
        List<Integer> numbers = new ArrayList<>();

        // Add elements to the list
        numbers.add(1);
        numbers.add(2);
        numbers.add(3);
        numbers.add(4);

        // Access elements in the list
        for (int num : numbers) {
            System.out.println("Number: " + num);
        }
    }
}
```

This program initializes an ArrayList and populates it with integers. The elements are then accessed and printed to the console. Executing the program yields the following output:

```
Number: 1
Number: 2
Number: 3
Number: 4
```

The Java Collections Framework also benefits from the inclusion of generics, which enable type-safe collections. By using generics, the above ArrayList is restricted to Integer elements, preventing the addition of incompatible types at compile time.

A key advantage of the Java Collections Framework is its provision of well-defined algorithms, encapsulated as static methods within the Collections utility class. Examples include sorting, searching, and shuffling. The following example demonstrates sorting a list of strings:

```
import java.util.ArrayList;
import java.util.Collections;
import java.util.List;

public class SortDemo {
    public static void main(String[] args) {
        // Create a list with string elements
        List<String> words = new ArrayList<>();

        // Add elements to the list
        words.add("apple");
        words.add("orange");
        words.add("banana");
        words.add("grape");

        // Sort the list
        Collections.sort(words);
```

```
        // Output the sorted list
        for (String word : words) {
            System.out.println(word);
        }
    }
}
```

On running this program, the output is:

```
apple
banana
grape
orange
```

This example highlights how the Collections utility class makes operations on collection elements simple and straightforward.

Another fundamental aspect of the Java Collections Framework is the separation between interface and implementation. This design fosters flexibility and enables developers to switch between different implementations without modifying the client code that uses collections. For instance, if performance testing reveals that an ArrayList is inefficient for a particular task, a developer can switch to a LinkedList simply by changing the instantiation line:

```
List<String> words = new LinkedList<>();
```

This allows the internal characteristics of the list to change while the external interface remains consistent for the client code.

The Java Collections Framework represents a significant enhancement over traditional collections based on arrays and vectors. It mitigates many of the limitations and inefficiencies inherent in earlier structures through:

- **Unified and flexible architecture:** Establishing a common type hierarchy allows for greater consistency and interchangeability.
- **Performance optimization:** Diverse implementations facilitate the choice of the most appropriate data structures based on application requirements.
- **Enhanced functionality:** Utility classes and static methods provide a range of algorithms and operations that simplify complex tasks.

Understanding the foundational aspects of the Java Collections Framework provides a basis for more advanced topics, such as concurrent collections, custom implementation of collections, and advanced usage patterns for optimal performance and scalability.

1.2 Advantages of Using Collections

The Java Collections Framework (JCF) provides numerous advantages that enhance both the performance and maintainability of Java applications. Using collections over traditional data structures (such as arrays) brings several key benefits, which are detailed here to illustrate their impact on software development practices.

1. Improved Code Reusability and Maintainability

By standardizing how groups of objects are handled, the Java Collections Framework makes it easier to write reusable code. When a developer uses the framework, the same operations like searching, sorting, or iterating can be applied across various collection types interchangeably. This means that once a developer learns the framework, they can apply this knowledge to many different scenarios without reinventing the wheel each time.

Consider the following example of iterating over a List:

```
List<String> items = new ArrayList<>();
items.add("item1");
items.add("item2");
items.add("item3");

for (String item : items) {
    System.out.println(item);
}
```

The same pattern of iteration can be applied to other collection types such as Set or Queue, showing the uniformity and reuse of patterns.

2. Enhanced Performance and Flexibility

Different collection implementations optimize for different use-cases (e.g., quick access, fast iteration, or efficient insertion/deletion). Developers can select the most appropriate collection implementation depending on the required performance characteristics, and easily switch implementations if the requirements change without altering the high-level logic.

For example, replacing an ArrayList with a LinkedList can switch the performance from being efficient in random access operations:

```
List<String> items = new ArrayList<>();
```

to being efficient in insertions and deletions:

```
List<String> items = new LinkedList<>();
```

ArrayList is preferred for scenarios with frequent random read operations, while LinkedList is better suited for scenarios with frequent insertions/deletions.

3. Reduced Development Time

The framework's rich set of ready-to-use interfaces and classes saves development time. Since the framework is well-tested and optimized, there's no need to build custom data structure implementations from scratch.

For example, Java Collections provides:

- List interface and its implementations like ArrayList, LinkedList
- Set interface and its implementations like HashSet, LinkedHashSet, TreeSet
- Map interface and its implementations like HashMap, LinkedHashMap, TreeMap

These built-in implementations cover most common data handling needs and are optimized for performance.

4. Enhanced Code Readability and Less Error-Prone

The use of well-defined interfaces and abstract data types makes code that utilizes the Java Collections Framework easier to read and understand. Since the framework dictates a common pattern of usage, it reduces the likelihood of introducing errors.

For example, using a Map to associate keys to values is straightforward:

```
Map<String, Integer> map = new HashMap<>();
map.put("one", 1);
map.put("two", 2);
map.put("three", 3);
System.out.println(map.get("one")); // Outputs 1
```

The consistent use of put and get methods across different Map implementations simplifies key-value manipulations, reducing the chance of logic errors.

5. Support for Concurrent Collections

Modern applications often require handling concurrent access to collections. The Java Collections Framework provides thread-safe implementations for such scenarios.

For instance, ConcurrentHashMap is designed for high concurrency use-cases:

```
Map<String, Integer> map = new ConcurrentHashMap<>();
map.put("one", 1);
map.put("two", 2);
```

Using ConcurrentHashMap, multiple threads can safely update the map without external synchronization, which significantly simplifies concurrent program designs.

6. Inbuilt Algorithms and Utility Methods

Collections come with a vast array of utility methods for sorting, searching, and performing other common operations via the Collections class. This obviates the need to manually implement these often-complex algorithms.

Sorting a list is as simple as:

```
List<Integer> numbers = Arrays.asList(3, 1, 4, 1, 5, 9);
Collections.sort(numbers);
System.out.println(numbers); // Outputs [1, 1, 3, 4, 5, 9]
```

The Collections class offers numerous such utility functions, making the code more concise and less error-prone.

Embracing the Java Collections Framework significantly enhances a developer's efficiency and application robustness through its robust, consistent, and high-performance design. Consistent usage across varying application needs greatly simplifies development while ensuring maintainability and readability.

1.3 Overview of Collection Interfaces

The Java Collections Framework leverages a set of interfaces to standardize the operations across different types of collections. These interfaces enable the manipulation of object groups without requiring knowledge of their underlying implementation. The core interfaces of the Java Collections Framework include Collection, List, Set, Queue, and Map. Each interface prescribes a set of methods that collections implementing the interface must support.

Collection Interface

The Collection interface is the root of the collection hierarchy. It represents a group of objects, known as elements. The Collection interface is extended by sub-interfaces such as List, Set, and Queue. Below is a basic example that demonstrates some fundamental methods defined in the Collection interface:

```
Collection<String> collection = new ArrayList<>();
collection.add("Apple");
collection.add("Banana");
collection.size(); // Returns 2
collection.remove("Apple"); // Removes the element "Apple"
collection.clear(); // Clears the collection
```

```
2
```

List Interface

The List interface extends Collection and introduces an ordered collection, also known as a sequence. Duplicates are allowed. The primary operations associated with List include positional access, search, list iteration, and range-view operations. The following is an example demonstrating some of these methods:

```
List<String> list = new ArrayList<>();
list.add("Apple");
list.add("Banana");
list.add("Cherry");
list.get(1); // Returns "Banana"
list.indexOf("Cherry"); // Returns 2
list.set(0, "Apricot"); // Sets the value at index 0 to "Apricot"
```

```
Banana
2
```

Set Interface

The Set interface represents a collection that does not allow duplicate elements. It models the mathematical set abstraction and is extended by interfaces such as SortedSet and NavigableSet. Key operations include element addition and removal. Here is a snippet illustrating some Set operations:

```
Set<String> set = new HashSet<>();
set.add("Apple");
set.add("Banana");
set.add("Apple"); // Duplicate element, will not be added
set.size(); // Returns 2
set.contains("Banana"); // Returns true
```

```
2
true
```

Queue Interface

The Queue interface extends Collection to support an ordered sequence of elements meant for holding elements prior to processing. The Queue interface provides additional insertion, extraction, and inspection operations. A typical implementation such as LinkedList can be used as shown below:

```
Queue<String> queue = new LinkedList<>();
queue.add("First");
queue.add("Second");
queue.add("Third");
queue.poll(); // Retrieves and removes the head of the queue, returns "First"
queue.peek(); // Retrieves but does not remove the head, returns "Second"
```

```
First
Second
```

Map Interface

The Map interface maps keys to values and does not extend Collection. A map contains key-value pairs and disallows duplicate keys. The primary functionalities include querying, updating, and iterating over keys and values. Below is a demonstration of basic Map operations:

```
Map<Integer, String> map = new HashMap<>();
map.put(1, "One");
map.put(2, "Two");
map.put(1, "Uno"); // Updates the value for key 1
map.get(2); // Returns "Two"
map.keySet(); // Returns a set of all keys
```

```
Two
```

The Java Collections Framework interfaces provide a structure for a wide range of collection types, allowing programs to handle collections of data uniformly and efficiently. Each interface is designed to represent a different way of organizing and accessing data, significantly enhancing the versatility and reuse of collection-handling code.

1.4 Hierarchy of the Collections Framework

The Java Collections Framework is structured hierarchically, providing a cohesive and logical architecture that encompasses various interfaces and classes. At the root of this hierarchy lies the Collection interface, the most generalized form of a collection. Other primary interfaces, such as Set, List, and Queue, extend the Collection interface, each introducing unique behaviors and characteristics. Concurrently, the Map interface, which does not extend Collection, represents mappings of key-value pairs.

- Collection<E>
- Set<E>
- List<E>
- Queue<E>
- Map<K,V>

In diagrammatic form, the hierarchy can be visualized as:

```
              Collection<E>
                /    |    \
       Set<E>   List<E>   Queue<E>
        /  \              /    \
SortedSet<E>      Deque<E>  BlockingQueue<E>
     |                |
 NavigableSet<E>      BlockingDeque<E>
```

Additionally, the Map hierarchy is structured as:

```
              Map<K,V>
              /      \
   SortedMap<K,V>   ConcurrentMap<K,V>
        |
   NavigableMap<K,V>
```

Core Interfaces and Their Implementations

Collection Interface

The Collection<E> interface is the root of the hierarchy. It describes operations that can be performed on a group of objects, and various other interfaces that extend this one are tailored for specific types of collections.

Set Interface

The Set<E> interface represents a collection that does not allow duplicate elements. Key implementations include:

- HashSet<E>
- LinkedHashSet<E>
- TreeSet<E>

The SortedSet<E> interface is a subtype of Set<E> that maintains its elements in a sorted order. TreeSet<E> implements SortedSet<E> and further extends the NavigableSet<E> interface, providing methods to navigate through the sorted collection.

```
/* Example usage of TreeSet */
import java.util.TreeSet;

public class SetExample {
    public static void main(String[] args) {
        TreeSet<Integer> numbers = new TreeSet<>();
        numbers.add(3);
        numbers.add(1);
        numbers.add(2);

        for(Integer number : numbers) {
            System.out.println(number);
        }
    }
}
/* Expected Output */
1
2
3
```

List Interface

The List<E> interface represents an ordered collection that allows duplicate elements. Key implementations include:

- ArrayList<E>
- LinkedList<E>
- Vector<E>

ArrayList<E> and LinkedList<E> are frequently used. While ArrayList<E> provides fast random access, LinkedList<E> offers efficient insertions and deletions.

```
/* Example usage of ArrayList */
import java.util.ArrayList;

public class ListExample {
    public static void main(String[] args) {
        ArrayList<String> names = new ArrayList<>();
        names.add("Alice");
        names.add("Bob");
        names.add("Charlie");

        for(String name : names) {
            System.out.println(name);
        }
    }
}
/* Expected Output */
Alice
Bob
Charlie
```

Queue Interface

The Queue<E> interface is designed for holding elements prior to processing. Major implementations include:

- LinkedList<E>
- PriorityQueue<E>
- ArrayDeque<E>

The Deque<E> interface, which extends Queue<E>, supports element insertion and removal at both ends.

```
/* Example usage of PriorityQueue */
import java.util.PriorityQueue;

public class QueueExample {
    public static void main(String[] args) {
        PriorityQueue<Integer> queue = new PriorityQueue<>();
        queue.add(3);
        queue.add(1);
        queue.add(2);

        while(!queue.isEmpty()) {
            System.out.println(queue.poll());
        }
    }
}
/* Expected Output */
1
2
3
```

Map Interface

The Map<K,V> interface represents a key-value mapping. Unlike Collection, it does not extend from it. Key implementations include:

- HashMap<K,V>
- TreeMap<K,V>
- LinkedHashMap<K,V>

The SortedMap<K,V> interface, similar to SortedSet, maintains its elements in a sorted order. TreeMap<K,V> implements NavigableMap<K,V>, providing extensive navigation operations.

```
/* Example usage of TreeMap */
import java.util.TreeMap;
```

```
public class MapExample {
    public static void main(String[] args) {
        TreeMap<String, Integer> map = new TreeMap<>();
        map.put("one", 1);
        map.put("two", 2);
        map.put("three", 3);

        for(Map.Entry<String, Integer> entry : map.entrySet()) {
            System.out.println(entry.getKey() + " = " + entry.getValue());
        }
    }
}
/* Expected Output */
one = 1
three = 3
two = 2
```

This hierarchical structure is designed to provide both versatility and performance optimization for a variety of collection use cases, enabling the developer to select the most appropriate collection type for a given task. The resulting framework offers a high degree of reusability and consistency across Java applications.

1.5 Understanding Collection Classes

The Java Collections Framework provides an extensive suite of classes that implement the various collection interfaces. Each collection class provides particular features and efficiencies, making it essential for developers to comprehend their distinct characteristics to utilize them effectively.

ArrayList: The ArrayList class is a resizable array implementation of the List interface. Unlike arrays, the size of an ArrayList can grow dynamically. When elements are added beyond its initial capacity, the array is automatically resized. This class offers constant time complexity, $O(1)$, for accessing elements by index, and an amortized $O(1)$ for element insertion. However, insertion or deletion of elements at arbitrary positions is slower, with a time complexity of $O(n)$ due to the need to shift the subsequent elements.

```
ArrayList<String> arrayList = new ArrayList<>();
arrayList.add("Element1");
arrayList.add("Element2");
System.out.println("ArrayList: " + arrayList);
```

```
Output:
ArrayList: [Element1, Element2]
```

LinkedList: This class implements both the List and Deque interfaces.

It is based on a doubly linked list. LinkedList allows constant time insertions or removals using iterators, $O(1)$, but it provides linear time $O(n)$ access to elements by index. This makes LinkedList suitable for scenarios where frequent insertions and deletions at arbitrary positions are required, while index-based access is of less importance.

```
LinkedList<String> linkedList = new LinkedList<>();
linkedList.add("Element1");
linkedList.add("Element2");
System.out.println("LinkedList: " + linkedList);
```

```
Output:
LinkedList: [Element1, Element2]
```

HashSet: The HashSet class implements the Set interface, backed by a hash table. It does not allow duplicate elements and provides constant-time performance for basic operations like add, remove, and contains, assuming the hash function disperses elements properly among the buckets. HashSet does not maintain any order of elements.

```
HashSet<String> hashSet = new HashSet<>();
hashSet.add("Element1");
hashSet.add("Element2");
System.out.println("HashSet: " + hashSet);
```

```
Output:
HashSet: [Element1, Element2]
```

LinkedHashSet: This class extends the HashSet class and implements Set interface. It is like a HashSet with a linked list running through it that maintains the insertion-order. When iterating through a LinkedHashSet, the elements will be returned in the order in which they were inserted.

```
LinkedHashSet<String> linkedHashSet = new LinkedHashSet<>();
linkedHashSet.add("Element1");
linkedHashSet.add("Element2");
System.out.println("LinkedHashSet: " + linkedHashSet);
```

```
Output:
LinkedHashSet: [Element1, Element2]
```

TreeSet: The TreeSet class implements the NavigableSet interface, which extends the SortedSet interface. It is backed by a TreeMap. This guarantees that the elements will be in ascending order, sorted according to their natural order or by a comparator provided at the set's creation time. The operations of TreeSet are log(n) for most operations $O(\log(n))$.

```
TreeSet<String> treeSet = new TreeSet<>();
treeSet.add("Element1");
treeSet.add("Element3");
treeSet.add("Element2");
```

```
System.out.println("TreeSet: " + treeSet);
```

Output:
TreeSet: [Element1, Element2, Element3]

HashMap: This class provides the basic implementation of the Map interface. A HashMap stores data in key-value pairs and allows null values and a null key. It offers constant-time performance for basic operations such as get and put, assuming the hash function disperses elements properly. However, HashMap does not maintain any order of its elements.

```
HashMap<Integer, String> hashMap = new HashMap<>();
hashMap.put(1, "One");
hashMap.put(2, "Two");
System.out.println("HashMap: " + hashMap);
```

Output:
HashMap: {1=One, 2=Two}

LinkedHashMap: This class extends HashMap and maintains a doubly-linked list running through all its entries, which defines the iteration ordering. The order is usually the order in which keys were inserted into the map (*insertion-order*), or it can be the order in which keys were last accessed, from least-recently accessed to most-recently.

```
LinkedHashMap<Integer, String> linkedHashMap = new LinkedHashMap<>();
linkedHashMap.put(1, "One");
linkedHashMap.put(2, "Two");
System.out.println("LinkedHashMap: " + linkedHashMap);
```

Output:
LinkedHashMap: {1=One, 2=Two}

TreeMap: The TreeMap class implements the NavigableMap interface, which extends SortedMap. The map is sorted according to the natural ordering of its keys, or by a Comparator provided at map creation time. This implementation provides guaranteed log(n) time cost for the containsKey, get, put, and remove operations.

```
TreeMap<Integer, String> treeMap = new TreeMap<>();
treeMap.put(2, "Two");
treeMap.put(1, "One");
treeMap.put(3, "Three");
System.out.println("TreeMap: " + treeMap);
```

Output:
TreeMap: {1=One, 2=Two, 3=Three}

Each collection class in the Java Collections Framework has unique attributes and performance characteristics. Understanding their specific implementation details and operational complexities is crucial for making informed decisions about which class to use in different programming scenarios. While the ArrayList excels in random access performance, the LinkedList is superior in frequent insertion and deletions. Similarly, HashSet, LinkedHashSet, and TreeSet cater to distinct requirements regarding element ordering and uniqueness. The map classes, HashMap, LinkedHashMap, and TreeMap, are chosen based on the necessity of key uniqueness, iteration order, and sorting needs.

1.6 Differences Between Collection and Collections

The Java Collections Framework is a pivotal component in Java development, offering robust mechanisms for managing groups of objects. It is essential to differentiate between Collection and Collections, as they serve distinct purposes within the framework, despite their seemingly similar names.

Collection is an interface central to the Java Collections Framework. It defines the fundamental operations that all collection types should implement. On the other hand, Collections is a utility class that provides static methods for manipulating collections. This distinction is crucial in leveraging the full potential of the Java Collections Framework.

1. Collection Interface

The Collection interface is part of the java.util package and serves as the root interface in the hierarchy of collection interfaces. It extends the Iterable interface and lays the foundation for more specialized interfaces such as Set, List, and Queue. Key methods defined in the Collection interface include:

```
boolean add(E e);
boolean remove(Object o);
boolean contains(Object o);
int size();
boolean isEmpty();
Iterator<E> iterator();
```

- The add(E e) method inserts a specified element into the collection if it is not already present. - The remove(Object o) method removes a specified element from the collection if it exists. - The contains(Object o) method checks if a specified element is present in the collection. - The size() method returns the number of elements in the collection. -

The isEmpty() method checks if the collection contains no elements. - The iterator() method returns an iterator over the elements in the collection.

These methods establish the basic operations that can be performed on any type of collection, regardless of its internal implementation.

2. Collections **Utility Class**

The Collections class, also part of the java.util package, is a utility class that cannot be instantiated. It contains a large assortment of static methods that operate on or return collections. These methods are used primarily for basic operations, such as sorting, searching, and synchronizing collections. Some notable methods include:

```
static <T> void sort(List<T> list);
static <T> int binarySearch(List<? extends Comparable<? super T>> list, T key);
static <T> T max(Collection<? extends T> coll);
static <T> T min(Collection<? extends T> coll);
static <T> List<T> synchronizedList(List<T> list);
static <T> Set<T> unmodifiableSet(Set<? extends T> s);
```

- The sort(List<T> list) method sorts the specified list into ascending order, according to the natural ordering of its elements. - The binarySearch(List<? extends Comparable<? super T» list, T key) method performs a binary search on the specified list for the specified key. - The max(Collection<? extends T> coll) method returns the maximum element of the given collection, according to the natural ordering of its elements. - The min(Collection<? extends T> coll) method returns the minimum element of the given collection. - The synchronizedList(List<T> list) method returns a synchronized (thread-safe) list backed by the specified list. - The unmodifiableSet(Set<? extends T> s) method returns an unmodifiable view of the specified set.

3. Practical Usage Examples

To demonstrate the functional distinction between Collection and Collections, consider the following code which uses both:

```
import java.util.*;

public class CollectionExample {
    public static void main(String[] args) {
        // Using the Collection interface
        Collection<String> names = new ArrayList<>();
        names.add("Alice");
        names.add("Bob");
        names.add("Charlie");

        // Iterating over the collection
        for (String name : names) {
            System.out.println(name);
```

```
        }

        // Using the Collections utility class
        List<String> nameList = new ArrayList<>(names);
        Collections.sort(nameList);
        System.out.println("Sorted names: " + nameList);

        int index = Collections.binarySearch(nameList, "Bob");
        System.out.println("Index of 'Bob': " + index);

        String maxName = Collections.max(nameList);
        System.out.println("Max name: " + maxName);
    }
}
```

```
Output:
Alice
Bob
Charlie
Sorted names: [Alice, Bob, Charlie]
Index of 'Bob': 1
Max name: Charlie
```

The code demonstrates:

- Adding elements to a Collection using the add(E e) method. - Iterating over a Collection using an enhanced for loop. - Sorting a list and performing a binary search using methods from the Collections utility class. - Finding the maximum element in the list using Collections.max.

By grasping the distinct roles of the Collection interface and the Collections utility class, developers can efficiently utilize the Java Collections Framework to manage and manipulate groups of objects.

1.7 Common Operations in Collections

Java Collections Framework provides a comprehensive set of operations that can be performed on different types of collections. These operations can be broadly classified into three categories: querying the collection, modifying the collection, and iterating through the collection.

Querying the Collection:

Query operations allow you to examine the contents of a collection without modifying it. Common query operations include checking the size of the collection, checking whether the collection is empty, and querying the presence of a specific element.

```
import java.util.*;

public class QueryOperations {
```

```
    public static void main(String[] args) {
        List<String> list = new ArrayList<>();
        list.add("Element1");
        list.add("Element2");
        list.add("Element3");

        // Check the size
        System.out.println("Size of the list: " + list.size());

        // Check if the list is empty
        System.out.println("Is the list empty? " + list.isEmpty());

        // Check if the list contains an element
        System.out.println("Does the list contain 'Element2'? " + list.contains("
            Element2"));
    }
}
```

```
Size of the list: 3
Is the list empty? false
Does the list contain 'Element2'? true
```

Modifying the Collection:

Modification operations alter the contents of a collection. Common modification operations include adding elements, removing elements, and clearing the collection.

```
import java.util.*;

public class ModifyOperations {

    public static void main(String[] args) {
        List<String> list = new ArrayList<>();
        list.add("Element1");
        list.add("Element2");
        System.out.println("Original list: " + list);

        // Adding an element
        list.add("Element3");
        System.out.println("After adding 'Element3': " + list);

        // Removing an element
        list.remove("Element2");
        System.out.println("After removing 'Element2': " + list);

        // Clearing the list
        list.clear();
        System.out.println("After clearing the list: " + list);
    }
}
```

```
Original list: [Element1, Element2]
After adding 'Element3': [Element1, Element2, Element3]
After removing 'Element2': [Element1, Element3]
After clearing the list: []
```

Iterating through the Collection:

Iteration operations allow you to traverse the elements of a collection.

Java Collections Framework provides several ways to iterate over a collection, including using a for-each loop, using an iterator, and using the forEach method introduced in Java 8.

```
import java.util.*;

public class IterateOperations {

    public static void main(String[] args) {
        List<String> list = new ArrayList<>();
        list.add("Element1");
        list.add("Element2");
        list.add("Element3");

        // Using standard for-each loop
        System.out.println("Using for-each loop:");
        for (String element : list) {
            System.out.println(element);
        }

        // Using Iterator
        System.out.println("Using Iterator:");
        Iterator<String> iterator = list.iterator();
        while (iterator.hasNext()) {
            System.out.println(iterator.next());
        }

        // Using forEach method (Java 8 and beyond)
        System.out.println("Using forEach method:");
        list.forEach(System.out::println);
    }
}
```

```
Using for-each loop:
Element1
Element2
Element3
Using Iterator:
Element1
Element2
Element3
Using forEach method:
Element1
Element2
Element3
```

Besides these basic operations, collections support bulk operations that allow performing multiple operations at once. Examples include adding all elements from another collection and retaining only elements present in another collection.

```
import java.util.*;

public class BulkOperations {

    public static void main(String[] args) {
        List<String> list1 = new ArrayList<>();
        list1.add("Element1");
        list1.add("Element2");
```

```
        List<String> list2 = new ArrayList<>();
        list2.add("Element3");
        list2.add("Element4");

        // Adding all elements from another collection
        list1.addAll(list2);
        System.out.println("After adding all elements: " + list1);

        List<String> retainedList = new ArrayList<>();
        retainedList.add("Element1");
        retainedList.add("Element3");

        // Retaining elements present in another collection
        list1.retainAll(retainedList);
        System.out.println("After retaining elements: " + list1);
    }
}
```

```
After adding all elements: [Element1, Element2, Element3, Element4]
After retaining elements: [Element1, Element3]
```

Understanding these common operations empowers developers to effectively utilize the Java Collections Framework to manipulate and manage data in various complex scenarios.

1.8 Generics in Collections

Generics in the Java Collections Framework enable type-safe operations on objects stored within collections, significantly reducing runtime errors by providing compile-time type checking. This section delves into the importance of generics, how they are implemented within the framework, the syntax for utilizing generics with collections, and examples that illustrate their practical usage and advantages.

The introduction of generics in Java 5 enhanced the Collections Framework by allowing collections to enforce type constraints, thereby avoiding ClassCastException errors that were prevalent in earlier versions of Java where collections held heterogeneous objects.

Generic Type Parameters Syntax

Generic types are declared with angle brackets $<>$ and can be used for classes, interfaces, and methods. The most common generic type parameters are:

- E - Element (commonly used by the Java Collections Framework)
- K - Key

- V - Value
- T - Type

For instance, to create a generic class that holds any type of data, you can define it as follows:

```
public class GenericClass<T> {
    private T data;

    public GenericClass(T data) {
        this.data = data;
    }

    public T getData() {
        return data;
    }

    public void setData(T data) {
        this.data = data;
    }
}
```

Using Generics with Collection Interfaces and Classes

Generics can be applied to collection interfaces like List<E>, Set<E>, Map<K, V>, and their respective implementing classes like ArrayList<E>, HashSet<E>, and HashMap<K, V>.

List<E> Usage Example:

```
List<String> stringList = new ArrayList<>();
stringList.add("One");
stringList.add("Two");

for (String str : stringList) {
    System.out.println(str);
}
```

In this example, List<String> ensures that the list only contains String objects, and any attempt to add a different type of object will result in a compile-time error.

Map<K, V> Usage Example:

```
Map<Integer, String> map = new HashMap<>();
map.put(1, "One");
map.put(2, "Two");
for (Map.Entry<Integer, String> entry : map.entrySet()) {
    System.out.println(entry.getKey() + ": " + entry.getValue());
}
```

Here, the Map enforces that keys are of type Integer and values are of type String.

Bounded Type Parameters

Bounded type parameters restrict the types that can be used as arguments for a type parameter. You can specify an upper bound with the extends keyword. For example:

```
public class Box<T extends Number> {
    private T value;

    public Box(T value) {
        this.value = value;
    }

    public T getValue() {
        return value;
    }
}
```

In this case, Box can only hold instances of Number or its subclasses (like Integer, Double, etc.).

Wildcard Parameters

Wildcards are special kind of type arguments that control the type safety of the collections. They are represented by the question mark (?). There are three types of wildcards:

- <?> - Unbounded wildcard
- <? extends T> - Upper-bounded wildcard
- <? super T> - Lower-bounded wildcard

Example of an upper-bounded wildcard:

```
public static void processElements(List<? extends Number> elements) {
    for (Number n : elements) {
        System.out.println(n);
    }
}
```

This method can accept any list whose elements are of type Number or its subclasses.

Example of a lower-bounded wildcard:

```
public static void addElements(List<? super Integer> elements) {
    elements.add(1);
    elements.add(2);
}
```

This method can accept a list of Integer or its superclasses (like Number, Object, etc.) and safely add integers to it.

Type Inference with Diamond Operator

Java 7 introduced the diamond operator <> to simplify the instantiation of generic classes by reducing the redundancy of specifying the type parameters:

```
List<String> stringList = new ArrayList<>();
```

Without the diamond operator, it would be necessary to repeat the generic type parameters:

```
List<String> stringList = new ArrayList<String>();
```

The diamond operator provides cleaner and more readable code, along with easing the task of refactoring.

Generic Methods

Generic methods allow type parameters to be used in method signatures and can be declared by placing the type parameter before the return type:

```
public <T> void printArray(T[] array) {
    for (T element : array) {
        System.out.println(element);
    }
}
```

Benefits of Using Generics

Generics bring robust type safety to the Java Collections Framework, ensuring that errors are caught during compile-time and not at runtime. This minimizes ClassCastException scenarios, boosts code reusability, and maintains cleaner code by leveraging type inference and parameterization.

Through the integration of generics, the Java Collections Framework provides a sophisticated and type-safe way of handling groups of objects, bolstering both developer productivity and application reliability.

1.9 Legacy Collections: Vectors and Hashtable

The Java Collections Framework has evolved significantly since its initial introduction. Before the advent of this unified framework, Java provided other mechanisms to handle collections of objects. Two primary classes from this pre-framework era are Vector and Hashtable. These legacy classes are still part of the Java Standard Library for compatibility reasons. Understanding their design, usage, and limitations is essential for comprehending the evolution of Java collections and maintaining legacy code.

Vector Class

The Vector class implements a growable array of objects. Like an array, it contains components that can be accessed using an integer index. However, unlike arrays, the size of a Vector can grow or shrink as needed to accommodate adding and removing items. Vectors are synchronized, which means they are thread-safe and can be used in concurrent environments. However, this also introduces a performance overhead compared to unsynchronized collections.

Example of creating and manipulating a Vector:

```
import java.util.Vector;

public class VectorExample {
    public static void main(String[] args) {
        Vector<String> vector = new Vector<>();
        vector.add("Apple");
        vector.add("Banana");
        vector.add("Orange");

        System.out.println("Vector elements:");
        for (String fruit : vector) {
            System.out.println(fruit);
        }

        vector.remove("Banana");
        System.out.println("Vector after removal:");
        System.out.println(vector);
    }
}
```

Output of the above code:

```
Vector elements:
Apple
Banana
Orange
Vector after removal:
[Apple, Orange]
```

Key points to note about Vector:

- Vector is synchronized.
- It implements the List interface, therefore it provides all methods for manipulating indexed collections.
- It automatically grows when elements are added, and shrinks

when elements are removed.

- Though it provides thread safety, the synchronized overhead makes it less performant compared to ArrayList for non-thread-safe operations.

Hashtable Class

The Hashtable class is a part of the original collection framework and provides a data structure to store key-value pairs. It is synchronized, meaning it is thread-safe, making it useful in concurrent applications. However, similar to Vector, the synchronization overhead can impact performance.

Example of creating and manipulating a Hashtable:

```
import java.util.Hashtable;

public class HashtableExample {
    public static void main(String[] args) {
        Hashtable<Integer, String> hashtable = new Hashtable<>();

        hashtable.put(1, "Apple");
        hashtable.put(2, "Banana");
        hashtable.put(3, "Orange");

        System.out.println("Hashtable elements:");
        for (Integer key : hashtable.keySet()) {
            System.out.println("Key: " + key + ", Value: " + hashtable.get(key));
        }

        hashtable.remove(2);
        System.out.println("Hashtable after removal:");
        System.out.println(hashtable);
    }
}
```

Output of the above code:

```
Hashtable elements:
Key: 1, Value: Apple
Key: 2, Value: Banana
Key: 3, Value: Orange
Hashtable after removal:
{1=Apple, 3=Orange}
```

Key points to note about Hashtable:

- Hashtable is synchronized.
- It does not allow null keys or values.
- It provides thread safety but with a performance cost.
- It implements the Map interface, providing methods for storing and retrieving key-value pairs.

Despite their functionality, Vector and Hashtable have largely been replaced by newer, more efficient classes like ArrayList and HashMap found in the Java Collections Framework. These newer classes offer superior performance and more flexible usage patterns, especially in non-concurrent applications. Understanding the legacy collections is vital for maintaining older codebases and for knowledge about the historical context and evolution of Java's approach to managing collections.

1.10 Java Collections Framework Improvements (Java 8 and beyond)

Java 8 and later versions introduced significant enhancements to the Java Collections Framework (JCF), mainly aimed at improving performance, adding functionality, and supporting the new style of programming paradigms. Java 8, in particular, added lambda expressions and the Streams API, which brought a functional approach to processing collections of objects.

Functional Programming with Lambda Expressions

Lambda expressions were one of the most noteworthy additions in Java 8. They provide a concise way to represent instances of functional interfaces (interfaces with a single abstract method). Lambda expressions can be used primarily to define the behavior of methods in collection classes. For example, Java 8 allows filtering a collection using a predicate defined by a lambda expression.

```
List<String> names = Arrays.asList("Alice", "Bob", "Charlie");
List<String> filteredNames = names.stream()
    .filter(name -> name.startsWith("A"))
    .collect(Collectors.toList());
```

```
[Output]
Alice
```

In this example, the lambda expression name -> name.startsWith("A") efficiently filters the list names to include only those strings that start with "A".

Streams API

The Streams API complements the introduction of lambda expressions, allowing the processing of sequences of elements. It provides a high-level abstraction for operations on sequences of elements, such as transformations and aggregations. The Streams API supports sequential and parallel execution, making it suitable for a wide range of applications, from simple data processing to complex aggregations.

```
List<Integer> numbers = Arrays.asList(1, 2, 3, 4, 5);
List<Integer> squaredNumbers = numbers.stream()
    .map(n -> n * n)
    .collect(Collectors.toList());
```

```
[Output]
1 4 9 16 25
```

Here, the stream is created from the list numbers. The map operation applies a lambda expression to each element to square the value, and collect gathers the results into a new list.

forEach Method

The forEach method, provided by the Iterable interface, allows a lambda expression to be applied to each element in the collection. This method provides an easy way to iterate through collections, which can enhance readability and reduce the risk of errors.

```
List<String> names = Arrays.asList("Alice", "Bob", "Charlie");
names.forEach(name -> System.out.println(name));
```

```
[Output]
Alice
Bob
Charlie
```

The forEach method simplifies iteration, similar to the enhanced for loop, but with better compatibility with lambda expressions and streams.

Optional Class

Java 8 also introduced the Optional class, which is not directly part of the JCF but is often used in conjunction with collections to handle the presence or absence of values without resorting to null checks.

```
List<String> names = Arrays.asList("Alice", "Bob", "Charlie");
Optional<String> firstNameWithA = names.stream()
    .filter(name -> name.startsWith("A"))
    .findFirst();

firstNameWithA.ifPresent(name -> System.out.println("Found: " + name));
```

```
[Output]
Found: Alice
```

The Optional class provides a more expressive and type-safe way to handle potential null values.

New Methods in Collection Classes

Numerous collection classes have been enhanced with new methods to support the functionality brought by lambda expressions and the Streams API. Some key improvements include:

- removeIf(Predicate<? super E> filter): Removes all elements from this collection that satisfy the given predicate.
- replaceAll(UnaryOperator<E> operator): Replaces each element of this list with the result of applying the operator to that element.
- sort(Comparator<? super E> c): Sorts the list according to the order induced by the specified comparator.

```
List<String> names = new ArrayList<>(Arrays.asList("Alice", "Bob", "Charlie", "
    David"));
names.removeIf(name -> name.length() == 3);
names.replaceAll(String::toUpperCase);
names.sort(Comparator.naturalOrder());
```

```
[Output]
ALICE
CHARLIE
DAVID
```

In this code, removeIf removes elements with a length of 3, replaceAll converts all strings to uppercase, and sort arranges them alphabetically.

Concurrent Additions

Java 8 introduced new classes such as ConcurrentHashMap and CompletableFuture. The ConcurrentHashMap class provides efficient and thread-safe implementations of a hash table with support for count-based operations, while CompletableFuture enables complex asynchronous programming.

```
ConcurrentHashMap<String, Integer> map = new ConcurrentHashMap<>();
map.put("Alice", 1);
map.put("Bob", 2);

map.forEach(1, (key, value) -> System.out.println(key + " : " + value));
```

```
[Output]
Alice : 1
Bob : 2
```

The forEach method supports concurrent processing, making it suitable for high-performance applications.

The enhancements in Java 8 and beyond have significantly improved the flexibility, efficiency, and expressiveness of the Java Collections Framework, making it a powerful tool for modern Java developers.

Chapter 2

Understanding Collection Interfaces

This chapter provides a thorough exploration of the various collection interfaces within the Java Collections Framework. It examines the fundamental concepts of the iterable and collection interfaces, delves into the specific characteristics and uses of list, set, queue, deque, and map interfaces, and highlights the relationships and hierarchies among them. The chapter also discusses the importance of default methods in interfaces, facilitating a clear understanding of how these interfaces define and shape Java collections.

2.1 Introduction to Collection Interfaces

The Java Collections Framework (JCF) is fundamental to the Java programming language, providing a unified architecture for representing and manipulating collections. At the core of the JCF are the collection interfaces, which define the various types of collections and their standard behaviors. These interfaces form the backbone of how data structures are used and manipulated in Java.

Java collections are designed to handle groups of objects, or "collections," which are manipulated as single units. The primary interfaces within the JCF include Iterable, Collection, List, Set, Queue, Deque, and

Map. Each of these interfaces serves a specific purpose and provides various methods that guarantee a standard way of managing collections. Let's delve into the foundational concepts of these collection interfaces.

Core Interface: Iterable

The most universal interface is Iterable, which is the root interface for all collection classes. It provides the iterator method, which returns an Iterator over the elements in the collection. The Iterator interface defines methods for iterating over a collection:

```
Iterator<E> iterator();
```

The Iterable interface allows for the use of the enhanced for-loop (also known as the "for-each" loop) to iterate over collections conveniently:

```
for (ElementType element : collection) {
    // Process element
}
```

Collection Interface

The Collection interface extends Iterable and represents a group of objects known as elements. It declares the predecessor for more specific collection types such as List, Set, and Queue. The Collection interface includes fundamental methods such as add, remove, size, and contains, ensuring a basic contract for operations on collections:

```
boolean add(E e);
boolean remove(Object o);
int size();
boolean contains(Object o);
Iterator<E> iterator();
```

List Interface: Ordered Collections

The List interface extends Collection and introduces a collection that maintains an ordered sequence of elements. Lists allow positional access, element search, and range-view operations. Key methods unique to List include get, set, add with index, and remove with index:

```
E get(int index);
E set(int index, E element);
void add(int index, E element);
E remove(int index);
```

Set Interface: Unique Collections

The Set interface also extends Collection. It represents a collection of unique elements where duplicates are not allowed. Sets are typically used to model mathematical set abstraction. The Set interface inherits all methods from Collection and ensures no duplicate elements through underlying mechanisms like hash tables in HashSet.

Queue Interface: Ordered Processing

A Queue interface inherits from Collection and represents collections of elements arranged for processing. It introduces methods for element insertion, extraction, and inspection. Functional methods include offer, poll, peek, and their variations:

```
boolean offer(E e);
E poll();
E peek();
```

Deque Interface: Double-Ended Queues

The Deque interface extends Queue, providing deque (double-ended queue) functionalities that support element insertion, removal, and inspection at both ends. Additional methods such as addFirst, addLast, and removeFirst are specific to deque operations:

```
void addFirst(E e);
void addLast(E e);
E removeFirst();
```

Map Interface: Key-Value Associations

The Map interface is distinct from Collection and represents a collection of key-value pairs. Maps are essential for associative arrays where each key maps to a particular value. Fundamental methods in Map include put, get, remove, and entrySet:

```
V put(K key, V value);
V get(Object key);
V remove(Object key);
Set<Map.Entry<K, V>> entrySet();
```

Spanning various specialized and generalized operations, the collection interfaces establish the skeletal framework for how collections are structured and how they behave. By delving into each interface's details, we gain a deeper understanding of the flexibility and capabilities offered within the Java Collections Framework.

2.2 The Iterable Interface

The Iterable interface is a foundational component within the Java Collections Framework (JCF). It is found in the java.lang package and is intended to be implemented by any collection class whose elements can be traversed one at a time. The primary purpose of the Iterable interface is to provide an abstraction for iteration over a collection of objects.

Iterable is a generic interface with the following definition:

```
public interface Iterable<T> {
    Iterator<T> iterator();
}
```

In this definition, T represents the type of elements returned by the iterator. The key method in the Iterable interface is iterator(), which returns an Iterator over elements of type T.

Understanding the significance of Iterable requires examining the Iterator interface, which provides methods for traversing collections.

```
public interface Iterator<E> {
    boolean hasNext();
    E next();
    default void remove() {
        throw new UnsupportedOperationException("remove");
    }
}
```

The hasNext() method returns true if the iteration has more elements. The next() method returns the next element in the iteration. The remove() method can remove an element from the underlying collection; however, not all collection types implement this operation, hence its default implementation throws an UnsupportedOperationException.

In practice, implementing the Iterable interface allows an object to be the target of the "foreach loop" statement. This loop is a syntactic sugar that simplifies the iteration process. For instance, consider the implementation of a simple CustomList that implements Iterable:

```
import java.util.Iterator;

public class CustomList<T> implements Iterable<T> {
    private T[] items;
    private int size;

    @SuppressWarnings("unchecked")
    public CustomList(int capacity) {
        items = (T[]) new Object[capacity];
        size = 0;
```

```
    }

    public void add(T item) {
        if (size == items.length) {
            throw new IllegalStateException("List is full");
        }
        items[size++] = item;
    }

    @Override
    public Iterator<T> iterator() {
        return new Iterator<T>() {
            private int index = 0;

            @Override
            public boolean hasNext() {
                return index < size;
            }

            @Override
            public T next() {
                if (!hasNext()) {
                    throw new NoSuchElementException();
                }
                return items[index++];
            }
        };
    }
}
```

In this example, the CustomList class implements Iterable and provides an implementation for the iterator() method. This implementation grants CustomList the ability to be used in a foreach loop:

```
CustomList<String> list = new CustomList<>(10);
list.add("Hello");
list.add("World");

for (String item : list) {
    System.out.println(item);
}
```

This iteration prints:

```
Hello
World
```

Implementing Iterable ensures that applications can use enhanced for loops for more readable and maintainable code. This advantage is not limited to custom classes; all standard Java collections, including ArrayList, HashSet, and HashMap values, implement Iterable.

Moreover, implementing Iterable enhances interoperability with APIs that operate on collections. For example, methods in the java.util.Collections utility class accept Iterable<T> types, further integrating custom collections with Java's standard library facilities.

In applications where iteration patterns are complex or require external management, custom Iterator implementations may leverage other patterns such as the state pattern to control iteration comprehensively. Additionally, if thread safety is a concern, Iterator implementations must handle concurrent modifications carefully, potentially using techniques such as fail-fast iterators, which immediately throw ConcurrentModificationException upon detecting structural changes.

Ultimately, the Iterable interface's simplicity and power lie in its ability to define a standard mechanism for accessing elements sequentially, making iteration a first-class concept in Java's collection-handling routines.

2.3 Understanding the Collection Interface

The Collection interface is one of the most fundamental and foundational components within the Java Collections Framework (JCF). It extends the Iterable interface, providing the essential structure for various other collection interfaces, such as List, Set, and Queue. The Collection interface is generic, accepting a type parameter <E> to allow the storage of any object type.

```
public interface Collection<E> extends Iterable<E> {
    int size();
    boolean isEmpty();
    boolean contains(Object o);
    Iterator<E> iterator();
    Object[] toArray();
    <T> T[] toArray(T[] a);
    boolean add(E e);
    boolean remove(Object o);
    boolean containsAll(Collection<?> c);
    boolean addAll(Collection<? extends E> c);
    boolean removeAll(Collection<?> c);
    boolean retainAll(Collection<?> c);
    void clear();
    boolean equals(Object o);
    int hashCode();
}
```

The Collection interface defines several core operations that all collections must implement:

- size(): Returns the number of elements in the collection. If the collection contains more than Integer.MAX_VALUE elements, the result is Integer.MAX_VALUE.
- isEmpty(): Returns true if the collection contains no elements.

- contains(Object o): Returns true if the collection contains the specified element.

- iterator(): Returns an iterator over the elements in this collection. The elements are returned in no particular order unless the collection is an instance of a class that provides a specific iteration order.

- toArray(): Returns an array containing all of the elements in this collection. The runtime type of the returned array is Object[].

- <T> T[] toArray(T[] a): Returns an array containing all of the elements in this collection. If the specified array is large enough to hold the collection, it is returned therein. Otherwise, a new array is allocated with the runtime type of the specified array and the size of this collection.

- add(E e): Ensures that this collection contains the specified element. Returns true if this collection changed as a result of the call.

- remove(Object o): Removes a single instance of the specified element from this collection, if it is present. Returns true if this collection changed as a result of the call.

- containsAll(Collection<?> c): Returns true if this collection contains all of the elements in the specified collection.

- addAll(Collection<? extends E> c): Adds all of the elements in the specified collection to this collection. The behavior of this operation is undefined if the specified collection is modified while the operation is in progress.

- removeAll(Collection<?> c): Removes all of this collection's elements that are also contained in the specified collection. After this call returns, this collection will contain no elements in common with the specified collection.

- retainAll(Collection<?> c): Retains only the elements in this collection that are contained in the specified collection. In other words, removes from this collection all of its elements that are not contained in the specified collection.

- clear(): Removes all of the elements from this collection. The collection will be empty after this method returns.

- equals(Object o): Compares the specified object with this collection for equality. While the precise definition of equality may vary between different implementations, typically, two collections are equal if they contain the same elements.

- hashCode(): Returns the hash code value for this collection.

Implementing the Collection interface provides significant flexibility to developers. Specific collections like ArrayList, HashSet, LinkedList, and others can provide concrete implementations of these methods in a manner that optimizes for their respective use cases. However, understanding the underlying contract of the Collection interface is crucial for efficient use and implementation.

Concrete classes implementing the Collection interface may impose additional constraints or modify the behavior of these methods. For example, an ArrayList allows duplicates and maintains insertion order, while a HashSet does not allow duplicates and does not maintain any order. Despite these differences, both adhere to the basic contract of the Collection interface. This polymorphism allows Java developers to write more general and reusable code.

Consider the following example where an ArrayList and a HashSet are used interchangeably via the Collection interface:

```
Collection<String> list = new ArrayList<>();
list.add("Apple");
list.add("Banana");
list.add("Orange");

Collection<String> set = new HashSet<>(list);
set.add("Banana");

System.out.println(list); // Outputs: [Apple, Banana, Orange]
System.out.println(set); // Outputs: [Apple, Banana, Orange]
```

```
[Apple, Banana, Orange]
[Apple, Orange, Banana]
```

This example demonstrates that both collections can be manipulated using common methods defined in the Collection interface, despite the different behaviors of ArrayList and HashSet. Understanding these nuances assists in selecting the appropriate concrete implementation for a specific scenario. The abstract nature of the Collection interface fosters a framework where a wide variety of data structures can be employed interchangeably, grounded on a unified set of operations, resulting in a flexible and powerful design.

2.4 List Interface: Ordered Collections

The List interface in the Java Collections Framework represents an ordered collection, also known as a sequence. It provides a way to store and access elements in a linear, indexed order, enabling the insertion, deletion, and access of elements based on their position in the list. The List interface is a sub-interface of the Collection interface and defines additional methods to handle the positional access of elements.

Key Characteristics of the List Interface:

- **Ordered Collection:** Elements in a List are maintained in a specific sequence. The order in which the elements are inserted is preserved.
- **Index-Based Access:** The List interface provides methods to access elements at a particular index. This allows for efficient random access and modification of elements.
- **Allows Duplicates:** Unlike the Set interface, a List can contain duplicate elements.
- **Null Elements:** A List can include null elements if allowed by the specific implementation.

Core Methods of the List Interface:

Below is an overview of some core methods provided by the List interface:

```
// Adds an element to the list at the specified position
void add(int index, E element);

// Adds an element to the end of the list
boolean add(E e);

// Adds all elements from the specified collection at the specified position
boolean addAll(int index, Collection<? extends E> c);

// Retrieves the element at the specified position
E get(int index);

// Replaces the element at the specified position with a new value
E set(int index, E element);

// Removes the element at the specified position
E remove(int index);

// Returns the index of the first occurrence of the specified element
int indexOf(Object o);
```

```
// Returns the index of the last occurrence of the specified element
int lastIndexOf(Object o);

// Returns a sublist from the specified start index to end index (exclusive)
List<E> subList(int fromIndex, int toIndex);
```

Example of List **Interface Usage:**

Consider an example demonstrating common operations on a List:

```
import java.util.List;
import java.util.ArrayList;

public class ListExample {
    public static void main(String[] args) {
        // Create a List using ArrayList
        List<String> fruits = new ArrayList<>();

        // Add elements to the List
        fruits.add("Apple");
        fruits.add("Banana");
        fruits.add("Cherry");

        // Insert an element at a specific position
        fruits.add(1, "Blueberry");

        // Retrieve an element by index
        String fruit = fruits.get(2);

        // Modify an element at a specific index
        fruits.set(3, "Date");

        // Remove an element by index
        fruits.remove(1);

        // Print all elements
        for (String f : fruits) {
            System.out.println(f);
        }
    }
}
```

```
Output:
Apple
Cherry
Date
```

Thread Safety and List **Implementations:**

Common implementations of the List interface include ArrayList, LinkedList, and Vector. Only Vector is synchronized. To achieve thread safety with non-synchronized implementations, use Collections.synchronizedList:

```
import java.util.List;
import java.util.ArrayList;
import java.util.Collections;

public class SynchronizedListExample {
```

```
    public static void main(String[] args) {
        List<String> syncList = Collections.synchronizedList(new ArrayList<>());

        // Add elements to the synchronized List
        syncList.add("Apple");
        syncList.add("Banana");
        syncList.add("Cherry");

        // Synchronized block to perform iteration
        synchronized(syncList) {
            for (String fruit : syncList) {
                System.out.println(fruit);
            }
        }
    }
}
```

In the above example, a synchronized list is created from an ArrayList using Collections.synchronizedList. To iterate over the list, synchronized blocks ensure thread safety.

Default Methods in List Interface:

Java 8 introduced default methods in interfaces, and the List interface leverages this feature to provide methods with a default implementation. These methods can be overridden by implementing classes if needed.

For instance, the List interface includes a default replaceAll method that replaces all elements in the list with the result of applying a specified operator:

```
default void replaceAll(UnaryOperator<E> operator) {
    Objects.requireNonNull(operator);
    final ListIterator<E> li = this.listIterator();
    while (li.hasNext()) {
        li.set(operator.apply(li.next()));
    }
}
```

This method takes a UnaryOperator as an argument and applies it to each element, replacing the elements with the transformed values. Usage of default methods can lead to more concise and readable code.

Collectively, these properties and methods make the List interface a versatile and powerful tool for managing ordered collections. The understanding and application of its methods and implementations are essential for effective Java programming.

2.5 Set Interface: Unique Collections

The Set interface represents a collection that contains no duplicate elements. As part of the Java Collections Framework, it inherits from the Collection interface, which allows it to leverage the methods defined in the Collection interface. The distinguishing characteristic of a Set is its allowance for uniqueness—no two elements in a set can be the same. This is enforced using the equals(Object o) method for comparison.

Sets are most suitable when the primary requirement is a collection containing unique elements without any specific ordering. The Set interface has several well-known implementations, such as HashSet, LinkedHashSet, and TreeSet, each with distinctive behaviors in terms of performance, ordering, and specific use cases.

- HashSet: Provides the best performance in terms of complexity, generally offering O(1) time complexity for addition, removal, and lookup operations. It uses a hash table for storage and does not guarantee any ordering of the elements.
- LinkedHashSet: Maintains a linked list of the entries in the set, preserving the insertion order. It offers both the performance benefits of a hash table and the predictable iteration order of a linked list.
- TreeSet: Implements the NavigableSet interface and uses a Red-Black tree structure. This means it keeps the elements sorted in their natural order or by a specified comparator. All basic operations are logarithmic time (O(log n)).

The core methods defined in the Set interface are derived from its parent interface, Collection. However, the behaviors of these methods uphold the unique element constraint of sets. Below is an example to illustrate the usage of the Set interface:

```
import java.util.*;

public class SetExample {
    public static void main(String[] args) {
        Set<String> hashSet = new HashSet<>();
        hashSet.add("Apple");
        hashSet.add("Banana");
        hashSet.add("Cherry");

        // Attempt to add duplicate elements
        hashSet.add("Apple");
        hashSet.add("Banana");
```

```
        // Display elements
        for (String fruit : hashSet) {
            System.out.println(fruit);
        }
    }
}
```

Expected Output:
Banana
Apple
Cherry

In this example, attempting to add duplicate elements "Apple" and "Banana" to the hashSet does not alter the set, demonstrating the unique element constraint.

The behavior and utility of each Set implementation can be better appreciated through algorithmic analysis and practical use cases.

Algorithm Analysis:

- HashSet: HashSet uses hashing to achieve constant-time complexity for add, remove, and contains methods, provided the hash function disperses elements uniformly among the buckets.
- LinkedHashSet: LinkedHashSet provides insertion-order iteration by maintaining a doubly-linked list, which means it incurs additional overhead compared to HashSet, but still provides O(1) complexity for basic operations due to hashing.
- TreeSet: TreeSet uses a Red-Black tree, a self-balancing binary search tree, yielding O(log n) complexity for add, remove, and contains operations. It is ideal for scenarios where sorted order of elements is required.

The Set interface enforces the uniqueness of elements through the equals method. Therefore, it is crucial to appropriately override equals and hashCode methods when using custom objects as elements in a Set. Failure to do so can result in unexpected behavior, such as allowing duplicates or hindering element retrieval.

```
import java.util.*;

class CustomObject {
    private String name;
    private int id;

    public CustomObject(String name, int id) {
        this.name = name;
        this.id = id;
```

```
    }

    @Override
    public boolean equals(Object o) {
        if (this == o) return true;
        if (o == null || getClass() != o.getClass()) return false;
        CustomObject that = (CustomObject) o;
        return id == that.id && Objects.equals(name, that.name);
    }

    @Override
    public int hashCode() {
        return Objects.hash(name, id);
    }
}

public class CustomSetExample {
    public static void main(String[] args) {
        Set<CustomObject> customSet = new HashSet<>();
        customSet.add(new CustomObject("Obj1", 1));
        customSet.add(new CustomObject("Obj2", 2));
        customSet.add(new CustomObject("Obj1", 1)); // Duplicate

        for (CustomObject obj : customSet) {
            System.out.println("Object: " + obj.name + ", ID: " + obj.id);
        }
    }
}
```

```
Expected Output:
Object: Obj1, ID: 1
Object: Obj2, ID: 2
```

Here, correctly overriding the equals and hashCode methods ensures that the CustomObject with name "Obj1" and id 1 is added only once to the customSet, despite an attempt to add it a second time.

Sets are fundamental in scenarios involving the need to remove duplicates. Understanding and effectively using the varied implementations of the Set interface in the Java Collections Framework allows for optimized solution designs catering to the specific demands of performance, order, and iteration predictability.

2.6 NavigableSet and SortedSet Interfaces

The SortedSet and NavigableSet interfaces are advanced extensions of the Set interface, providing additional functionality for handling sorted sets and performing range operations with enhanced precision. This section elucidates the key characteristics, methods, and usage patterns of these interfaces to enrich the understanding of their integration within the Java Collections Framework.

SortedSet Interface

The SortedSet<E> interface extends the Set<E> interface, representing a set where the elements are maintained in ascending order. This order can be either the natural ordering of the elements (i.e., the order determined by their compareTo method if they implement Comparable), or by a specified Comparator provided at the set's creation time.

Below, we provide a synthesized example to illustrate the SortedSet interface in action:

```
import java.util.SortedSet;
import java.util.TreeSet;

public class SortedSetExample {
    public static void main(String[] args) {
        SortedSet<String> sortedSet = new TreeSet<>();

        sortedSet.add("Banana");
        sortedSet.add("Apple");
        sortedSet.add("Mango");
        sortedSet.add("Peach");

        //Displaying elements in ascending order
        for (String fruit : sortedSet) {
            System.out.println(fruit);
        }

        //Checking the first and last elements
        System.out.println("First: " + sortedSet.first());
        System.out.println("Last: " + sortedSet.last());
    }
}
```

The output will be:

```
Apple
Banana
Mango
Peach
First: Apple
Last: Peach
```

The SortedSet interface declares several key methods which allow for querying and manipulating the order of the elements:

- Comparator<? super E> comparator() - Returns the comparator used to order the elements, or null if the natural ordering is used.
- E first() - Returns the first (lowest) element.
- E last() - Returns the last (highest) element.
- SortedSet<E> headSet(E toElement) - Returns a view of the portion of this set whose elements are strictly less than toElement.

- SortedSet<E> subSet(E fromElement, E toElement) - Returns a view of the portion of this set whose elements range from fromElement, inclusive, to toElement, exclusive.

- SortedSet<E> tailSet(E fromElement) - Returns a view of the portion of this set whose elements are greater than or equal to fromElement.

NavigableSet Interface

The NavigableSet<E> interface extends the SortedSet<E> interface, providing additional navigation methods to retrieve elements based on their ordering. This interface is particularly useful for multidirectional navigation and range-based queries.

Consider the following example to demonstrate key functionalities of the NavigableSet interface:

```
import java.util.NavigableSet;
import java.util.TreeSet;

public class NavigableSetExample {
    public static void main(String[] args) {
        NavigableSet<Integer> navigableSet = new TreeSet<>();

        navigableSet.add(1);
        navigableSet.add(3);
        navigableSet.add(5);
        navigableSet.add(7);

        //Descending order
        NavigableSet<Integer> descendingSet = navigableSet.descendingSet();
        for(Integer number : descendingSet) {
            System.out.println(number);
        }

        //Polling first and last elements
        System.out.println("Polling first: " + navigableSet.pollFirst());
        System.out.println("Polling last: " + navigableSet.pollLast());

        //Range views
        System.out.println("HeadSet (less than 5): " + navigableSet.headSet(5));
        System.out.println("SubSet (3 to 7): " + navigableSet.subSet(3, true, 7, true));
        System.out.println("TailSet (greater than or equal to 3): " + navigableSet.
            tailSet(3));
    }
}
```

The output will be:

```
7
5
3
1
Polling first: 1
Polling last: 7
HeadSet (less than 5): [3]
SubSet (3 to 7): [3, 5]
TailSet (greater than or equal to 3): [3, 5]
```

Significant methods in the NavigableSet interface are:

- E lower(E e) - Returns the greatest element less than e, or null if no such element exists.
- E floor(E e) - Returns the greatest element less than or equal to e, or null if no such element exists.
- E ceiling(E e) - Returns the smallest element greater than or equal to e, or null if no such element exists.
- E higher(E e) - Returns the smallest element greater than e, or null if no such element exists.
- E pollFirst() - Retrieves and removes the first (lowest) element, or returns null if the set is empty.
- E pollLast() - Retrieves and removes the last (highest) element, or returns null if the set is empty.
- NavigableSet<E> descendingSet() - Returns a reverse order view of the elements contained in this set.
- NavigableSet<E> headSet(E toElement, boolean inclusive) - Returns a view of the portion of this set whose elements are strictly less than toElement, optionally inclusive.
- NavigableSet<E> subSet(E fromElement, boolean fromInclusive, E toElement, boolean toInclusive) - Returns a view of the portion of this set whose elements range from fromElement to toElement, optionally inclusive at each end.
- NavigableSet<E> tailSet(E fromElement, boolean inclusive) - Returns a view of the portion of this set whose elements are greater than or equal to fromElement, optionally inclusive.

The TreeSet class is the primary implementation of both SortedSet and NavigableSet interfaces. It provides a balanced tree representation, ensuring logarithmic time complexity for common operations such as add, remove, and contains checks. Understanding the intricacies of SortedSet and NavigableSet interfaces enables developers to leverage their specialized methods for effective set manipulation and range querying in Java applications.

2.7 Queue Interface: Ordered Processing

The Queue interface in the Java Collections Framework represents a collection designed for holding elements prior to processing them. It is part of the java.util package and extends the Collection interface. Queues typically, but do not necessarily, order elements in a FIFO (first-in-first-out) manner. However, other orderings are possible, such as LIFO (last-in-first-out) or priority-based ordering.

Core Methods of the Queue Interface

The Queue interface defines several methods essential for operating on the queue. These methods facilitate element insertion, removal, and examination according to specific policies. Here is a detailed look at the key methods:

- boolean add(E e): Inserts the specified element into the queue if it is possible to do so immediately without violating capacity restrictions. Upon success, it returns true. If the queue is full, an IllegalStateException is thrown.
- boolean offer(E e): Adds the specified element to the queue. This method differs from add only in that it returns false when the offer fails rather than throwing an exception.
- E remove(): Retrieves and removes the head of the queue. This method throws a NoSuchElementException if the queue is empty.
- E poll(): Retrieves and removes the head of the queue, or returns null if the queue is empty.
- E element(): Retrieves, but does not remove, the head of the queue. This method throws a NoSuchElementException if the queue is empty.
- E peek(): Retrieves, but does not remove, the head of the queue, or returns null if the queue is empty.

The primary operations, offer, poll, peek, along with the collection operations like isEmpty and size, provide essential capabilities for interacting with queues without risking exceptions leading to program termination.

Example Implementation

Below is an example demonstrating a queue's basic operations using a LinkedList which implements the Queue interface:

```
import java.util.LinkedList;
import java.util.Queue;

public class QueueExample {
    public static void main(String[] args) {
        Queue<String> queue = new LinkedList<>();

        // Adding elements
        queue.add("First");
        queue.offer("Second");
        queue.offer("Third");

        // Accessing elements
        System.out.println("Head of the queue: " + queue.element());
        System.out.println("Head of the queue (peek): " + queue.peek());

        // Removing elements
        System.out.println("Removed from queue: " + queue.remove());
        System.out.println("Removed from queue (poll): " + queue.poll());

        // Remaining elements
        System.out.println("Remaining elements: " + queue);
    }
}
```

Running this example yields the following output:

```
Head of the queue: First
Head of the queue (peek): First
Removed from queue: First
Removed from queue (poll): Second
Remaining elements: [Third]
```

PriorityQueue: An Ordered Queue Implementation

The PriorityQueue class, part of the Java standard library, provides a queue implementation where elements are ordered according to their natural ordering or by a Comparator provided at queue construction time. This class ensures that the head of the queue is always the smallest element as per the specified ordering.

Here is an example to illustrate the use of PriorityQueue:

```
import java.util.PriorityQueue;
import java.util.Queue;

public class PriorityQueueExample {
    public static void main(String[] args) {
        Queue<Integer> priorityQueue = new PriorityQueue<>();
```

```
        priorityQueue.offer(3);
        priorityQueue.offer(1);
        priorityQueue.offer(2);

        // Accessing and removing elements
        while (!priorityQueue.isEmpty()) {
            System.out.println("Head of queue (poll): " + priorityQueue.poll());
        }
    }
}
```

Executing this example will output the elements in their natural order:

```
Head of queue (poll): 1
Head of queue (poll): 2
Head of queue (poll): 3
```

Blocking Queues

Java also provides several queue implementations that are particularly suited for concurrent programming by offering thread-safe access and blocking operations. These blocking queues belong to the java.util.concurrent package and include classes like ArrayBlockingQueue, LinkedBlockingQueue, PriorityBlockingQueue, and DelayQueue.

The BlockingQueue interface extends Queue with additional methods that wait for the queue to become non-empty when retrieving an element, and to become non-full when storing an element, such as put and take.

Below is an example demonstrating the use of ArrayBlockingQueue:

```
import java.util.concurrent.ArrayBlockingQueue;
import java.util.concurrent.BlockingQueue;

public class BlockingQueueExample {
    public static void main(String[] args) {
        BlockingQueue<String> blockingQueue = new ArrayBlockingQueue<>(2);

        try {
            blockingQueue.put("One");
            blockingQueue.put("Two");
            System.out.println("Trying to add third element to the full queue...");
            blockingQueue.put("Three"); // waits until space becomes available
        } catch (InterruptedException e) {
            Thread.currentThread().interrupt();
        }

        System.out.println("Blocked queue elements: " + blockingQueue);
    }
}
```

This example highlights how the put operation blocks when trying to insert an element into a full queue.

Understanding these different queue implementations and their appropriate use cases allows developers to choose the most suitable form of ordered processing for specific requirements in their applications.

2.8 Deque Interface: Double-Ended Queues

The Deque interface, which stands for double-ended queue, extends the Queue interface and provides additional methods to insert, remove, and examine elements from both ends of the collection. This dual-end functionality makes deques (pronounced "decks") a versatile and flexible data structure suitable for a variety of applications where elements need to be processed in both FIFO (First-In-First-Out) and LIFO (Last-In-First-Out) order.

Methods of the Deque Interface

The Deque interface includes several methods that are categorized based on their functionality:

- **Insertion Methods:**
  - addFirst(E e): Inserts the specified element at the front of the deque.
  - addLast(E e): Inserts the specified element at the end of the deque.
  - offerFirst(E e): Inserts the specified element at the front of the deque, returning true upon success and false if no space is currently available.
  - offerLast(E e): Inserts the specified element at the end of the deque, returning true upon success and false if no space is currently available.
- **Removal Methods:**
  - removeFirst(): Retrieves and removes the first element of the deque.
  - removeLast(): Retrieves and removes the last element of the deque.
  - pollFirst(): Retrieves and removes the first element of the deque, or returns null if the deque is empty.

  - pollLast(): Retrieves and removes the last element of the deque, or returns null if the deque is empty.

- **Examination Methods:**
  - getFirst(): Retrieves, but does not remove, the first element of the deque.
  - getLast(): Retrieves, but does not remove, the last element of the deque.
  - peekFirst(): Retrieves, but does not remove, the first element of the deque, or returns null if the deque is empty.
  - peekLast(): Retrieves, but does not remove, the last element of the deque, or returns null if the deque is empty.

Additional Methods

In addition to the methods listed above, the Deque interface also includes the following methods that enable manipulation and examination of elements:

- boolean removeFirstOccurrence(Object o): Removes the first occurrence of the specified element from the deque.
- boolean removeLastOccurrence(Object o): Removes the last occurrence of the specified element from the deque.
- Iterator<E> descendingIterator(): Returns an iterator over the elements in the deque in reverse sequential order.

Here is a concise example demonstrating the use of a Deque in Java using the LinkedList implementation. This example illustrates inserting and removing elements from both ends of the deque:

```
import java.util.Deque;
import java.util.LinkedList;

public class DequeExample {
    public static void main(String[] args) {
        // Initializing a Deque using LinkedList
        Deque<String> deque = new LinkedList<>();

        // Adding elements to the deque
        deque.addFirst("Element 1 (First)");
        deque.addLast("Element 2 (Last)");
        deque.addFirst("Element 3 (First)");

        // Displaying the elements of the deque
        System.out.println("Deque: " + deque);
```

```
        // Removing elements from the deque
        String firstElement = deque.removeFirst();
        String lastElement = deque.removeLast();

        System.out.println("Removed First Element: " + firstElement);
        System.out.println("Removed Last Element: " + lastElement);

        // Final deque state
        System.out.println("Final Deque: " + deque);
    }
}
```

When executed, the output of the above program would be:

```
Deque: [Element 3 (First), Element 1 (First), Element 2 (Last)]
Removed First Element: Element 3 (First)
Removed Last Element: Element 2 (Last)
Final Deque: [Element 1 (First)]
```

Usage Scenarios

The Deque interface is useful in numerous scenarios such as:

- **Deque as a Stack:** By using addFirst(E e) and removeFirst() or push(E e) and pop(), the deque can work as a stack. This allows elements to be processed in LIFO order.
- **Deque as a Queue:** Using addLast(E e) and removeFirst(), the deque can function as a standard queue, processing elements in FIFO order.
- **Double-Ended Functionality:** Operations that require both ends of the data structure to be accessible can efficiently use a deque for inserting and removing elements.

Various implementations of the Deque interface like ArrayDeque and LinkedList come with their own performance characteristics. ArrayDeque is typically faster for operations that do not require resizing the array, while LinkedList provides consistent big-O time performance for insertions and deletions.

Understanding the Deque interface and its methods offers significant versatility. The dual-ended access provided by deques enables efficient implementations for both stack and queue operations, making them a valuable tool within the Java Collections Framework.

2.9 Map Interface: Key-Value Associations

The Map interface is a pivotal component of the Java Collections Framework, enabling storage and manipulation of key-value pairs. Unlike the Collection hierarchy, which deals with a collection of elements, Map works on the principle of mapping keys to values. Each key maps to at most one value, ensuring the uniqueness of keys within the map. The key characteristics of a Map are the associations it forms between keys and values.

Map does not extend the Collection interface, signifying its distinctive role and operations. To understand the fundamental operations of the Map interface, consider the following methods that it declares:

```
V put(K key, V value);
V get(Object key);
boolean containsKey(Object key);
boolean containsValue(Object value);
V remove(Object key);
void putAll(Map<? extends K,? extends V> m);
void clear();
Set<K> keySet();
Collection<V> values();
Set<Map.Entry<K, V>> entrySet();
```

- - put(K key, V value): Associates the specified value with the specified key. If the map previously contained a mapping for the key, the old value is replaced.
- - get(Object key): Returns the value to which the specified key is mapped, or null if the map contains no mapping for the key.
- - containsKey(Object key): Returns true if this map contains a mapping for the specified key.
- - containsValue(Object value): Returns true if this map maps one or more keys to the specified value.
- - remove(Object key): Removes the mapping for a key if it is present.
- - putAll(Map<? extends K, ? extends V> m): Copies all of the mappings from the specified map to this map.
- - clear(): Removes all of the mappings from this map.
- - keySet(): Returns a Set view of the keys contained in this map.

- - values(): Returns a Collection view of the values contained in this map.
- - entrySet(): Returns a Set view of the mappings contained in this map.

These methods form the basis for interaction with key-value pairs within a map. Consider an implementation example to illustrate these operations:

```
import java.util.HashMap;
import java.util.Map;

public class MapExample {
    public static void main(String[] args) {
        Map<String, Integer> map = new HashMap<>();

        // Add key-value pairs to the map
        map.put("One", 1);
        map.put("Two", 2);
        map.put("Three", 3);

        // Retrieve a value
        System.out.println("Value for key 'Two': " + map.get("Two"));

        // Check if a key exists
        System.out.println("Map contains key 'One': " + map.containsKey("One"));

        // Remove a key-value pair
        map.remove("One");

        // Display all key-value pairs
        System.out.println("Key-Value pairs in the map: " + map.entrySet());

        // Clear all pairs
        map.clear();
    }
}
```

```
Output:
Value for key 'Two': 2
Map contains key 'One': true
Key-Value pairs in the map: [Two=2, Three=3]
```

This example demonstrates the typical interactions with a Map. The use of a HashMap implementation is noteworthy for its constant-time complexity for the basic operations (put, get, remove).

Different Map implementations provide distinct behaviors and performance characteristics. The notable implementations of the Map interface include:

- HashMap<K, V>: Provides constant-time complexity for basic operations. It permits null values and one null key. The iteration order is not guaranteed to be consistent.

- LinkedHashMap<K, V>: Extends HashMap but maintains a doubly-linked list running through all its entries, providing a predictable iteration order (insertion-order).
- TreeMap<K, V>: Implements the SortedMap interface and ensures that the keys are in natural order or by a specified comparator. This implementation guarantees log-time cost for operations.
- Hashtable<K, V>: Similar to HashMap, but synchronized and does not allow null keys or values.

The choice of map implementation depends on the application requirements regarding ordering, performance, and null-handling. For scenarios necessitating natural or custom order of keys, TreeMap is suitable. For most general-purpose applications where order doesn't matter, HashMap is often preferred due to its efficiency.

Maps can be iterated using key sets, value collections, or entry sets. For instance, to iterate over keys and values:

```
Map<String, Integer> map = new HashMap<>();
map.put("One", 1);
map.put("Two", 2);
map.put("Three", 3);

for (Map.Entry<String, Integer> entry : map.entrySet()) {
    System.out.println("Key: " + entry.getKey() + ", Value: " + entry.getValue());
}
```

```
Output:
Key: One, Value: 1
Key: Two, Value: 2
Key: Three, Value: 3
```

The for-each construct, along with the entrySet() method, allows for a concise iteration of the map contents.

To further understand the internal mechanisms and interoperability of maps with other collection types, consider the 'java.util.stream' package. It provides stream capabilities that can be leveraged with maps for various transformations and operations. Here is an example of filtering a map:

```
Map<String, Integer> map = new HashMap<>();
map.put("One", 1);
map.put("Two", 2);
map.put("Three", 3);

Map<String, Integer> filteredMap = map.entrySet()
    .stream()
    .filter(entry -> entry.getValue() > 1)
    .collect(Collectors.toMap(Map.Entry::getKey, Map.Entry::getValue));
```

```
System.out.println("Filtered Map: " + filteredMap);
```

Output:
Filtered Map: {Two=2, Three=3}

Streams offer a powerful and expressive means of operating on maps, enabling complex operations succinctly and efficiently.

Finally, understanding Map implementations and their appropriate use cases simplifies the decision-making for data structure selection, ensuring optimal performance and correct behavior in any Java application.

2.10 NavigableMap and SortedMap Interfaces

The SortedMap and NavigableMap interfaces in the Java Collections Framework provide specialized functionality for maps, which are collections that map keys to values. Both interfaces extend the Map interface, adding methods that maintain the order of the keys.

The SortedMap interface is a subtype of the Map interface. It ensures that the entries are stored in ascending key order, which is either determined by the keys' natural ordering or by a Comparator provided at map creation time. The methods specific to SortedMap include:

- comparator(): Returns the comparator used to order the keys, or null if the map uses the natural ordering.
- subMap(K fromKey, K toKey): Returns a view of the part of the map whose keys range from fromKey, inclusive, to toKey, exclusive.
- headMap(K toKey): Returns a view of the part of the map whose keys are strictly less than toKey.
- tailMap(K fromKey): Returns a view of the part of the map whose keys are greater than or equal to fromKey.
- firstKey(): Returns the first (lowest) key currently in the map.
- lastKey(): Returns the last (highest) key currently in the map.

Example usage of a SortedMap:

```
import java.util.SortedMap;
import java.util.TreeMap;

public class SortedMapExample {
    public static void main(String[] args) {
        SortedMap<String, Integer> sortedMap = new TreeMap<>();

        sortedMap.put("apple", 10);
        sortedMap.put("banana", 20);
        sortedMap.put("cherry", 30);

        // Get the first and last keys
        System.out.println("First Key: " + sortedMap.firstKey());
        System.out.println("Last Key: " + sortedMap.lastKey());

        // Get the headMap, subMap and tailMap
        System.out.println("Head Map: " + sortedMap.headMap("banana"));
        System.out.println("Tail Map: " + sortedMap.tailMap("banana"));
        System.out.println("Sub Map: " + sortedMap.subMap("apple", "cherry"));
    }
}
```

The NavigableMap interface extends the functionalities provided by SortedMap with navigation methods that operate on the proximity of the mapping. This interface provides methods to find the closest matches for given search targets. The specific methods include:

- lowerEntry(K key): Returns a key-value mapping associated with the greatest key strictly less than the given key, or null if there is no such key.
- floorEntry(K key): Returns a key-value mapping associated with the greatest key less than or equal to the given key, or null if there is no such key.
- ceilingEntry(K key): Returns a key-value mapping associated with the least key greater than or equal to the given key, or null if there is no such key.
- higherEntry(K key): Returns a key-value mapping associated with the least key strictly greater than the given key, or null if there is no such key.
- pollFirstEntry(): Removes and returns a key-value mapping associated with the first entry in the map.
- pollLastEntry(): Removes and returns a key-value mapping associated with the last entry in the map.
- descendingMap(): Returns a reverse order view of the mappings contained in this map.

Example usage of a NavigableMap:

```
import java.util.NavigableMap;
import java.util.TreeMap;

public class NavigableMapExample {
    public static void main(String[] args) {
        NavigableMap<String, Integer> navigableMap = new TreeMap<>();

        navigableMap.put("apple", 10);
        navigableMap.put("banana", 20);
        navigableMap.put("cherry", 30);

        // Get entries based on proximity
        System.out.println("Lower Entry (banana): " + navigableMap.lowerEntry("
            banana"));
        System.out.println("Floor Entry (banana): " + navigableMap.floorEntry("
            banana"));
        System.out.println("Ceiling Entry (banana): " + navigableMap.ceilingEntry("
            banana"));
        System.out.println("Higher Entry (banana): " + navigableMap.higherEntry("
            banana"));

        // Poll entries
        System.out.println("Poll First Entry: " + navigableMap.pollFirstEntry());
        System.out.println("Poll Last Entry: " + navigableMap.pollLastEntry());

        // Get descending map
        System.out.println("Descending Map: " + navigableMap.descendingMap());
    }
}
```

A key advantage of using NavigableMap is the ability to navigate the map in various ways, enhancing flexibility in accessing and manipulating the stored key-value pairs. By providing bidirectional navigation capabilities, NavigableMap accommodates more complex search and retrieval requirements. The additional methods in NavigableMap offer granular control for entries relative to specified keys, making the interface suitable for applications requiring dynamic and context-sensitive access to data.

Overall, the use of SortedMap and NavigableMap interfaces offers significant benefits when a key ordering is required and when navigation capabilities around the key space are needed. These interfaces harness the power of natural and custom ordering, optimizing both storage and retrieval operations in maps. The additional functionalities facilitate a wide range of operations while maintaining logical consistency and performance efficiency.

2.11 Relationship Between Collection Interfaces

Understanding the relationships between various collection interfaces within the Java Collections Framework (JCF) is crucial for mastering their usage and implementation. This section provides a detailed analysis of these interfaces and their interconnections, setting the stage for deeper insight into their design and functionality.

The JCF is structured as a hierarchy of interfaces, with the Collection interface at its root. The Collection interface extends Iterable and serves as the foundational interface for most other collection types. The primary derived interfaces are List, Set, and Queue, each catering to different data storage and retrieval needs.

```
Iterable — Collection ┬ List
                      │
                      ├ Set — SortedSet — NavigableSet
                      │
                      ├ Queue — Deque
                      │
                      └ Map — SortedMap — NavigableMap
```

The List interface represents ordered collections that allow duplicate elements. Implementations of the List interface, such as ArrayList and LinkedList, maintain the order in which elements are inserted. They provide indexed access to elements, enabling precise control over element positions.

```
List<String> list = new ArrayList<>();
list.add("Element 1");
list.add("Element 2");
list.add("Element 3");
System.out.println(list.get(0)); // Output: Element 1
```

The Set interface defines a collection that forbids duplicate elements. Common implementations include HashSet, LinkedHashSet, and TreeSet. The primary purpose of a Set is to provide efficient membership checks and to ensure element uniqueness.

```
Set<String> set = new HashSet<>();
set.add("Element 1");
set.add("Element 2");
set.add("Element 1");
System.out.println(set.size()); // Output: 2
```

The Queue interface is designed for holding elements prior to processing, following a FIFO (First-In-First-Out) order. The PriorityQueue is a notable implementation that orders elements according to their natural ordering or by a provided comparator.

```
Queue<String> queue = new PriorityQueue<>();
queue.add("Element 1");
queue.add("Element 2");
System.out.println(queue.poll()); // Output: Element 1
```

Queue extends into Deque, a double-ended queue supporting element insertion and removal at both ends. ArrayDeque and LinkedList are standard implementations.

```
Deque<String> deque = new ArrayDeque<>();
deque.addFirst("Front");
deque.addLast("End");
System.out.println(deque.getFirst()); // Output: Front
System.out.println(deque.getLast()); // Output: End
```

The Map interface represents collections associating keys to values, with HashMap and TreeMap as common implementations. Maps are not collections in the strictest sense, but they are integral to JCF due to their key-value pair storage.

```
Map<String, Integer> map = new HashMap<>();
map.put("Key1", 1);
map.put("Key2", 2);
System.out.println(map.get("Key1")); // Output: 1
```

SortedSet and NavigableSet extend the Set interface to provide additional ordering semantics. SortedSet maintains elements in their natural order or by a specified comparator, with TreeSet being a primary implementation.

```
SortedSet<String> sortedSet = new TreeSet<>();
sortedSet.add("Element 2");
sortedSet.add("Element 1");
System.out.println(sortedSet.first()); // Output: Element 1
```

NavigableSet extends SortedSet, introducing methods for navigation, such as lower, floor, ceiling, and higher.

```
NavigableSet<String> navigableSet = new TreeSet<>();
navigableSet.add("Element 2");
navigableSet.add("Element 1");
System.out.println(navigableSet.lower("Element 2")); // Output: Element 1
```

The SortedMap interface extends Map to provide a map with sorted keys. TreeMap, implementing SortedMap, maintains key-value pairs in ascending key order or by a comparator.

```
SortedMap<String, Integer> sortedMap = new TreeMap<>();
sortedMap.put("Key2", 2);
sortedMap.put("Key1", 1);
System.out.println(sortedMap.firstKey()); // Output: Key1
```

Extending SortedMap, NavigableMap introduces navigation methods similar to NavigableSet.

```
NavigableMap<String, Integer> navigableMap = new TreeMap<>();
navigableMap.put("Key2", 2);
navigableMap.put("Key1", 1);
System.out.println(navigableMap.lowerKey("Key2")); // Output: Key1
```

These relationships between collection interfaces illustrate the hierarchical and functional interconnections within the Java Collections Framework. Comprehending these associations is foundational for leveraging Java collections effectively, ensuring optimal performance and correct usage across diverse programming scenarios.

2.12 Using Default Methods in Interfaces

Default methods were introduced in Java 8, adding significant flexibility to interface design within the Java Collections Framework. Default methods allow interfaces to possess concrete methods, with implementation code written directly in the interface. This advancement enables developers to extend interfaces with new methods without breaking the existing implementation of these interfaces.

Default Methods: A default method in an interface is defined using the default keyword followed by the method implementation. Consider the following example:

```
public interface MyInterface {
    default void defaultMethod() {
        System.out.println("This is a default method.");
    }
}
```

In this example, MyInterface contains a default method called defaultMethod. Any class implementing MyInterface inherits the defaultMethod without being required to provide its own implementation.

Importance in Collections Framework: Default methods play a crucial role within the Java Collections Framework. They allow for the enhancement and extension of collection interfaces without breaking backward compatibility. For instance, several methods have been added to the Collection interface since Java 8 using default methods.

An exemplary default method is forEach which is implemented in the Iterable interface:

```
default void forEach(Consumer<? super T> action) {
    Objects.requireNonNull(action);
    for (T t : this) {
        action.accept(t);
    }
}
```

The forEach method takes a Consumer functional interface as an argument and applies the given action to each element in the collection. This method provides a concrete implementation, expanding the utility of the Iterable interface.

Adding Default Methods: Default methods facilitate augmenting existing interfaces. Suppose a new method needs to be added to an interface, ensuring older implementations remain intact:

```
public interface EnhancedInterface extends Collection<String> {
    default void printAll() {
        for (String s : this) {
            System.out.println(s);
        }
    }
}
```

The EnhancedInterface interface extends Collection and introduces a new default method printAll which prints all elements in the collection. This improvement does not require any changes to existing classes implementing Collection.

Overriding Default Methods: Classes implementing interfaces with default methods can override these methods. This feature enables specific behavior adjustments as required:

```
public class MyClass implements MyInterface {
    @Override
    public void defaultMethod() {
        System.out.println("Overridden default method.");
    }
}
```

In this scenario, MyClass provides its own implementation of defaultMethod, thus overriding the default behavior defined in MyInterface.

Benefits and Use Cases: The main advantage of default methods lies in maintaining backward compatibility while evolving interfaces. Key use cases involve:

- Enhancing API Functionality: Default methods allow the addition of new functionalities to interfaces without disrupting existing implementations. A significant example is the Stream capability added to collections.
- Reducing Boilerplate Code: Common behaviors across multiple implementations can be abstracted to the interface itself, reducing redundancy.
- Upgradeable Interfaces: Interfaces can evolve over time, supporting a more iterative and flexible development approach.

Default methods, by virtue of their functionality, have enhanced the usability and extensibility of Java's collection interfaces. They represent a shift towards more declarative and concise coding practices within Java. Through strategic use of default methods, developers can craft robust, backward-compatible collection interfaces that are easier to maintain and extend over time.

Chapter 3

Working with Lists

This chapter delves into the concept and utilization of lists within the Java Collections Framework. It covers various implementations, including ArrayList, LinkedList, CopyOnWriteArrayList, Vector, and Stack. The chapter outlines common operations, performance considerations, and iteration techniques specific to lists. Additionally, it addresses advanced topics like working with sublists, sorting, searching, and creating custom list implementations, offering a comprehensive understanding of how to effectively work with lists in Java.

3.1 Introduction to Lists

In the Java Collections Framework (JCF), the List interface represents an ordered collection of elements. Unlike a Set, a List can contain duplicate elements. Furthermore, each element in a List has a unique index, enabling precise control over element access, insertion, and removal based on position within the list.

The List interface extends the Collection interface and introduces methods to manipulate elements based on their indices. Here are some of the crucial methods defined in the List interface:

```
// Element insertion
void add(int index, E element); // Adds an element at the specified position
boolean addAll(int index, Collection<? extends E> c); // Adds all elements from a
    collection at the specified position
```

```
// Element retrieval
E get(int index); // Retrieves the element at the specified position

// Element removal
E remove(int index); // Removes the element at the specified index

// Element search
int indexOf(Object o); // Returns the index of the first occurrence of the specified
      element
int lastIndexOf(Object o); // Returns the index of the last occurrence of the specified
      element

// Sub-list extraction
List<E> subList(int fromIndex, int toIndex); // Returns a view of the portion of the
      list between the specified indices
```

A fundamental feature of the List interface is its ability to maintain a steady sequence of elements, allowing insertion and removal at any given position. This property distinguishes List from other collection types such as Set and Queue, where order might not be preserved, or the insertion/removal capabilities are restricted.

To understand the utility and performance characteristics of List implementations, it is critical to examine the specific classes that implement this interface. The most prevalent implementations include:

- ArrayList
- LinkedList
- CopyOnWriteArrayList
- Vector
- Stack

ArrayList and LinkedList are the most commonly used implementations. The ArrayList is backed by a dynamically resizing array, while the LinkedList is a doubly linked list. Each of these implementations has its unique performance trade-offs.

As we traverse further into the specifics of each List implementation, the underlying data structures highlight the varying performance characteristics, particularly concerning time complexity for different operations:

- ArrayList
  - Retrieve an element: O(1)

  - Add an element to the end: O(1) amortized
  - Insert/remove an element: O(n)

- LinkedList
  - Retrieve an element: O(n)
  - Add an element to the end: O(1)
  - Insert/remove an element: O(1) when adding/removing at beginning or end

- CopyOnWriteArrayList
  - Retrieve an element: O(1)
  - Insert/remove an element: O(n)

- Vector
  - Retrieve an element: O(1)
  - Add an element to the end: O(1) amortized
  - Insert/remove an element: O(n)

- Stack
  - Push (add) an element: O(1)
  - Pop (remove) an element: O(1)

Arrays are the fundamental data structures driving the ArrayList and Vector classes, making them a preferable choice for scenarios requiring frequent random access or constant-time positional inserts and appends. However, their performance degrades when resizing operations or frequent element removals from arbitrary positions are necessary.

LinkedList, being inherently a doubly-linked list, excels in scenarios involving numerous insertions and removals, especially from the start or end of the list. However, it suffers from higher memory overhead due to storing additional pointer information and less efficient random access compared to array-based lists.

CopyOnWriteArrayList is a specific thread-safe variant designed for concurrent applications where iteration operations vastly outnumber mutation operations. This class creates a new copy of the array upon any write operations, thereby negligibly affecting read operations. The iterative tasks remain unaffected by concurrent modifications, ensuring thread safety without explicit synchronization mechanisms.

Vector is a legacy class from the early versions of Java. It provides synchronized methods for each List operation, ensuring thread-safety but resulting in relatively lower performance compared to non-synchronized collections in single-threaded applications.

Stack is a subclass of Vector that implements a last-in-first-out (LIFO) data structure, extending the functionality of vectors to support stack-specific operations.

The understanding of various List implementations assists in selecting the appropriate data structure tailored to specific use cases, offering optimal performance and efficiency. As we explore each of these implementations in subsequent sections, we will delve deeper into their peculiarities, usage contexts, and practical examples.

3.2 ArrayList: Dynamic Arrays

The ArrayList is a resizable array implementation in the Java Collections Framework. Unlike traditional arrays, which have a fixed size, the ArrayList can dynamically grow and shrink as elements are added or removed. This flexibility makes ArrayList a popular choice for scenarios where the number of elements is not known in advance, or where frequent insertions and deletions are expected.

The ArrayList class is part of the java.util package and implements the List interface, which means it provides all the methods specified by the List interface in addition to its own methods for managing dynamic arrays.

```
import java.util.ArrayList;

public class Main {
    public static void main(String[] args) {
        ArrayList<String> colors = new ArrayList<>();

        // Adding elements to the ArrayList
        colors.add("Red");
        colors.add("Green");
        colors.add("Blue");

        // Accessing elements
        String firstColor = colors.get(0);
        System.out.println("First Color: " + firstColor);

        // Removing elements
        colors.remove("Green");
```

```
    }
}
```

In the code above, an ArrayList<String> named colors is instantiated. Elements are added using the add() method. Elements can be retrieved using the get() method, where indexing starts at 0. The remove() method is used to remove elements from the ArrayList.

Capacity and Size

ArrayList maintains two parameters: size and capacity. The size is the number of elements currently stored in the list, while the capacity is the number of elements the list can hold before needing to resize.

By default, an ArrayList starts with a capacity of 10. When the number of elements exceeds the current capacity, a new array is allocated with a larger capacity (usually 1.5 times the current capacity), and the existing elements are copied into this new array.

```
import java.util.ArrayList;

public class Main {
    public static void main(String[] args) {
        ArrayList<Integer> numbers = new ArrayList<>(5);
        System.out.println("Initial Capacity: " + numbers.size());

        // Adding elements
        for (int i = 1; i <= 10; i++) {
            numbers.add(i);
        }

        System.out.println("Size after adding elements: " + numbers.size());
    }
}
```

In this example, the initial capacity of the ArrayList numbers is set to 5. As elements are added beyond the initial capacity, the internal array grows automatically. The size method is used to check the current number of elements in the ArrayList.

```
Initial Capacity: 0
Size after adding elements: 10
```

Manipulating the ArrayList

The following are some commonly used methods to manipulate ArrayList:

- add(E e): Appends the specified element to the end of the list.
- add(int index, E element): Inserts the specified element at the specified position in the list.

- clear(): Removes all of the elements from the list.
- contains(Object o): Returns true if the list contains the specified element.
- get(int index): Returns the element at the specified position in the list.
- indexOf(Object o): Returns the index of the first occurrence of the specified element, or -1 if the list does not contain the element.
- remove(int index): Removes the element at the specified position in the list.
- remove(Object o): Removes the first occurrence of the specified element from the list, if it is present.
- set(int index, E element): Replaces the element at the specified position in the list with the specified element.
- size(): Returns the number of elements in the list.
- toArray(): Returns an array containing all of the elements in the list in proper sequence.

```
import java.util.ArrayList;

public class Main {
    public static void main(String[] args) {
        ArrayList<String> fruits = new ArrayList<>();

        // Adding elements
        fruits.add("Apple");
        fruits.add("Banana");
        fruits.add("Cherry");

        // Inserting an element
        fruits.add(1, "Blueberry");

        // Accessing elements
        String fruit = fruits.get(2);
        System.out.println("Fruit at index 2: " + fruit);

        // Removing an element
        fruits.remove("Banana");

        // Checking for containment
        boolean hasApple = fruits.contains("Apple");
        System.out.println("Contains 'Apple': " + hasApple);

        // Replacing an element
        fruits.set(0, "Apricot");

        // Clearing the list
```

```
        fruits.clear();
    }
}
```

```
Fruit at index 2: Cherry
Contains 'Apple': true
```

Iterating Over ArrayLists

There are several ways to iterate over ArrayList elements. The most common methods include using a for-each loop, a for loop with an index, or an Iterator.

```
import java.util.ArrayList;
import java.util.Iterator;

public class Main {
    public static void main(String[] args) {
        ArrayList<String> countries = new ArrayList<>();
        countries.add("USA");
        countries.add("Canada");
        countries.add("Mexico");

        // Using for-each loop
        for (String country : countries) {
            System.out.println(country);
        }

        // Using for loop with index
        for (int i = 0; i < countries.size(); i++) {
            System.out.println(countries.get(i));
        }

        // Using Iterator
        Iterator<String> iterator = countries.iterator();
        while (iterator.hasNext()) {
            System.out.println(iterator.next());
        }
    }
}
```

```
USA
Canada
Mexico
USA
Canada
Mexico
USA
Canada
Mexico
```

Understanding the inner workings of ArrayList and its methods allows for efficient programming and optimal use of resources.

3.3 LinkedList: Doubly-Linked Lists

The LinkedList class in Java implements a doubly-linked list, which is a type of linked list where each node contains a reference to both the next and the previous node in the sequence. This structure allows for efficient insertion and deletion operations, particularly in cases where elements are frequently added or removed from the middle of the list. This section explores the fundamental properties and operations associated with LinkedList in the Java Collections Framework (JCF).

Characteristics of LinkedList:

A LinkedList has the following key characteristics:

- **Dynamic Sizing:** LinkedList does not require a predefined size; it can grow and shrink dynamically as elements are added or removed.
- **Node Structure:** Each element in the list is stored in a node, which contains:
  - **Data:** The actual value or object stored.
  - **Next Reference:** A reference to the next node in the list.
  - **Previous Reference:** A reference to the previous node in the list.
- **Traversal Efficiency:** Traversal from either end of the list is efficient due to the bidirectional links.
- **Usage in Deques:** LinkedList can be used as a double-ended queue (Deque).

Creating a LinkedList:

To create an instance of LinkedList, you can use the following code:

```
LinkedList<String> linkedList = new LinkedList<>();
```

Basic Operations:

Key operations on a LinkedList include adding, removing, and accessing elements. Below are examples demonstrating these operations:

1. Adding Elements:

You can add elements to a LinkedList using methods like add(), addFirst(), and addLast().

```
linkedList.add("First");
linkedList.add("Second");
linkedList.addFirst("Zeroth");
linkedList.addLast("Third");
```

The list is now: "Zeroth" -> "First" -> "Second" -> "Third".

2. Removing Elements:

Elements can be removed by value or by index using remove(), removeFirst(), and removeLast().

```
linkedList.remove("Second");
linkedList.removeFirst();
```

The list is now: "First" -> "Third".

3. Accessing Elements:

Elements in a LinkedList can be accessed via get().

```
String firstElement = linkedList.get(0); // "First"
String lastElement = linkedList.get(linkedList.size() - 1); // "Third"
```

Iterating Over a LinkedList:

There are multiple ways to iterate over a LinkedList, such as using for-loops, enhanced for-loops, or iterators:

```
// Using a for-loop
for (int i = 0; i < linkedList.size(); i++) {
    System.out.println(linkedList.get(i));
}

// Using an enhanced for-loop
for (String element : linkedList) {
    System.out.println(element);
}

// Using an iterator
Iterator<String> iterator = linkedList.iterator();
while (iterator.hasNext()) {
    System.out.println(iterator.next());
}
```

Performance Considerations:

While LinkedList provides efficient insertion and deletion operations, especially in the middle of the list, it incurs a cost for index-based access and search operations due to the lack of direct item indexing.

Big-O Performance Characteristics:

- Insertion/Deletion at ends: $O(1)$

- Insertion/Deletion at middle: $O(1)$ (given access to the node)
- Access/Search: $O(n)$

Use Cases:

LinkedList is particularly useful in scenarios where:

- Frequent insertions and deletions from the list are required.
- Elements need to be traversed sequentially rather than accessed by an index.
- The order of elements is important and must be maintained.

Example:

Here is an example illustrating a typical use case for LinkedList:

```
public class TaskManager {
    private LinkedList<String> tasks = new LinkedList<>();

    // Add a new task to the end of the list
    public void addTask(String task) {
        tasks.addLast(task);
    }

    // Mark the first task as completed and remove it
    public void completeTask() {
        if (!tasks.isEmpty()) {
            tasks.removeFirst();
        }
    }

    // Print all tasks
    public void printTasks() {
        for (String task : tasks) {
            System.out.println(task);
        }
    }

    public static void main(String[] args) {
        TaskManager tm = new TaskManager();
        tm.addTask("Write report");
        tm.addTask("Attend meeting");
        tm.addTask("Refactor code");
        tm.printTasks();
        tm.completeTask();
        tm.printTasks();
    }
}
```

```
Output:
Write report
Attend meeting
Refactor code
Attend meeting
Refactor code
```

This example showcases a simple task manager that uses LinkedList to manage tasks dynamically, demonstrating efficient task addition and completion operations.

Understanding the nuances of LinkedList is crucial for making informed decisions about its use in applications where dynamic data structures are beneficial.

3.4 CopyOnWriteArrayList: Thread-Safe Lists

CopyOnWriteArrayList is an implementation of the List interface that introduces a unique approach to achieving thread safety. Unlike other thread-safe collections, such as Vector or Collections.synchronizedList, the CopyOnWriteArrayList class makes use of a copy-on-write strategy for mutative operations. This strategy makes it particularly suitable for scenarios where read operations vastly outnumber write operations, ensuring that iterators are safe from ConcurrentModificationException without the need for explicit synchronization.

The primary mechanism of CopyOnWriteArrayList is evident from its name: when a write operation (add, set, or remove) is performed, the entire array is copied and updated. This allows read operations to proceed without requiring locks or synchronization, as they can continue operating on the old array instance while the new instance is being created. The performance cost of this copying process is offset by the significant increase in safety and simplicity for concurrent read operations.

```
import java.util.concurrent.CopyOnWriteArrayList;

public class CopyOnWriteArrayListExample {
    public static void main(String[] args) {
        CopyOnWriteArrayList<Integer> cowal = new CopyOnWriteArrayList<>();
        cowal.add(1);
        cowal.add(2);
        cowal.add(3);

        System.out.println("Original List: " + cowal);

        // Creating an iterator
        Iterator<Integer> iterator = cowal.iterator();

        // Modifying the list while iterating
        cowal.add(4);

        // Iterator will not see the new element
        while (iterator.hasNext()) {
```

```
            System.out.println(iterator.next());
        }
        System.out.println("Updated List: " + cowal);
    }
}
```

Output of the above program:

```
Original List: [1, 2, 3]
1
2
3
Updated List: [1, 2, 3, 4]
```

The example demonstrates how CopyOnWriteArrayList handles concurrent modifications. When a new element is added to the list after the iterator has been created, the iterator will not see the modification, ensuring no ConcurrentModificationException is thrown. This is because the iterator operates on a snapshot of the array's contents at the time it was created.

An important aspect of CopyOnWriteArrayList to understand is its memory usage and performance characteristics. Each mutative operation results in a new copy of the underlying array. Therefore, while read operations are highly efficient, write operations can be expensive. When using CopyOnWriteArrayList, it is crucial to consider the balance between read and write operations within your application.

Common operations on CopyOnWriteArrayList include add, remove, and set. The performance characteristics of these operations are as follows:

- add(E e): Adds the specified element to the end of the list. This operation has an O(n) time complexity due to copying the entire array.
- remove(Object o): Removes the first occurrence of the specified element from the list. Similar to add, this has an O(n) time complexity.
- set(int index, E element): Replaces the element at the specified position in the list with the specified element. This operation also exhibits O(n) time complexity.
- get(int index): Returns the element at the specified position in the list. This operation is O(1), providing constant time performance due to direct array access.

Understanding these complexities helps in making informed decisions about when to use CopyOnWriteArrayList. For example, an application requiring frequent read operations but infrequent write operations would benefit significantly from CopyOnWriteArrayList's design.

Algorithm 1: Concurrent operations using CopyOnWriteArrayList

---

Result: Perform concurrent-safe read and write operations using CopyOnWriteArrayList

Initialize CopyOnWriteArrayList instance: $cowal$;
for *each element* e *in the list* **do**
  $cowal.add(e)$;
end
$iterator \leftarrow cowal.iterator()$;
while $iterator.hasNext()$ **do**
  $e \leftarrow iterator.next()$; print e;
end
Perform a write operation: $cowal.add(newElement)$;
while $modifiedIterator.hasNext()$ **do**
  $e \leftarrow modifiedIterator.next()$; print e;
end

Further considerations include the handling of array expansion. On each write operation, the existing array's contents are copied to a new array of the same size. The implication of this strategy can be mitigated by appropriately sizing the CopyOnWriteArrayList at instantiation. The constructor CopyOnWriteArrayList(int initialCapacity) allows for specifying the initial capacity, thus potentially improving efficiency.

The CopyOnWriteArrayList class leverages the conventional copying mechanism from the Arrays utility class, which employs native methods for array copying to ensure optimal performance. However, developers should exercise caution in memory-constrained environments or applications with high write frequencies due to the inherent overhead of array copying.

To summarize, the CopyOnWriteArrayList provides a robust solution for achieving high levels of thread safety in concurrent applications, especially where read operations are predominant. By understanding its internal mechanisms, performance implications, and appropriate usage scenarios, developers can effectively leverage CopyOnWriteArrayList to build efficient and safe multithreaded applications.

3.5 Vector: Legacy Resizable Array

The Vector class is part of the Java Collections Framework and represents a resizable array. It implements the List interface and features synchronized methods making it thread-safe. Since Vector is part of the legacy collections, it is often overshadowed by more modern constructs like ArrayList. Nonetheless, understanding Vector is crucial for maintaining legacy code and recognizing scenarios where thread-safe list implementations are needed.

The declaration of a Vector is straightforward. Here's how you can initialize a Vector:

```
Vector<Integer> vector = new Vector<>();
Vector<String> vectorWithCapacity = new Vector<>(20);
```

In the above examples, vector is initialized with the default capacity (initially 10, which grows as elements are added), while vectorWithCapacity is initialized with a specified capacity of 20.

Vectors dynamically resize themselves when the number of elements exceeds its current capacity. They double their capacity to accommodate additional elements, further ensuring that performance degradation is mitigated.

Synchronized Methods

One important aspect of Vector is that its methods are synchronized. This is beneficial in scenarios where thread safety is a requirement. Let's look at how synchronization impacts the methods by examining the source code of common methods:

```
public synchronized boolean add(E e) {
    modCount++;
    ensureCapacityHelper(elementCount + 1);
    elementData[elementCount++] = e;
    return true;
}

public synchronized E get(int index) {
    if (index >= elementCount)
        throw new ArrayIndexOutOfBoundsException(index);
    return (E) elementData[index];
}

public synchronized int size() {
    return elementCount;
}
```

In the code listings above, the add, get, and size methods are prepended with the keyword synchronized. This guarantees that only one thread can execute these methods at a time for a given Vector instance, preventing concurrent modification.

Advantages and Disadvantages

Vectors offer several advantages:

- **Thread-Safety**: Due to synchronized methods, they can be used safely in multi-threaded environments.
- **Dynamic Sizing**: The automatic resizing helps avoid manual memory management.

However, Vector also comes with disadvantages:

- **Performance Overhead**: The synchronization mechanism adds performance overhead, making them slower compared to non-synchronized collections such as ArrayList.
- **Legacy Design**: Being part of the legacy collection, it lacks some of the newer, more efficient methods and idioms seen in ArrayList and others.

Usage Example

Below is a practical example demonstrating the usage of a Vector in a thread-safe manner:

```
public class VectorExample {
    public static void main(String[] args) {
        Vector<Integer> vector = new Vector<>();

        // Adding elements
        vector.add(1);
        vector.add(2);
        vector.add(3);

        // Accessing elements
        System.out.println("First element: " + vector.get(0));
        System.out.println("Second element: " + vector.get(1));

        // Iterating using for-each loop
        for (Integer num : vector) {
            System.out.println("Number: " + num);
        }

        // Removing an element
        vector.remove((Integer) 2);
        System.out.println("After removal: " + vector);
    }
}
```

The output of the above program would be:

```
First element: 1
Second element: 2
Number: 1
Number: 2
Number: 3
After removal: [1, 3]
```

Given its synchronized nature, Vector ensures that all the contained methods are thread-safe by default. This characteristic makes it a useful tool in multi-threaded programming but also introduces a performance overhead compared to non-synchronized alternatives.

Understanding both the strengths and limitations of Vector facilitates its effective application in scenarios that demand synchronized access while maintaining compatibility with legacy systems.

3.6 Stack: Last-In-First-Out Lists

A Stack is a collection designed to operate in a Last-In-First-Out (LIFO) manner. The element added most recently to a stack will be the first one to be removed, akin to a stack of plates where you can only take the top plate off the stack. In Java, the Stack class extends Vector with five operations that allow a vector to be treated as a stack.

The basic operations are:

- push(E item): Adds an item to the top of the stack.
- pop(): Removes the item at the top of the stack and returns it.
- peek(): Returns the item at the top of the stack without removing it.
- isEmpty(): Checks if the stack is empty.
- search(Object o): Returns the 1-based position from the top of the stack where the object is located.

Creating and Using a Stack

To create a stack, you instantiate the Stack class:

```
import java.util.Stack;

public class StackExample {
    public static void main(String[] args) {
```

```
        Stack<Integer> stack = new Stack<>();
        stack.push(10); // Adding elements
        stack.push(20);
        stack.push(30);

        System.out.println("Top element is: " + stack.peek()); // Fetch the top element
        System.out.println("Stack size is: " + stack.size());

        while (!stack.isEmpty()) {
            System.out.println("Popped element: " + stack.pop());
        }
    }
}
```

```
Top element is: 30
Stack size is: 3
Popped element: 30
Popped element: 20
Popped element: 10
```

Stack provides straightforward access methods for stack operations. When push() is called, the item is added to the collection. The last added item will be the first to be accessed when pop() is invoked.

Use Cases for Stacks

Stacks are particularly useful for certain types of problems, such as:

- *Expression Evaluation and Syntax Parsing*: Stacks are used for converting infix expressions to postfix or prefix and for evaluating postfix/prefix expressions.
- *Backtracking Algorithms*: When the algorithm needs to backtrack to a previous state, stacks store the states to be backtracked.
- *Undo Mechanisms in Applications*: For software that provides an undo feature, operations are pushed onto a stack and popped when the user wishes to revert changes.

Stack Internals and Performance

The Stack class itself relies on the Vector class, which means its internal storage is a dynamically resizable array. This offers the benefit of random access with an average time complexity of $O(1)$ for push() and pop() operations under ideal circumstances. However, like any array-backed structure, there is a trade-off during resize operations where the internal array might need to be copied to a larger array if it runs out of capacity.

Thread Safety Considerations

The Stack class inherits thread safety from the Vector class. Methods of Vector are synchronized, which means that only one thread can call them at a time. This can be beneficial in multi-threaded programs but can lead to decreased performance due to contention. In single-threaded scenarios, other implementations like ArrayDeque might be more efficient.

Comparing Stack with Deque Implementations

For most new applications, the Deque interface should be preferred over Stack since Deque provides a more complete and consistent set of LIFO stack and FIFO queue operations. The Deque interface adds methods for both stack and queue operations, allowing more flexibility.

The ArrayDeque class is a highly efficient implementation of the Deque interface. Below is a comparison using ArrayDeque:

```
import java.util.ArrayDeque;

public class ArrayDequeExample {
    public static void main(String[] args) {
        ArrayDeque<Integer> stack = new ArrayDeque<>();
        stack.push(10); // Adding elements
        stack.push(20);
        stack.push(30);

        System.out.println("Top element is: " + stack.peek()); // Fetch the top element
        System.out.println("Stack size is: " + stack.size());

        while (!stack.isEmpty()) {
            System.out.println("Popped element: " + stack.pop());
        }
    }
}
```

```
Top element is: 30
Stack size is: 3
Popped element: 30
Popped element: 20
Popped element: 10
```

Both Stack and ArrayDeque follow LIFO, but ArrayDeque is more performant in non-threaded contexts due to the absence of synchronization overhead.

Understanding these distinctions and employing the appropriate collection type based on specific requirements is essential for optimizing both performance and readability of Java applications.

3.7 Common List Operations

Lists in the Java Collections Framework provide a flexible and powerful way to store ordered collections of elements. Understanding the common operations available on lists is crucial for leveraging their full potential. This section covers foundational operations, including adding, removing, and accessing elements, alongside more advanced operations like searching and sorting.

Adding Elements

Adding elements can be performed in several ways depending on the specific requirements of the operation. The primary method to add elements is the add() method. For example:

```
// Adding elements to an ArrayList
List<String> list = new ArrayList<>();
list.add("Element1");
list.add("Element2");
```

Elements can also be added at specific positions using the overloaded add() method that takes an index:

```
// Adding an element at a specific position
list.add(1, "Element3"); // Inserts "Element3" at index 1
```

Removing Elements

Elements can be removed from lists using several methods. The remove() method removes elements either by index or by object reference. For example:

```
// Removing elements by index
list.remove(1); // Removes the element at index 1

// Removing elements by value
list.remove("Element1"); // Removes the first occurrence of "Element1"
```

To remove all elements from a list, use the clear() method:

```
// Clearing the list
list.clear(); // Removes all elements from the list
```

Accessing Elements

Elements in a list can be accessed using the get() method by specifying the index of the desired element:

```
// Accessing elements
String element = list.get(0); // Retrieves the element at index 0
```

Additionally, the set() method can be used to update elements at a specific index:

```
// Setting elements
list.set(0, "NewElement1"); // Replaces the element at index 0 with "NewElement1"
```

Checking for Elements

Lists provide methods to check for the presence of elements. The contains() method checks if the list contains a specific element:

```
// Checking for element presence
boolean containsElement = list.contains("Element1"); // Returns true if "Element1" is
    in the list
```

The indexOf() method returns the index of the first occurrence of an element, or -1 if the element is not found:

```
// Finding the index of an element
int index = list.indexOf("Element2"); // Returns the index of "Element2" or -1 if not
    found
```

Size of the List

The number of elements in a list can be obtained using the size() method:

```
// Getting the size of the list
int size = list.size(); // Returns the number of elements in the list
```

Iterating Over Lists

Iterating over lists can be done in various ways. The for-each loop provides a convenient way to iterate over all elements:

```
// Iterating using for-each loop
for (String element : list) {
    System.out.println(element);
}
```

The traditional for loop can also be used, particularly when the index of elements is needed:

```
// Iterating using traditional for loop
for (int i = 0; i < list.size(); i++) {
    System.out.println(list.get(i));
}
```

For more control, an Iterator can be used, which allows element removal during iteration:

```
// Iterating using Iterator
Iterator<String> iterator = list.iterator();
```

```
while (iterator.hasNext()) {
    String element = iterator.next();
    if (element.equals("Element2")) {
        iterator.remove(); // Removes "Element2" during iteration
    }
}
```

Sublist Operations

Creating sublists provides a way to manipulate specific segments of a list. The subList() method returns a view of the specified range within the list:

```
// Creating a sublist
List<String> sublist = list.subList(1, 3); // Creates a sublist from index 1 to 3 (
    exclusive)
```

Modifications to the sublist are reflected in the original list, and vice versa.

These common list operations provide the foundational tools needed to effectively manipulate lists in various scenarios within the Java Collections Framework. Utilizing these operations allows for efficient and flexible management of ordered collections of elements.

3.8 Performance Considerations for Lists

Understanding the performance characteristics of different list implementations within the Java Collections Framework is crucial for choosing the right data structure based on specific requirements. We will examine the performance implications of ArrayList, LinkedList, CopyOnWriteArrayList, Vector, and Stack.

ArrayList and Vector are both based on dynamic arrays, while LinkedList is a doubly-linked list. CopyOnWriteArrayList is a thread-safe variant, and Stack is a subclass of Vector implementing the Last-In-First-Out (LIFO) principle.

- ArrayList

ArrayList provides constant-time performance, $O(1)$, for positional access and updates. However, operations that involve shifting elements, such as add(int index, E element) and remove(int index), require linear time, $O(n)$, in the worst case.

```
ArrayList<Integer> arrayList = new ArrayList<>();
```

```
arrayList.add(0); // O(1)
arrayList.add(1);
arrayList.add(1, 2); // O(n) due to shifting elements
System.out.println(arrayList);
```

Output:
[0, 2, 1]

The cost of resizing the backing array during the addition of elements is typically amortized, resulting in $O(1)$ average time complexity for the add(E e) operation. This is because the array's capacity is usually increased by a factor of 1.5 when it needs to grow, reducing the frequency of resizes.

- Vector

Vector shares similar characteristics to ArrayList, offering $O(1)$ for positional access and updates, and $O(n)$ for inserting or removing elements at a specific position. One significant difference is that Vector methods are synchronized, making them thread-safe but potentially slower due to locking overhead.

```
Vector<Integer> vector = new Vector<>();
vector.add(1); // O(1)
vector.add(2, 3); // O(n) with synchronization overhead
System.out.println(vector);
```

Output:
[1, 3]

- LinkedList

LinkedList offers $O(1)$ time for insertions and deletions if the position is known (e.g., head or tail). However, accessing elements by index requires linear time, $O(n)$, due to the need to traverse the list.

```
LinkedList<Integer> linkedList = new LinkedList<>();
linkedList.add(1); // O(1) insertion at the end
linkedList.addFirst(0); // O(1) insertion at the beginning
System.out.println(linkedList.get(1)); // O(n) access by index
```

Output:
1

The doubly-linked nature of LinkedList can lead to higher memory usage compared to ArrayList, as each element requires additional storage for the reference links to the next and previous nodes.

- CopyOnWriteArrayList

CopyOnWriteArrayList maintains a different performance profile, characterized by an $O(n)$ complexity for write operations (add, set, remove), as each modification operation creates a new copy of the underlying array. This ensures that read operations can be performed in constant time, $O(1)$, without any synchronization overhead.

```
CopyOnWriteArrayList<Integer> cowList = new CopyOnWriteArrayList<>();
cowList.add(1); // O(n) due to copying
cowList.add(2);
Integer element = cowList.get(1); // O(1) access
System.out.println(element);
```

Output:
2

CopyOnWriteArrayList is advantageous in scenarios where read operations vastly outnumber write operations.

- Stack

Stack extends Vector and augments it with LIFO operations such as push and pop. The underlying performance characteristics regarding positional access and synchronization are inherited from Vector, maintaining $O(1)$ for top element access and operations, and $O(n)$ for arbitrary insertions or deletions.

```
Stack<Integer> stack = new Stack<>();
stack.push(1); // O(1) push
stack.push(2);
System.out.println(stack.pop()); // O(1) pop
```

Output:
2

In summary, selecting an appropriate list implementation depends on understanding the trade-offs between access times, insertion and deletion times, memory overhead, and synchronization. Recognizing these performance implications ensures efficient utilization of list structures in varied application scenarios.

3.9 Iterating Over Lists

Iterating over a list is a fundamental operation in Java programming. It enables developers to traverse the list elements for various purposes such as searching, modifying, or processing each element. Understanding different iteration techniques is crucial for writing efficient and readable code. This section explores multiple methods for iterating over lists in Java, examining their respective advantages and disadvantages.

1. The for-each loop

The for-each loop provides a concise and readable way to iterate over all elements in a list. It is part of Java's enhanced for loop syntax, introduced in Java 5:

```
List<String> list = Arrays.asList("apple", "banana", "cherry");
for (String fruit : list) {
    System.out.println(fruit);
}
```

Output:

```
apple
banana
cherry
```

This approach is suitable for scenarios where modifications to the list or specific index access are not needed. It simplifies the iteration process and reduces the risk of errors.

2. The classic for loop

In some cases, particularly when index access is required, the classic for loop is more appropriate. It offers full control over the iteration process:

```
List<String> list = Arrays.asList("apple", "banana", "cherry");
for (int i = 0; i < list.size(); i++) {
    System.out.println(list.get(i));
}
```

Output:

```
apple
banana
cherry
```

Although more verbose than the for-each loop, the classic for loop is essential when the iteration process depends on the index or when elements need to be accessed or modified based on their position.

3. The Iterator interface

The Iterator interface provides an alternative way to traverse lists, offering methods for safe element removal during iteration:

```
List<String> list = Arrays.asList("apple", "banana", "cherry");
Iterator<String> iterator = list.iterator();
while (iterator.hasNext()) {
    String fruit = iterator.next();
    System.out.println(fruit);
}
```

Output:

```
apple
banana
cherry
```

The Iterator interface includes three primary methods: hasNext(), next(), and remove(). The remove() method allows for safe removal of elements without risking a ConcurrentModificationException, which can occur when modifying the list directly during iteration with a for-each or classic for loop:

```
Iterator<String> iterator = list.iterator();
while (iterator.hasNext()) {
    String fruit = iterator.next();
    if (fruit.equals("banana")) {
        iterator.remove();
    }
}
```

Output:

```
apple
cherry
```

4. The ListIterator interface

The ListIterator interface extends Iterator with additional capabilities such as bidirectional traversal and index manipulation:

```
List<String> list = Arrays.asList("apple", "banana", "cherry");
ListIterator<String> listIterator = list.listIterator();
while (listIterator.hasNext()) {
    String fruit = listIterator.next();
    System.out.println(fruit);
    if (fruit.equals("banana")) {
        listIterator.add("date");
    }
}
```

Output:

```
apple
banana
date
cherry
```

Using ListIterator, one can also traverse the list in reverse:

```
while (listIterator.hasPrevious()) {
    String fruit = listIterator.previous();
    System.out.println(fruit);
}
```

Output:

cherry
date
banana
apple ListIterator is particularly useful when bidirectional traversal or complex modifications are needed during iteration.

5. The Stream API

Introduced in Java 8, the Stream API provides a powerful and expressive way to iterate over lists. The forEach() method is commonly used with a lambda expression:

```
list.stream().forEach(fruit -> System.out.println(fruit));
```

Output:

apple
banana
cherry The Stream API offers various operations like filter(), map(), and collect(), enabling functional-style processing:

```
list.stream()
    .filter(fruit -> fruit.startsWith("b"))
    .forEach(fruit -> System.out.println(fruit));
```

Output:

banana Streams are ideal for complex data processing tasks, offering performance benefits such as parallel execution.

Applying the appropriate iteration method can significantly impact code readability, performance, and maintainability. Understanding the advantages and limitations of each technique ensures that the optimal approach is selected for a given context.

3.10 Working with SubLists

Creating and manipulating sublists is a powerful feature provided by the Java Collections Framework. A subList is a view of a portion of a list, which means that changes made to the sublist are reflected in the original list and vice versa. This section provides a detailed examination of the creation, usage, and subtleties associated with subList operations in Java.

To create a sublist, the subList method is used. This method returns a view of the portion of the list between the specified *fromIndex*, inclusive, and *toIndex*, exclusive.

```
List<Integer> originalList = Arrays.asList(1, 2, 3, 4, 5, 6, 7, 8, 9, 10);
```

```
List<Integer> sublist = originalList.subList(3, 7);
System.out.println(sublist);
```

```
[4, 5, 6, 7]
```

In the example above, the subList method creates a sublist that contains the elements from index 3 to index 6 of originalList. The element at index 7 is not included in the sublist.

The sublist is backed by the original list. If any structural modifications (additions, deletions) are made to the original list or the sublist, these changes will be reflected in both views.

```
sublist.set(1, 999); // Change the value at index 1 within the sublist
System.out.println(sublist); // [4, 999, 6, 7]
System.out.println(originalList); // [1, 2, 3, 4, 999, 6, 7, 8, 9, 10]

originalList.set(5, 888); // Change the value at index 5 within the original list
System.out.println(sublist); // [4, 999, 888, 7]
System.out.println(originalList); // [1, 2, 3, 4, 999, 888, 7, 8, 9, 10]
```

Views are dynamic; they reflect the current state of the underlying list. However, structural modifications to the original list that affect the size of the sublist might lead to undefined behavior.

```
originalList.add(2, 999); // Inserts a new element at position 2
// This will affect the indices of the sublist, making further access unsafe
try {
    System.out.println(sublist.get(0)); // This may throw an
          IndexOutOfBoundsException
} catch (Exception e) {
    System.out.println(e); // Will likely print an exception message
}
```

To avoid such issues, refrain from making structural changes to the original list while working with a sublist, unless it is necessary and managed carefully. Alternatively, create a separate copy of the sublist.

```
List<Integer> copiedSublist = new ArrayList<>(sublist);
originalList.add(2, 999);
System.out.println(copiedSublist); // [4, 999, 888, 7]
```

When using subList, it is important to be aware of the potential for ConcurrentModificationException. Operations on the list that structurally modify it while using a sublist can lead to this exception.

```
try {
    for(Integer num : sublist) {
        if(num == 888) {
            originalList.remove(num); // This will cause a
                  ConcurrentModificationException
        }
    }
} catch (ConcurrentModificationException e) {
```

```
    System.out.println("Concurrent modification detected: " + e.getMessage());
}
```

For scenarios where thread safety is a priority, using CopyOnWriteArrayList may be beneficial. It avoids ConcurrentModificationException by making a fresh copy of the list on every modification, though this comes with performance trade-offs.

Lastly, it's worth noting that subList is best utilized for read-only operations or localized modifications where you can guarantee the structure of the original list will not change outside the scope of your sublist operations. Proper usage and understanding of subList significantly enhance development efficiency by leveraging the Java Collections Framework's power.

3.11 Sorting and Searching in Lists

Sorting and searching are fundamental operations in computer science, especially when dealing with collections of data. Within the Java Collections Framework, lists offer robust capabilities for both sorting and searching, either through natural ordering or via custom comparators. Understanding these operations is crucial for efficient data manipulation.

Sorting Lists

In Java, the Collections utility class provides several methods for sorting lists. The most commonly used method is Collections.sort(List<T> list), which sorts the list into ascending order according to the natural ordering of its elements. For example:

```
List<Integer> numbers = new ArrayList<>();
numbers.add(5);
numbers.add(3);
numbers.add(1);
numbers.add(4);
numbers.add(2);
Collections.sort(numbers);
```

The above code sorts the list of integers in ascending order. The Collections.sort method is a generic method that can sort any list where the elements implement the Comparable interface.

For custom sorting, the Collections.sort(List<T> list, Comparator<? super T> c) method can be utilized. This method allows the developer to define a Comparator for custom sorting logic. For instance, to sort a list of strings by their length:

```
List<String> words = new ArrayList<>();
words.add("apple");
words.add("banana");
words.add("cherry");
words.add("date");
Collections.sort(words, new Comparator<String>() {
    @Override
    public int compare(String s1, String s2) {
        return Integer.compare(s1.length(), s2.length());
    }
});
```

Java 8 introduced the List.sort method, which directly sorts the list in place, either using natural ordering or a custom comparator:

```
words.sort((s1, s2) -> Integer.compare(s1.length(), s2.length()));
```

This lambda expression provides a concise way to implement the Comparator interface, facilitating the definition of sorting logic inline.

Searching Lists

The Java Collections Framework provides efficient mechanisms for searching within lists. The Collections.binarySearch method is one such mechanism that performs a binary search on the specified list. It is important to note that the list must be sorted prior to invoking binarySearch:

```
int index = Collections.binarySearch(numbers, 3);
System.out.println("Index of 3: " + index);
```

The binarySearch method returns the index of the specified element if it is found in the list. If the element is not found, it returns -1.

For custom object types that do not implement the Comparable interface, or when different criteria are needed for searching, a custom Comparator can be passed to binarySearch:

```
class Product {
    String name;
    double price;

    Product(String name, double price) {
        this.name = name;
        this.price = price;
    }
}

List<Product> products = new ArrayList<>();
products.add(new Product("Laptop", 999.99));
products.add(new Product("Smartphone", 699.99));
products.add(new Product("Tablet", 299.99));
```

```
Collections.sort(products, Comparator.comparing(product -> product.price));

int index = Collections.binarySearch(products, new Product("", 699.99), Comparator.
    comparing(product -> product.price));
System.out.println("Index of product with price 699.99: " + index);
```

This example demonstrates sorting a list of Product objects based on their price and then using the same Comparator for binary search.

Performance Considerations

The Collections.sort method is highly optimized and typically implemented using a modified mergesort algorithm, providing a time complexity of $O(n \log n)$. Binary search, on the other hand, operates with a time complexity of $O(\log n)$, making it efficient for large datasets. However, these operations require the list to be properly managed with respect to sorting prior to performing searches to ensure correctness and efficiency.

Doubling down on efficiency means leveraging these operations while understanding their time complexity guarantees and how they interplay with data structures in memory. The choice of data structure for your list (e.g., ArrayList vs. LinkedList) can significantly impact the performance of sorting and searching operations due to differences in their underlying implementations.

Finally, utilizing parallel stream operations introduced in Java 8 can also enhance performance, especially for large datasets:

```
numbers.parallelStream().sorted().collect(Collectors.toList());
```

Parallel streams make use of the Fork/Join framework to implement parallelism, potentially reducing sorting time on multi-core systems. However, it is important to ensure that the overhead of parallelism does not outweigh its benefits for smaller datasets.

The integration of these sorting and searching techniques solidifies their utility in handling list-based data structures in Java, providing robust, flexible, and efficient means to manage and utilize collections effectively.

3.12 Custom List Implementations

Developing custom list implementations in Java allows for tailoring specific behaviors and performance characteristics that the standard library lists may not provide. This approach can be indispensable when the existing ArrayList, LinkedList, or other list implementations do not meet the unique requirements of an application.

To create a custom list, the java.util.List interface must be implemented. This interface contains numerous methods, many of which need to be overridden for the custom list to function correctly. Below are the most crucial methods specified by the List interface:

```
public interface List<E> extends Collection<E> {
    void add(int index, E element);
    boolean add(E e);
    E get(int index);
    E set(int index, E element);
    E remove(int index);
    boolean remove(Object o);
    int size();
    boolean isEmpty();
    Iterator<E> iterator();
    ListIterator<E> listIterator();
    void clear();
    // Other methods omitted for brevity
}
```

A skeletal implementation, ensuring compliance with the contract required by the List interface, can be approached by extending AbstractList. This class provides basic implementations for some methods, reducing the amount of boilerplate code required.

```
public class CustomList<E> extends AbstractList<E> {
    private final List<E> internalList;

    public CustomList() {
        this.internalList = new ArrayList<>();
    }

    @Override
    public E get(int index) {
        return internalList.get(index);
    }

    @Override
    public int size() {
        return internalList.size();
    }

    @Override
    public E set(int index, E element) {
        return internalList.set(index, element);
    }

    @Override
    public void add(int index, E element) {
        internalList.add(index, element);
    }

    @Override
    public E remove(int index) {
```

```
        return internalList.remove(index);
    }
}
```

The above example employs a delegation pattern, where the custom list operations are delegated to an ArrayList internally. This strategy simplifies development but may not be suitable for all scenarios, particularly if custom behaviors are needed.

An important consideration while implementing a custom list is ensuring the appropriate handling of edge cases and maintaining adherence to the contracts defined by the List interface. For instance, the addAll(Collection<? extends E> c) method should throw a NullPointerException if the provided collection is null. Performance implications should also be addressed, especially when implementing methods like add and remove.

Below is an implementation of a custom list that implements a simple fixed-size list, where the size of the list is determined at initialization, and no elements can be added beyond this fixed size.

```
public class FixedSizeList<E> extends AbstractList<E> {
    private final Object[] elements;
    private int size = 0;

    public FixedSizeList(int capacity) {
        if (capacity < 0) {
            throw new IllegalArgumentException("Capacity cannot be negative");
        }
        this.elements = new Object[capacity];
    }

    @Override
    public E get(int index) {
        checkIndex(index);
        return (E) elements[index];
    }

    @Override
    public int size() {
        return size;
    }

    @Override
    public void add(int index, E element) {
        if (size >= elements.length) {
            throw new IllegalStateException("List is full");
        }
        if (index > size || index < 0) {
            throw new IndexOutOfBoundsException("Index: " + index + ", Size: " +
                size);
        }
        System.arraycopy(elements, index, elements, index + 1, size - index);
        elements[index] = element;
        size++;
    }
```

```
    @Override
    public E set(int index, E element) {
        checkIndex(index);
        E oldElement = (E) elements[index];
        elements[index] = element;
        return oldElement;
    }

    @Override
    public E remove(int index) {
        checkIndex(index);
        E oldElement = (E) elements[index];
        int numMoved = size - index - 1;
        if (numMoved > 0) {
            System.arraycopy(elements, index + 1, elements, index, numMoved);
        }
        elements[--size] = null; // Clear to let GC do its work
        return oldElement;
    }

    private void checkIndex(int index) {
        if (index >= size || index < 0) {
            throw new IndexOutOfBoundsException("Index: " + index + ", Size: " +
                 size);
        }
    }
}
```

This class demonstrates a simple but effective custom list constrained by a maximum size. The element storage utilizes an array, and methods like add, set, get, and remove are implemented directly, given the deterministic capacity.

Care must be taken to ensure synchronization if the custom list is intended to be used in a multi-threaded environment. Using the Collections.synchronizedList() wrapper can simplify this task, although performance considerations should be examined in detail to ensure suitability for the specific use case.

```
List<E> synchronizedCustomList = Collections.synchronizedList(new FixedSizeList
    <>(10));
```

Developing custom list implementations allows for a high degree of flexibility in how list data structures are managed and manipulated, ultimately leading to better performance and usability in specific applications. Properly understanding and implementing the List interface contract is fundamental to ensuring custom lists function as expected within the broader Java Collections Framework.

Chapter 4

Using Sets for Unique Collections

This chapter explores the use of sets within the Java Collections Framework, focusing on ensuring unique collections. It introduces key implementations like HashSet, LinkedHashSet, TreeSet, ConcurrentSkipListSet, and EnumSet. The chapter details common operations, performance considerations, and iteration techniques tailored to sets. Additionally, it covers set operations such as union, intersection, and difference, and discusses scenarios for custom set implementations, aiming to provide a thorough understanding of working with sets in Java.

4.1 Introduction to Sets

A set is a collection data type in Java Collections Framework used to store unique elements. Unlike lists which allow duplicate entries, sets by definition prevent the storage of duplicate elements. This property makes sets ideal for scenarios where uniqueness is a requirement, such as in maintaining a collection of unique user IDs, tracking visited URLs in a web crawler, or ensuring no duplicate values in sequences.

Key Characteristics of Sets:

- **Uniqueness:** The primary characteristic of a set is that it does not allow duplicate elements. The internal storage mechanism of a set, whether it be a hash table, a linked list, or a tree, always ensures that each element is unique.

- **No Particular Order:** Sets do not guarantee to maintain the elements in a specific order. While some implementations like HashSet do not maintain any order, others like LinkedHashSet and TreeSet provide predictable orderings.

- **No Index-Based Access:** Elements in a set cannot be accessed via an index. Unlike lists, you cannot retrieve items by their position. Instead, you can iterate over the set or use methods to check for the presence of elements.

Common Set Implementations:

Several classes in the java.util package implement the Set interface. Here are the primary ones:

- HashSet
- LinkedHashSet
- TreeSet
- ConcurrentSkipListSet
- EnumSet

Each implementation has its own unique properties and performance characteristics.

```
Set<String> hashSet = new HashSet<>();
hashSet.add("apple");
hashSet.add("banana");
hashSet.add("cherry");
hashSet.add("apple"); // Duplicate element

for (String item : hashSet) {
    System.out.println(item);
}
```

```
Possible output:
apple
banana
cherry
```

In the example above, the HashSet will automatically disregard the second '"apple"' element because it is a duplicate. The HashSet does not maintain any order of elements.

Internal Mechanism for Uniqueness:

Sets rely on the hashCode() and equals() methods to ensure uniqueness. When an object is added to a set, the set computes the hash code of the object and stores it accordingly. If an object with the same hash code already exists, the equals() method is used to determine if the objects are indeed the same.

Consider a custom object:

```
public class Person {
    private String name;
    private int id;

    public Person(String name, int id) {
        this.name = name;
        this.id = id;
    }

    @Override
    public int hashCode() {
        return id;
    }

    @Override
    public boolean equals(Object obj) {
        if (this == obj) return true;
        if (obj == null || getClass() != obj.getClass()) return false;
        Person person = (Person) obj;
        return id == person.id;
    }
}

Set<Person> personSet = new HashSet<>();
personSet.add(new Person("Alice", 1));
personSet.add(new Person("Bob", 2));
personSet.add(new Person("Alice", 1)); // Duplicate id

for (Person p : personSet) {
    System.out.println(p.getName());
}
```

```
Possible output:
Alice
Bob
```

In this case, the second 'Person' object with the same 'id' as the first one will be considered a duplicate and will not be added to the set. The methods 'hashCode()' and 'equals()' are crucial to maintaining this behavior.

Efficiency Considerations:

The efficiency of various set operations like add, remove, and contains can vary significantly based on the set implementation. For example, 'HashSet' generally offers constant time performance for basic operations, assuming the hash function disperses elements properly among the buckets. In contrast, 'TreeSet' operations have logarithmic time complexity because of its underlying red-black tree structure.

- HashSet offers average-case constant time complexity O(1) for add, remove, and contains.
- LinkedHashSet maintains insertion order and has similar performance characteristics to HashSet, but with additional cost for maintaining a linked list.
- TreeSet guarantees that the set will be in ascending order, based on its natural order or a custom comparator if provided. Operations like add, remove, and contains have O(log n) complexity.
- ConcurrentSkipListSet provides concurrent access and also maintains order with logarithmic time performance.
- EnumSet is highly optimized for sets of enumerated types, providing extremely high-performance operations.

Understanding which set implementation to use requires analyzing the specific needs in terms of ordering, performance, and concurrency for your application. The subsequent sections will delve deeper into the specifics of each of these implementations, exploring their internal mechanisms and use cases.

4.2 HashSet: Unordered Collections

The HashSet is a fundamental implementation of the Set interface within the Java Collections Framework. As an unordered collection, it guarantees neither the order of the elements nor the persistence of any specific ordering over time. The HashSet is backed by a hash table (actually a HashMap instance), and it allows operations like add, remove, and contains to run in constant time, on average.

```
import java.util.HashSet;

public class HashSetExample {
    public static void main(String[] args) {
        HashSet<String> set = new HashSet<>();

        // Add elements to the HashSet
        set.add("Element1");
        set.add("Element2");
```

```
        set.add("Element3");

        // Check for the presence of an element
        boolean contains = set.contains("Element2");

        // Remove an element
        set.remove("Element2");

        // Size of the HashSet
        int size = set.size();

        // Iterating over the elements
        for (String element : set) {
            System.out.println(element);
        }
    }
}
```

The HashSet implementation offers several benefits and considerations:

Uniqueness: A HashSet automatically manages the uniqueness of its elements. If an attempt is made to add a duplicate element, the existing element remains unchanged, and the new element is ignored.

Null Elements: HashSet allows a single null element. If multiple null elements are added, only one is retained in the set.

Order of Elements: Elements in a HashSet are not ordered, and the order can change over time. Consequently, when iterating over a HashSet, the sequence of elements may vary between iterations.

The HashSet is typically implemented by wrapping a HashMap instance. Each element in the HashSet corresponds to a key in the underlying HashMap, with a constant dummy value associated with each key.

Let's execute the provided code to see the output:

```
Element3
Element1
```

This example demonstrates the basic usage of a HashSet. It shows how to add elements, check for their presence, remove them, and iterate over the set's elements. Observe that the output does not maintain any specific order, underscoring the unordered nature of HashSet.

Time Complexity: The average-case time complexity for basic operations like add, remove, and contains is $O(1)$. This efficiency stems from the underlying hash table structure, which allows for direct index computation and element access. However, in the worst-case scenario, where hash collisions are excessive, the time complexity can degrade to $O(n)$.

Capacity and Load Factor: The capacity of a HashSet refers to the number of elements it can hold before it needs to resize. The load factor is a measure of how full the set can get before its capacity is automatically increased. By default, the load factor is 0.75, meaning that when a HashSet reaches 75% of its capacity, it will be resized. This automatic resizing helps maintain average-case time complexity while balancing efficient memory usage.

```
HashSet<String> customSet = new HashSet<>(initialCapacity, loadFactor);
```

This allows developers to adjust the initial capacity and load factor according to specific requirements, enabling fine-tuning for performance optimization.

Hash Function and Collision Handling: The effectiveness of a HashSet heavily depends on the correctness and efficiency of the hashCode() and equals() methods. A well-designed hashCode() function minimizes collisions, thereby maintaining the set's performance. When hash collisions occur, the HashSet handles them internally, typically through chaining or open addressing, based on the HashMap's implementation.

```
import java.util.HashSet;

public class CustomObject {
    private int id;
    private String name;

    public CustomObject(int id, String name) {
        this.id = id;
        this.name = name;
    }

    @Override
    public int hashCode() {
        return id;
    }

    @Override
    public boolean equals(Object obj) {
        if (this == obj) return true;
        if (obj == null || getClass() != obj.getClass()) return false;
        CustomObject that = (CustomObject) obj;
        return id == that.id && name.equals(that.name);
    }

    public static void main(String[] args) {
        HashSet<CustomObject> set = new HashSet<>();
        set.add(new CustomObject(1, "Object1"));
        set.add(new CustomObject(2, "Object2"));
    }
}
```

This example demonstrates a custom object within a HashSet. The CustomObject class overrides the hashCode() and equals() methods to ensure that objects with the same id and name are considered equal and hash to the same bucket.

Trade-offs: While HashSet offers $O(1)$ average time complexity, it does not maintain any order among elements. For scenarios where element order matters, other implementations like LinkedHashSet or TreeSet might be more appropriate. Additionally, frequent resizing due to load factor adjustments can incur overhead, which should be balanced against memory constraints and performance requirements.

4.3 LinkedHashSet: Ordered Sets

The LinkedHashSet class, part of the Java Collections Framework, extends the capabilities of HashSet by maintaining a doubly-linked list running through all of its entries. This linked list defines the iteration ordering, which is the order in which elements were inserted into the set (insertion-order). This aspect of LinkedHashSet can prove beneficial for scenarios where the predictable iteration order is required, unlike the HashSet, which does not guarantee any specific order of iteration.

LinkedHashSet implementation follows these inheritance:

```
public class LinkedHashSet<E> extends HashSet<E> implements Set<E>, Cloneable,
      Serializable
```

The above class declaration indicates that LinkedHashSet inherits the properties of HashSet and implements the Set, Cloneable, and Serializable interfaces. Here, E is a type parameter that denotes the type of elements maintained by this set.

LinkedHashSet relies heavily on LinkedHashMap, which indeed backs the LinkedHashSet. The primary purpose of LinkedHashSet is maintaining a consistent order of elements and eliminating duplicates, making it particularly useful in applications where order and uniqueness are critical.

Constructors

LinkedHashSet provides several constructors to accommodate different initialization needs:

- LinkedHashSet(): Constructs a new, empty set; the backing HashMap instance has default initial capacity (16) and load factor

(0.75).

- LinkedHashSet(int initialCapacity): Constructs a new, empty set with the specified initial capacity; the backing HashMap instance has the default load factor (0.75).

- LinkedHashSet(int initialCapacity, float loadFactor): Constructs a new set with the specified initial capacity and load factor.

- LinkedHashSet(Collection<? extends E> c): Constructs a new set containing the elements in the specified collection.

Usage and Examples

To illustrate the usage of LinkedHashSet, consider the following example where elements are inserted and the iteration order is demonstrated:

```
import java.util.LinkedHashSet;

public class LinkedHashSetDemo {
    public static void main(String[] args) {
        LinkedHashSet<String> linkedHashSet = new LinkedHashSet<>();

        // Adding elements to LinkedHashSet
        linkedHashSet.add("Element1");
        linkedHashSet.add("Element2");
        linkedHashSet.add("Element3");
        linkedHashSet.add("Element4");

        // Iterating over LinkedHashSet
        for (String element : linkedHashSet) {
            System.out.println(element);
        }
    }
}
```

Given the above code, the output will maintain the insertion order of elements:

```
Element1
Element2
Element3
Element4
```

Key Properties and Behaviors

- **Order Maintenance:** LinkedHashSet maintains a doubly-linked list running through all of its entries, preserving the insertion order.

- **Performance:** Performance-wise, the LinkedHashSet incurs slightly higher overhead compared to HashSet due to the additional linked list that maintains order. However, the amortized time complexity for basic operations such as add, remove, and contains remains O(1).

- **Null Elements:** Similar to HashSet, LinkedHashSet allows for the inclusion of a null element. It can only contain no more than one null element.

Considerations for Use

When deciding between HashSet and LinkedHashSet, developers must consider the necessity of maintaining order:

- **Iteration Order:** If the order of elements is important, LinkedHashSet is preferable.

- **Non-Deterministic Order Acceptable:** For scenarios where order does not matter, using HashSet can be more efficient in terms of memory and slight performance overhead reductions.

In contexts where elements must be accessed in the order of their insertion without allowing duplicates, LinkedHashSet offers a robust solution, extending functionality beyond the basic capabilities of HashSet. The examples and considerations provided should help delineate its appropriate applications.

4.4 TreeSet: Sorted Sets

The TreeSet class in the Java Collections Framework is an implementation of the Set interface that uses a tree for storage. Objects in a TreeSet are stored in a sorted and ascending order as defined by their natural ordering or by a custom comparator provided at set creation time. This makes TreeSet an essential tool for scenarios where the ordering of elements is necessary, such as in priority queues, ensuring uniqueness while automatically maintaining order.

Creating a TreeSet

A TreeSet can be instantiated in different ways to accommodate various requirements. Typically, it is initialized either using the default natural ordering of its elements or a supplied Comparator. The following examples illustrate these methods:

```
import java.util.TreeSet;
import java.util.Comparator;

public class Main {
    public static void main(String[] args) {
        // Default natural ordering
        TreeSet<Integer> naturalOrderingSet = new TreeSet<>();
        naturalOrderingSet.add(5);
        naturalOrderingSet.add(1);
        naturalOrderingSet.add(3);
        System.out.println(naturalOrderingSet); // Output: [1, 3, 5]

        // Custom comparator for descending order
        Comparator<Integer> descendingOrder = (i1, i2) -> i2 - i1;
        TreeSet<Integer> customOrderingSet = new TreeSet<>(descendingOrder);
        customOrderingSet.add(5);
        customOrderingSet.add(1);
        customOrderingSet.add(3);
        System.out.println(customOrderingSet); // Output: [5, 3, 1]
    }
}
```

```
Output:
[1, 3, 5]
[5, 3, 1]
```

Behavior and Characteristics

TreeSet implements the SortedSet interface, and therefore it provides several methods specific to this interface, such as first(), last(), headSet(), tailSet(), and subSet().

```
import java.util.TreeSet;

public class TreeSetExample {
    public static void main(String[] args) {
        TreeSet<String> treeSet = new TreeSet<>();
        treeSet.add("Apple");
        treeSet.add("Banana");
        treeSet.add("Mango");
        treeSet.add("Peach");

        // Accessing the first and last elements
        System.out.println("First: " + treeSet.first()); // Output: Apple
        System.out.println("Last: " + treeSet.last()); // Output: Peach

        // Getting a subset from the TreeSet
        System.out.println("HeadSet: " + treeSet.headSet("Mango")); // Output: [
            Apple, Banana]
```

```
        System.out.println("TailSet: " + treeSet.tailSet("Mango")); // Output: [Mango,
            Peach]
        System.out.println("SubSet: " + treeSet.subSet("Banana", "Peach")); // Output
            : [Banana, Mango]
    }
}
```

```
Output:
First: Apple
Last: Peach
HeadSet: [Apple, Banana]
TailSet: [Mango, Peach]
SubSet: [Banana, Mango]
```

NavigableSet Interface

The TreeSet class also implements the NavigableSet interface, which provides additional navigation methods. These include lower(), floor(), ceiling(), and higher().

```
import java.util.TreeSet;

public class NavigableSetExample {
    public static void main(String[] args) {
        TreeSet<Integer> treeSet = new TreeSet<>();
        treeSet.add(10);
        treeSet.add(20);
        treeSet.add(30);
        treeSet.add(40);

        System.out.println("Lower than 30: " + treeSet.lower(30)); // Output: 20
        System.out.println("Floor of 30: " + treeSet.floor(30)); // Output: 30
        System.out.println("Ceiling of 25: " + treeSet.ceiling(25));// Output: 30
        System.out.println("Higher than 30: " + treeSet.higher(30));// Output: 40
    }
}
```

```
Output:
Lower than 30: 20
Floor of 30: 30
Ceiling of 25: 30
Higher than 30: 40
```

Performance Considerations

TreeSet, backed by a TreeMap, provides guaranteed log(n) time cost for the basic operations – add, remove, and contains. This performance characteristic makes TreeSet suitable for use cases requiring fast retrieval and maintenance of the sorted order. The elements must be mutually comparable, implying that the elements need to implement the Comparable interface or be supplied with an appropriate Comparator.

```
import java.util.TreeSet;

public class PerformanceExample {
    public static void main(String[] args) {
        TreeSet<Integer> treeSet = new TreeSet<>();
        for (int i = 0; i < 1000; i++) {
            treeSet.add((int)(Math.random() * 2000));
        }
        System.out.println("TreeSet size: " + treeSet.size());
        System.out.println("Contains 500? " + treeSet.contains(500));
    }
}
```

```
Output:
TreeSet size: Varies
Contains 500? true/false
```

TreeSet ensures that elements are unique based on their comparison results, not equals(), and will not allow the insertion of elements that consider each other equal when compared.

Custom Comparator Example

When natural ordering is not suitable or available, using a custom comparator is necessary. This example demonstrates a TreeSet of a user-defined class sorted by a custom comparator.

```
import java.util.Comparator;
import java.util.TreeSet;

class Person {
    String name;
    int age;
    Person(String name, int age) {
        this.name = name;
        this.age = age;
    }
    @Override
    public String toString() {
        return name + ": " + age;
    }
}

public class CustomComparatorExample {
    public static void main(String[] args) {
        Comparator<Person> personComparator = Comparator.comparingInt(p -> p.
            age);
        TreeSet<Person> personSet = new TreeSet<>(personComparator);
        personSet.add(new Person("Alice", 30));
        personSet.add(new Person("Bob", 25));
        personSet.add(new Person("Charlie", 35));

        for (Person person : personSet) {
            System.out.println(person);
        }
    }
```

```
}
```

Output:
Bob: 25
Alice: 30
Charlie: 35

The TreeSet class is a powerful tool within the Java Collections Framework, providing an efficient means to maintain a fully ordered set of elements. The flexibility of using natural ordering or custom comparators ensures that TreeSet can be adapted to many different use cases, making it an indispensable part of Java's utility library.

4.5 ConcurrentSkipListSet: Thread-Safe Sorted Sets

The ConcurrentSkipListSet class, part of the java.util.concurrent package, provides a thread-safe, scalable alternative to other sorted set implementations. This class implements the NavigableSet interface and is backed by a ConcurrentSkipListMap, which is a concurrent variant of TreeMap. The key property of ConcurrentSkipListSet is its inherent thread-safety, meaning it is designed to be used concurrently by multiple threads without requiring explicit synchronization.

```
import java.util.concurrent.ConcurrentSkipListSet;

public class ConcurrentSkipListSetExample {
    public static void main(String[] args) {
        ConcurrentSkipListSet<Integer> set = new ConcurrentSkipListSet<>();

        set.add(3);
        set.add(1);
        set.add(2);

        System.out.println(set);
    }
}
```

Output:
[1, 2, 3]

The core advantage of ConcurrentSkipListSet is that it provides expected average $\log(n)$ time complexity for most operations like add, remove, and contains. This is achieved using a data structure called the skip list, which allows for efficient concurrent modifications.

Consider the underlying structure of a skip list. A skip list comprises multiple layers of linked lists, where the bottom layer is an ordinary sorted linked list. Each higher layer acts as an express lane, potentially skipping multiple elements of the list below. Search, insert, and delete operations are performed by traversing down from the topmost layer while moving across similar to a multi-level linked list.

The ConcurrentSkipListSet maintains all elements in a sorted order, which grants it the ability to efficiently implement the NavigableSet interface. This interface provides valuable methods for navigating through the set, finding entries relative to given keys, and retrieving subsets of the set. Examples include methods like headSet(E toElement), tailSet(E fromElement), and subSet(E fromElement, E toElement).

```
import java.util.concurrent.ConcurrentSkipListSet;

public class NavigableSetExample {
    public static void main(String[] args) {
        ConcurrentSkipListSet<Integer> set = new ConcurrentSkipListSet<>();
        set.add(1);
        set.add(3);
        set.add(5);
        set.add(7);

        System.out.println("HeadSet (less than 5): " + set.headSet(5));
        System.out.println("TailSet (greater than or equal to 5): " + set.tailSet(5));
        System.out.println("SubSet (3 to 7): " + set.subSet(3, 7));
    }
}
```

```
Output:
HeadSet (less than 5): [1, 3]
TailSet (greater than or equal to 5): [5, 7]
SubSet (3 to 7): [3, 5]
```

Given its concurrent nature, ConcurrentSkipListSet is particularly useful in multi-threaded environments where read and write operations need to be executed concurrently without explicit locks. For instance, high-throughput systems like real-time analytics platforms can benefit greatly from the concurrent capabilities of ConcurrentSkipListSet.

When designing algorithms that leverage ConcurrentSkipListSet, it is critical to understand both its performance characteristics and potential limitations. The expected $\log(n)$ time complexity holds under ordinary circumstances, but worst-case scenarios degrade to linear time. However, such scenarios are unlikely due to the probabilistic balancing of skip lists.

Additionally, ConcurrentSkipListSet does not support null elements. Attempting to add null will result in a NullPointerException. This design choice ensures reliable and predictable behavior across concurrent operations.

To illustrate the concurrent nature of ConcurrentSkipListSet, consider a scenario where multiple threads are inserting elements into the set simultaneously. The following example showcases a simple multi-threaded insertion.

```
import java.util.concurrent.ConcurrentSkipListSet;

public class ConcurrentInsertionExample {
    public static void main(String[] args) throws InterruptedException {
        ConcurrentSkipListSet<Integer> set = new ConcurrentSkipListSet<>();

        Runnable inserter = () -> {
            for (int i = 0; i < 5; i++) {
                set.add(i);
                System.out.println(Thread.currentThread().getName() + " added: " + i);
            }
        };

        Thread t1 = new Thread(inserter);
        Thread t2 = new Thread(inserter);

        t1.start();
        t2.start();

        t1.join();
        t2.join();

        System.out.println("Final set: " + set);
    }
}
```

```
Output:
Thread-0 added: 0
Thread-1 added: 0
Thread-0 added: 1
Thread-0 added: 2
Thread-1 added: 1
Thread-1 added: 2
Thread-0 added: 3
Thread-0 added: 4
Thread-1 added: 3
Thread-1 added: 4
Final set: [0, 1, 2, 3, 4]
```

The above example demonstrates that ConcurrentSkipListSet can handle concurrent insertions gracefully, maintaining thread-safety and the sorted property of the set. Each thread's output indicates the elements it added, and the final set reflects a combined, sorted collection.

Thread-safe collections such as ConcurrentSkipListSet are indispensable for designing robust multi-threaded applications. They abstract away the complexities of synchronization, allowing developers to focus on higher-level algorithmic concerns. The skip list data structure provides an efficient and scalable foundation, ensuring that operations on the set remain performant under concurrent access patterns.

4.6 EnumSet: Specialized Set for Enums

EnumSet is a specialized Set implementation specifically designed for use with enum types. It provides an efficient and compact representation that leverages the unique properties of enumerations. Unlike other set implementations such as HashSet or TreeSet, an EnumSet requires that all elements be of the same enum type, making it both type-safe and highly optimized. This section delves into the details of EnumSet, its usage, and the benefits it offers.

EnumSet is part of the java.util package and implements the Set interface. It is an abstract class with two concrete implementations: RegularEnumSet and JumboEnumSet. The choice between these implementations is determined automatically based on the size of the enum type.

```
import java.util.EnumSet;

enum Day {
    MONDAY, TUESDAY, WEDNESDAY, THURSDAY, FRIDAY, SATURDAY,
        SUNDAY
}

public class EnumSetExample {
    public static void main(String[] args) {
        EnumSet<Day> weekend = EnumSet.of(Day.SATURDAY, Day.SUNDAY);
        System.out.println("Weekend days: " + weekend);

        EnumSet<Day> workdays = EnumSet.range(Day.MONDAY, Day.FRIDAY);
        System.out.println("Workdays: " + workdays);

        EnumSet<Day> allDays = EnumSet.allOf(Day.class);
        System.out.println("All days: " + allDays);

        EnumSet<Day> noDays = EnumSet.noneOf(Day.class);
        System.out.println("No days: " + noDays);
    }
}
```

```
Weekend days: [SATURDAY, SUNDAY]
Workdays: [MONDAY, TUESDAY, WEDNESDAY, THURSDAY, FRIDAY]
All days: [MONDAY, TUESDAY, WEDNESDAY, THURSDAY, FRIDAY, SATURDAY, SUNDAY]
No days: []
```

Creating an EnumSet

There are several ways to create an EnumSet, each tailored to different requirements:

- EnumSet.of(E first, E... rest): Creates an EnumSet with the specified elements.
- EnumSet.noneOf(Class<E> elementType): Creates an empty

EnumSet.

- EnumSet.allOf(Class<E> elementType): Creates an EnumSet containing all the elements of the specified enum type.
- EnumSet.range(E from, E to): Creates an EnumSet containing all of the elements in the specified range.
- EnumSet.copyOf(Collection<E> c): Creates an EnumSet with the same elements as the specified collection.

Benefits of EnumSet

EnumSet offers numerous benefits:

- Compact Representation: Since EnumSet internally uses bit vectors, it is extremely memory-efficient compared to other Set implementations.
- High Performance: Operations on EnumSet (e.g., add, remove, contains) are constant time, O(1), and are generally faster than those on HashSet.
- Type Safety: EnumSet ensures that all elements belong to the same enum type, catching type errors at compile time.

Use Cases for EnumSet

Due to its specialized nature, EnumSet is particularly suited for scenarios involving enum types, such as:

- State Management: Representing and managing states or modes in finite state machines or UI components.
- Feature Flags: Enabling or disabling sets of features in software applications.
- Permissions and Roles: Representing sets of user permissions or roles in security/authentication modules.

Common Operations in EnumSet

Enumerating and performing operations in EnumSet mirrors those in other sets. Below are illustrative examples:

```
import java.util.EnumSet;

enum Feature {
    LOGIN, REGISTER, SEARCH, EDIT, DELETE
}

public class FeatureFlags {
    public static void main(String[] args) {
        EnumSet<Feature> enabledFeatures = EnumSet.of(Feature.LOGIN, Feature.
            SEARCH);

        // Adding features
        enabledFeatures.add(Feature.REGISTER);
        System.out.println("Enabled features: " + enabledFeatures);

        // Removing features
        enabledFeatures.remove(Feature.LOGIN);
        System.out.println("Enabled features after removal: " + enabledFeatures);

        // Checking if a feature is enabled
        boolean isSearchEnabled = enabledFeatures.contains(Feature.SEARCH);
        System.out.println("Is SEARCH enabled? " + isSearchEnabled);

        // Iterating over features
        for (Feature feature : enabledFeatures) {
            System.out.println("Enabled feature: " + feature);
        }
    }
}
```

```
Enabled features: [LOGIN, SEARCH, REGISTER]
Enabled features after removal: [SEARCH, REGISTER]
Is SEARCH enabled? true
Enabled feature: SEARCH
Enabled feature: REGISTER
```

These examples underscore the versatility and efficiency of EnumSet in managing sets of enum types. It stands out as uniquely suited for this purpose, providing both performance enhancements and type-safety guarantees that are unparalleled by other Set implementations.

Understanding the underlying mechanics and appropriate use cases of EnumSet equips one with the nuanced skills required to leverage its full potential, making it an indispensable tool in Java collections. Such knowledge extends beyond basic usage, enabling the development of sophisticated, optimized, and maintainable code.

4.7 Common Set Operations

Sets in the Java Collections Framework provide a variety of operations that allow for efficient manipulation and querying of unique elements. Understanding these common set operations is crucial for using sets effectively. This section will cover essential methods available for sets, illustrated with detailed Java code examples.

Adding Elements: To add an element to a set, the add method is used. This operation returns a boolean indicating whether the set did not already contain the specified element.

```
// Creating a HashSet to store Integer values
Set<Integer> integerSet = new HashSet<>();

// Adding an element to the set
boolean isAdded = integerSet.add(10); // returns true, 10 is added
boolean isAddedAgain = integerSet.add(10); // returns false, 10 is already present
```

Removing Elements: To remove an element, the remove method is employed. It also returns a boolean, indicating the success of the removal operation.

```
// Removing an element from the set
boolean isRemoved = integerSet.remove(10); // returns true, 10 is removed
boolean isRemovedAgain = integerSet.remove(10); // returns false, 10 is no longer
    present
```

Checking for Containment: The contains method checks if an element is present in the set, returning a boolean result.

```
// Checking if an element is in the set
boolean containsElement = integerSet.contains(10); // returns false, as 10 was removed
```

Size and Emptiness: To get the number of elements in the set, the size method is used, and to check if the set is empty, the isEmpty method is available.

```
// Checking the size of the set
int setSize = integerSet.size(); // returns 0, as the set is empty

// Checking if the set is empty
boolean isSetEmpty = integerSet.isEmpty(); // returns true
```

Clearing the Set: The clear method removes all elements from the set.

```
// Adding elements to the set
integerSet.add(20);
integerSet.add(30);

// Clearing the set
integerSet.clear(); // removes all elements
int clearedSetSize = integerSet.size(); // returns 0, as the set is now empty
```

Bulk Operations: Sets support bulk operations to perform tasks on multiple elements simultaneously. These include addAll, retainAll, and removeAll methods.

```
// Bulk addition of elements to the set
Set<Integer> anotherSet = new HashSet<>();
anotherSet.add(40);
anotherSet.add(50);

integerSet.addAll(anotherSet); // adds all elements from anotherSet to integerSet
boolean containsAll = integerSet.containsAll(anotherSet); // returns true

// Bulk removal of elements from the set
integerSet.removeAll(anotherSet); // removes elements present in anotherSet from
    integerSet
boolean containsAfterRemoval = integerSet.containsAll(anotherSet); // returns false

// Retaining common elements in the set
Set<Integer> yetAnotherSet = new HashSet<>();
yetAnotherSet.add(60);
yetAnotherSet.add(70);

integerSet.addAll(yetAnotherSet);
integerSet.add(80);
integerSet.add(90);

anotherSet.add(80);

integerSet.retainAll(anotherSet); // modifies integerSet to keep only common elements
    with anotherSet
boolean containsRetained = integerSet.contains(80); // returns true
boolean containsRemoved = integerSet.contains(90); // returns false, as 90 is not in
    anotherSet
```

Comparing and Subsetting: The equals and containsAll methods help compare sets and verify subset relationships respectively.

```
// Comparing two sets for equality
Set<Integer> comparisonSet1 = new HashSet<>(Arrays.asList(1, 2, 3));
Set<Integer> comparisonSet2 = new HashSet<>(Arrays.asList(1, 2, 3));

boolean areEqual = comparisonSet1.equals(comparisonSet2); // returns true

// Checking if one set is a subset of another
Set<Integer> subset = new HashSet<>(Arrays.asList(1, 2));
boolean isSubset = comparisonSet1.containsAll(subset); // returns true
```

Iterating Over Elements: While iteration techniques are covered in detail in a separate section, it's important to mention that sets can be iterated using enhanced for loops and iterators.

```
// Iterating using enhanced for loop
for (Integer element : integerSet) {
    System.out.println(element);
}

// Iterating using iterator
Iterator<Integer> iterator = integerSet.iterator();
while (iterator.hasNext()) {
    Integer element = iterator.next();
    System.out.println(element);
}
```

These common operations form the backbone of manipulating sets in Java, enabling users to build complex logic atop these fundamental methods.

4.8 Performance Considerations for Sets

Understanding the performance implications of different Set implementations is crucial for optimizing Java applications that require unique collections. Each implementation in the Java Collections Framework offers distinct performance characteristics in terms of time complexity for various operations like add, remove, contains, and iterate.

HashSet: This implementation provides the best performance for add, remove, and contains operations due to its underlying hash table structure. These operations generally have a time complexity of $O(1)$, assuming a good hash function that evenly distributes objects across the bucket array. However, in the worst-case scenario, where all elements hash to the same bucket, the time complexity can degrade to $O(n)$. Iteration over a $\mathrm{HashSet}$ depends on the capacity of the hash table, not the actual set size, making its performance less predictable.

```
HashSet<Integer> hashSet = new HashSet<>();
hashSet.add(1);
hashSet.add(2);
hashSet.add(3);
System.out.println(hashSet.contains(2)); // true
hashSet.remove(3);
```

```
true
```

LinkedHashSet: Extending $\mathrm{HashSet}$, this implementation maintains a doubly-linked list across all entries, preserving insertion order. The time complexity for add, remove, and contains operations remains $O(1)$, akin to $\mathrm{HashSet}$, as it also utilizes a hash table. However, the additional overhead of maintaining the linked list can lead to slightly decreased performance compared to $\mathrm{HashSet}$.

```
LinkedHashSet<Integer> linkedHashSet = new LinkedHashSet<>();
linkedHashSet.add(1);
linkedHashSet.add(2);
linkedHashSet.add(3);
System.out.println(linkedHashSet.contains(2)); // true
linkedHashSet.remove(3);
```

```
true
```

TreeSet: A $\mathrm{TreeSet}$ employs a Red-Black tree to store its elements, ensuring that the set remains sorted. This results in $O(\log n)$ time complexity for add, remove, and contains operations. The sorted nature of TreeSet makes it ideal for scenarios where order is paramount. While TreeSet offers logarithmic performance, it introduces more overhead compared to the constant-time complexity of hash-based sets.

```
TreeSet<Integer> treeSet = new TreeSet<>();
treeSet.add(1);
treeSet.add(2);
treeSet.add(3);
System.out.println(treeSet.contains(2)); // true
treeSet.remove(3);
```

```
true
```

ConcurrentSkipListSet: This implementation is engineered for concurrent environments, providing thread-safe access without requiring external synchronization. Internally, ConcurrentSkipListSet employs a skip list, offering $O(\log n)$ time complexity for add, remove, and contains operations similar to TreeSet, but optimized for concurrent modification. This makes it suitable for applications requiring high concurrency levels, where multiple threads can operate on the set without performance degradation.

```
ConcurrentSkipListSet<Integer> concurrentSet = new ConcurrentSkipListSet<>();
concurrentSet.add(1);
concurrentSet.add(2);
concurrentSet.add(3);
System.out.println(concurrentSet.contains(2)); // true
concurrentSet.remove(3);
```

```
true
```

EnumSet: Designed specifically for enums, EnumSet provides an exceptionally high-performance implementation. The behind-the-scenes representation of an EnumSet as a bit vector allows it to offer near constant-time performance for all basic operations. The performance of EnumSet is generally superior to that of other set implementations, making it the optimal choice when dealing with enum types.

```
enum Days { MONDAY, TUESDAY, WEDNESDAY, THURSDAY, FRIDAY }

EnumSet<Days> enumSet = EnumSet.of(Days.MONDAY, Days.FRIDAY);
System.out.println(enumSet.contains(Days.FRIDAY)); // true
enumSet.remove(Days.MONDAY);
```

```
true
```

Choosing the appropriate set implementation depends on specific application requirements and constraints like order preservation, concurrency, and the nature of stored elements. For unordered collections, HashSet offers excellent performance. If insertion order matters, LinkedHashSet is preferable. When sorting is necessary, TreeSet is beneficial, and for high-concurrency demands, ConcurrentSkipListSet is ideal. For enum types, EnumSet is the most efficient choice.

4.9 Iterating Over Sets

Iterating over elements in a set is a fundamental operation when working with collections in Java. Java provides several ways to traverse a set, each with its specific use cases and benefits. Understanding these methods is crucial for performing efficient data manipulation tasks.

The primary methods for iterating over a set are:

- Iterator
- Enhanced for loop
- forEach method with lambda expressions

Using an Iterator

The Iterator interface provides a standard way to traverse a collection. The iterator method returns an instance of Iterator, which allows you to traverse the set using hasNext() and next() methods. The following example demonstrates this approach.

```
import java.util.HashSet;
import java.util.Iterator;
import java.util.Set;

public class SetIterationExample {
    public static void main(String[] args) {
        Set<String> set = new HashSet<>();
        set.add("Element1");
        set.add("Element2");

        Iterator<String> iterator = set.iterator();
        while (iterator.hasNext()) {
            String element = iterator.next();
            System.out.println(element);
        }
    }
}
```

```
Element1
Element2
```

The key advantage of using an Iterator is that it allows you to safely remove elements from the set during iteration using the remove method. This is not possible with other traversal methods, which can result in a ConcurrentModificationException.

Using the Enhanced for Loop

The enhanced for loop, also known as the "foreach" loop, is a simpler and more readable way to iterate over a set. This loop is syntactic sugar for the Iterator approach, and it is suitable for most scenarios where you do not need to modify the set during iteration.

```
import java.util.HashSet;
import java.util.Set;

public class SetIterationExample {
    public static void main(String[] args) {
        Set<String> set = new HashSet<>();
        set.add("Element1");
        set.add("Element2");

        for (String element : set) {
            System.out.println(element);
        }
    }
}
```

```
Element1
Element2
```

This approach is concise and expressive, making the code easier to read and maintain. However, the enhanced for loop does not provide a direct way to remove elements during iteration, as it lacks direct access to the Iterator instance.

Using the forEach Method with Lambda Expressions

Java 8 introduced the forEach method in the Iterable interface, which allows for more functional-style operations using lambda expressions or method references. This method accepts a Consumer functional interface as its parameter.

```
import java.util.HashSet;
import java.util.Set;

public class SetIterationExample {
    public static void main(String[] args) {
        Set<String> set = new HashSet<>();
        set.add("Element1");
        set.add("Element2");

        set.forEach(element -> System.out.println(element));
    }
}
```

```
Element1
Element2
```

For scenarios requiring more complex operations, you can enhance this approach by defining custom lambda expressions or using method references for greater code reuse and readability.

Removing Elements During Iteration

As previously mentioned, the Iterator approach is the only safe and supported way to remove elements from the set during iteration. The following example illustrates the removal of elements that satisfy certain conditions.

```
import java.util.HashSet;
import java.util.Iterator;
import java.util.Set;

public class SetRemoveExample {
    public static void main(String[] args) {
        Set<String> set = new HashSet<>();
        set.add("Element1");
        set.add("Element2");
        set.add("RemoveMe");

        Iterator<String> iterator = set.iterator();
        while (iterator.hasNext()) {
            String element = iterator.next();
            if (element.equals("RemoveMe")) {
                iterator.remove();
            }
        }

        set.forEach(System.out::println);
    }
}
```

```
Element1
Element2
```

This method ensures that the underlying data structure remains consistent and free of ConcurrentModificationException.

Iterating Over Sorted Sets

For sorted set implementations like TreeSet or ConcurrentSkipListSet, iteration order is guaranteed by the natural ordering of elements or by a custom comparator. The iteration techniques remain the same, but the predictability of the order can be useful for certain applications.

```
import java.util.Set;
import java.util.TreeSet;

public class SortedSetIterationExample {
    public static void main(String[] args) {
        Set<String> sortedSet = new TreeSet<>();
        sortedSet.add("Banana");
```

```
        sortedSet.add("Apple");
        sortedSet.add("Cherry");

        for (String element : sortedSet) {
            System.out.println(element);
        }
    }
}
```

```
Apple
Banana
Cherry
```

The consistent order provided by sorted sets can be beneficial for applications requiring ordered traversal.

When iterating over sets, choosing the appropriate method based on the specific requirements and context ensures efficient and clear code. Understanding these different techniques and their characteristics enriches the ability to manipulate set collections effectively within Java applications.

4.10 Set Operations: Union, Intersection, Difference

In this section, we delve into the fundamental set operations: union, intersection, and difference. These operations are crucial for manipulating and comparing datasets, providing a basis for many algorithmic and data-processing tasks.

Union: The union of two sets results in a set containing all the distinct elements from both sets. The union operation is commutative and associative, which means the order of the sets does not affect the result.

Intersection: The intersection of two sets yields a set containing only the elements that are present in both sets. The intersection operation is also commutative and associative.

Difference: The difference between two sets results in a set containing elements that are in the first set but not in the second. Unlike union and intersection, the difference operation is neither commutative nor associative.

Here are Java code examples that illustrate how to perform these operations using the HashSet class, one of the most commonly used set implementations.

```
import java.util.HashSet;
import java.util.Set;

public class SetOperations {
    public static void main(String[] args) {
        Set<Integer> setA = new HashSet<>();
        Set<Integer> setB = new HashSet<>();

        setA.add(1);
        setA.add(2);
        setA.add(3);

        setB.add(3);
        setB.add(4);
        setB.add(5);

        // Union
        Set<Integer> union = new HashSet<>(setA);
        union.addAll(setB);
        System.out.println("Union: " + union);

        // Intersection
        Set<Integer> intersection = new HashSet<>(setA);
        intersection.retainAll(setB);
        System.out.println("Intersection: " + intersection);

        // Difference
        Set<Integer> difference = new HashSet<>(setA);
        difference.removeAll(setB);
        System.out.println("Difference (setA - setB): " + difference);
    }
}
```

```
Union: [1, 2, 3, 4, 5]
Intersection: [3]
Difference (setA - setB): [1, 2]
```

Union Operation:

To perform a union operation, the addAll method is used. Here, union.addAll(setB); combines the elements of setA and setB. This action results in a set containing all unique elements from both sets.

Intersection Operation:

For the intersection operation, the retainAll method is applied. The line intersection.retainAll(setB); modifies the intersection set to contain only those elements that are present in both setA and setB.

Difference Operation:

The difference operation utilizes the removeAll method. In difference.removeAll(setB);, the difference set is updated to exclude any elements that are also present in setB.

Algorithmic Implementation:

While Java's built-in methods perform these operations efficiently, understanding their underlying mechanisms is beneficial. Below is a simplified algorithmic approach to these operations, using pseudocode for better comprehension:

Algorithm 2: Union, Intersection, and Difference Algorithms

Input: Two sets, A and B
Output: Union set U, Intersection set I, Difference set D

```
U ← new set;
I ← new set;
D ← new set;
foreach element e in A do
    U.add(e);
    D.add(e);
end
foreach element e in B do
    U.add(e);
end
foreach element e in A do
    if B.contains(e) then
        I.add(e);
    end
end
foreach element e in B do
    D.remove(e);
end
return U, I, D
```

This pseudocode demonstrates the steps described previously—iterating through sets to construct union, intersection, and difference sets manually.

Special Cases and Considerations:

- - Empty Sets: Any operation with an empty set yields predictable results, e.g., the union of a set with an empty set returns the set itself.
- - Duplicates: Since sets inherently disallow duplicates, the union operation automatically handles multiplicities by including each element only once.
- - Performance: The time complexity of these operations is largely influenced by the size of the sets and the efficiency of the un-

derlying set implementation (usually O(1) for hash-based sets in average cases).

The reader should practice implementing and testing these operations to understand their behavior thoroughly. These fundamental set operations form the backbone of more complex data manipulation tasks and are widely used in various algorithmic problems and real-world applications. Their efficient and correct use is essential for robust Java application development.

4.11 Custom Set Implementations

When the standard implementations provided by the Java Collections Framework (JCF) do not meet specific performance or functional requirements, it may be beneficial to create a custom set implementation. This section covers how to design and implement a custom set by extending the AbstractSet class and adhering to the Set interface. A firm understanding of the equals(Object o) and hashCode() methods is also crucial, as these methods ensure the integrity of set operations, particularly for ensuring uniqueness.

To illustrate the process, we will implement a custom set that uses a simple array for storing elements. This example, while not optimal for real-world applications, highlights the fundamental principles of creating a custom set.

```
import java.util.AbstractSet;
import java.util.Iterator;
import java.util.NoSuchElementException;

public class ArraySet<E> extends AbstractSet<E> {
    private Object[] elements;
    private int size;

    public ArraySet() {
        elements = new Object[10];
        size = 0;
    }

    public boolean add(E e) {
        if (contains(e)) {
            return false;
        }

        if (size == elements.length) {
            Object[] newElements = new Object[size * 2];
            System.arraycopy(elements, 0, newElements, 0, size);
            elements = newElements;
        }
```

```
        elements[size] = e;
        size++;
        return true;
    }

    // Other methods omitted for brevity
}
```

In the initial implementation above, the ArraySet class extends AbstractSet and provides basic support for adding elements. The array backing the set, elements, starts with a length of 10, automatically expanding when full. This expansion is crucial to handle an arbitrary number of elements.

To ensure that only unique elements are added, the add method first checks if the element already exists in the set using the contains method before adding it. The contains method needs to be implemented next.

```
@Override
public boolean contains(Object o) {
    for (int i = 0; i < size; i++) {
        if (elements[i].equals(o)) {
            return true;
        }
    }
    return false;
}
```

The contains method iterates through the current elements to check if the object o is already present. This simple iteration satisfies the condition for small sets, but more efficient search mechanisms like hash tables are recommended for large datasets to optimize performance.

Next, we will implement the iterator method to iterate over the elements in the custom set.

```
@Override
public Iterator<E> iterator() {
    return new Iterator<E>() {
        private int index = 0;

        @Override
        public boolean hasNext() {
            return index < size;
        }

        @Override
        public E next() {
            if (!hasNext()) {
                throw new NoSuchElementException();
            }
            return (E) elements[index++];
        }
    };
```

```
}
```

The iterator provided by the ArraySet class implements the Iterator interface, offering hasNext and next methods essential for proper iteration. This simplistically iterates over the array, returning elements in the order they were added.

Finally, the size method, returning the number of elements in the set, ensures compliance with the Set interface.

```
@Override
public int size() {
    return size;
}
```

A comprehensive custom set implementation must handle several other details, such as removing elements, ensuring thread safety, and providing efficient storage and retrieval mechanisms. The provided ArraySet class is a simplified example demonstrating core principles. Advanced implementations, like those based on hash tables or balanced trees, offer better performance characteristics and should be explored for more demanding applications.

When designing custom set implementations, it is also essential to consider the implications of element ordering, thread safety, and memory overhead. Employing data structures like HashMap, or concurrent structures provided in java.util.concurrent, can alleviate many challenges associated with manual management.

The following is a more advanced skeleton of a set implementation based on hash tables, illustrating the leap from conceptual design to practical application in environments where performance and scalability are key concerns.

```
public class HashTableSet<E> extends AbstractSet<E> {
    private static final int DEFAULT_CAPACITY = 16;
    private LinkedList<E>[] table;
    private int size;

    public HashTableSet() {
        table = new LinkedList[DEFAULT_CAPACITY];
        size = 0;
    }

    private int hash(Object o) {
        return (o == null) ? 0 : Math.abs(o.hashCode() % table.length);
    }

    @Override
    public boolean add(E e) {
        int index = hash(e);
        if (table[index] == null) {
```

```
            table[index] = new LinkedList<E>();
        } else if (table[index].contains(e)) {
            return false;
        }
        table[index].add(e);
        size++;
        return true;
    }

    @Override
    public boolean contains(Object o) {
        int index = hash(o);
        return table[index] != null && table[index].contains(o);
    }

    @Override
    public Iterator<E> iterator() {
        return new HashTableIterator();
    }

    @Override
    public int size() {
        return size;
    }

    private class HashTableIterator implements Iterator<E> {
        private int index = 0;
        private Iterator<E> current;

        @Override
        public boolean hasNext() {
            if (current != null && current.hasNext()) {
                return true;
            }
            while (index < table.length && (table[index] == null || !table[index].iterator
                ().hasNext())) {
                index++;
            }
            if (index < table.length) {
                current = table[index].iterator();
                return current.hasNext();
            }
            return false;
        }

        @Override
        public E next() {
            if (!hasNext()) {
                throw new NoSuchElementException();
            }
            return current.next();
        }
    }
}
```

Developing custom set implementations allows tailored handling of specific needs and can optimize performance when the default implementations in the Java Collections Framework do not suffice. Understanding and applying these concepts is crucial for advanced Java development, particularly in high-performance or specialized domains.

Chapter 5

Exploring Maps: Key-Value Pairs

This chapter provides an in-depth look at maps within the Java Collections Framework, which handle key-value pair associations. It covers various implementations including HashMap, LinkedHashMap, TreeMap, ConcurrentHashMap, WeakHashMap, IdentityHashMap, and EnumMap. The chapter outlines common map operations, performance considerations, and iteration techniques. It also discusses practical use cases and custom map implementations, offering a comprehensive understanding of how to effectively utilize different map types in Java for various application needs.

5.1 Introduction to Maps

Maps represent a crucial component in the Java Collections Framework (JCF), designed for handling associations between unique keys and their corresponding values. The concept of a map allows for efficient data retrieval, insertion, and deletion, distinguishing it from other collection types such as lists and sets. Understanding the fundamentals of maps is essential for leveraging their capabilities to solve various programming challenges.

A Map in Java is an interface that represents a collection of key-value pairs where each key is associated with exactly one value. Keys must be unique within a map, but values can be duplicated. The primary objective of a Map is to provide a mechanism for finding a value based on its key efficiently.

The Java Collections Framework provides several implementations of the Map interface, each with distinct characteristics and use cases. Some of the most commonly used implementations are HashMap, LinkedHashMap, TreeMap, ConcurrentHashMap, WeakHashMap, IdentityHashMap, and EnumMap. Each of these implementations offers different performance trade-offs and memory usage considerations.

The basic operations supported by the Map interface include the following:

- put(K key, V value): Associates the specified value with the specified key in the map. If the key already exists, the old value is replaced by the new value.
- get(Object key): Returns the value to which the specified key is mapped or null if the map contains no mapping for the key.
- remove(Object key): Removes the mapping for the specified key from this map if present.
- containsKey(Object key): Returns true if this map contains a mapping for the specified key.
- containsValue(Object value): Returns true if this map maps one or more keys to the specified value.
- keySet(): Returns a Set view of the keys contained in this map.
- values(): Returns a Collection view of the values contained in this map.
- entrySet(): Returns a Set view of the mappings contained in this map.

Here is an example demonstrating the use of the HashMap class, a widely utilized implementation of the Map interface.

```
import java.util.HashMap;
import java.util.Map;

public class MapExample {
    public static void main(String[] args) {
        // Creating a HashMap
```

```
        Map<String, Integer> map = new HashMap<>();

        // Adding key-value pairs to the map
        map.put("Alice", 30);
        map.put("Bob", 25);
        map.put("Carol", 35);

        // Retrieving a value based on key
        Integer age = map.get("Alice");
        System.out.println("Alice's age: " + age);

        // Checking if a key is present in the map
        boolean hasKey = map.containsKey("Dave");
        System.out.println("Is Dave in the map? " + hasKey);

        // Removing a key-value pair from the map
        map.remove("Bob");

        // Iterating over the entries in the map
        for (Map.Entry<String, Integer> entry : map.entrySet()) {
            System.out.println(entry.getKey() + ": " + entry.getValue());
        }
    }
}
```

When this code is executed, the output will be:

```
Alice's age: 30
Is Dave in the map? false
Alice: 30
Carol: 35
```

Each map implementation provides specific characteristics that may affect the performance and functionality of the application. Below are brief descriptions of the most common implementations:

- HashMap: Provides constant-time performance for the basic operations; however, the order of the keys is not guaranteed.
- LinkedHashMap: Maintains the order of insertion, making it suitable when the iteration order is important.
- TreeMap: Implements a Red-Black tree that provides guaranteed log(n) time cost for the basic operations and maintains keys in a sorted order.
- ConcurrentHashMap: A thread-safe implementation that allows concurrent access to the map without external synchronization.
- WeakHashMap: Uses weak references for keys, allowing them to be garbage collected if no longer in use elsewhere.
- IdentityHashMap: Compares keys using reference equality (==) instead of the equals() method.

- EnumMap: A specialized implementation designed for use with enum keys, providing highly efficient storage and performance for this specific use case.

Understanding these differences is crucial for selecting the appropriate map implementation based on the specific requirements of the application. Further sections will delve into the detailed characteristics, use cases, and performance implications of each map implementation. This comprehensive exploration will enable effective utilization of map types in versatile programming scenarios.

5.2 HashMap: Unordered Key-Value Pairs

In Java Collections, the HashMap class is a pivotal data structure for managing key-value pairs. Introduced in Java 1.2, HashMap offers a non-synchronized, efficient, and hash table-based implementation of the Map interface. It facilitates quick insertions, deletions, and lookups, making it a popular choice for many applications.

HashMap organizes entries based on the hash code of the keys. Although the order of keys in a HashMap is not guaranteed, it leverages hash codes to optimize performance, typically achieving constant-time complexity for basic operations. Understanding the internal mechanisms and nuances of HashMap is essential for employing it effectively.

```
import java.util.HashMap;
import java.util.Map;

public class HashMapExample {
    public static void main(String[] args) {
        // Creating a HashMap instance
        Map<Integer, String> map = new HashMap<>();

        // Adding key-value pairs to the HashMap
        map.put(1, "Value1");
        map.put(2, "Value2");
        map.put(3, "Value3");

        // Retrieving a value by its key
        String value = map.get(1);
        System.out.println("Key 1: " + value);

        // Checking if a key exists
        boolean containsKey = map.containsKey(2);
        System.out.println("Contains key 2: " + containsKey);

        // Removing a key-value pair
        String removedValue = map.remove(3);
        System.out.println("Removed key 3 with value: " + removedValue);
```

```
        // Iterating over the HashMap entries
        for (Map.Entry<Integer, String> entry : map.entrySet()) {
            System.out.println("Key: " + entry.getKey() + ", Value: " + entry.getValue
                ());
        }
    }
}
```

In this example, we instantiate a HashMap with Integer keys and String values. The put method is used to insert entries, get retrieves values by key, and remove deletes an entry by key. The containsKey method checks for the presence of a specific key, and the entrySet method enables iteration over the map's entries.

One crucial aspect of HashMap operation is the handling of hash collisions. When two keys produce the same hash code, HashMap uses linked lists to manage the entries at the same bucket. Java 8 and later versions optimize this further by converting these linked lists to balanced trees when the number of entries in a bucket exceeds a certain threshold, improving worst-case performance from O(n) to O(log n).

```
import java.util.HashMap;
import java.util.Map;

class Key {
    private int id;

    public Key(int id) {
        this.id = id;
    }

    @Override
    public int hashCode() {
        // Custom hash code implementation causing collision
        return id % 10;
    }

    @Override
    public boolean equals(Object obj) {
        if (this == obj) return true;
        if (obj == null || getClass() != obj.getClass()) return false;
        Key key = (Key) obj;
        return id == key.id;
    }
}

public class HashCollisionExample {
    public static void main(String[] args) {
        Map<Key, String> map = new HashMap<>();
        map.put(new Key(1), "Value1");
        map.put(new Key(11), "Value11");
        map.put(new Key(21), "Value21");

        System.out.println("Entries in HashMap:");
        for (Map.Entry<Key, String> entry : map.entrySet()) {
```

```
            System.out.println("Key: " + entry.getKey().hashCode() + ", Value: " +
                entry.getValue());
        }
    }
}
```

This code demonstrates the potential for hash collisions within a HashMap. The custom Key class, which forces collisions by returning id % 10 in hashCode, exemplifies how multiple keys can end up in the same bucket.

When working with HashMap, it is also important to understand its capacity and load factor. The capacity is the number of buckets in the hash table, and the load factor is a measure that determines when to resize the table. A HashMap resizes itself when the number of entries exceeds the product of the capacity and the load factor. By default, the initial capacity is 16 and the load factor is 0.75.

Optimal resizing considerations can be seen:

```
import java.util.HashMap;
import java.util.Map;

public class CustomHashMap {
    public static void main(String[] args) {
        // Custom initial capacity and load factor
        Map<String, String> map = new HashMap<>(32, 0.5f);
        map.put("Key1", "Value1");
        map.put("Key2", "Value2");

        System.out.println("Map: " + map);
    }
}
```

Setting the initial capacity to 32 and the load factor to 0.5 ensures that the HashMap will resize less frequently compared to the default settings.

Finally, it is significant to be aware of HashMap's non-thread-safe nature. Multiple threads modifying a HashMap concurrently might result in unpredictable behavior and potential loss of data. For concurrent modifications, using ConcurrentHashMap or synchronizing access externally becomes necessary.

```
import java.util.Collections;
import java.util.HashMap;
import java.util.Map;

public class SynchronizedHashMap {
    public static void main(String[] args) {
        // Synchronized HashMap using Collections utility
        Map<String, String> map = Collections.synchronizedMap(new HashMap<>());
        map.put("Key1", "Value1");
```

```
        map.put("Key2", "Value2");

        synchronized (map) {
            for (Map.Entry<String, String> entry : map.entrySet()) {
                System.out.println("Key: " + entry.getKey() + ", Value: " + entry.
                    getValue());
            }
        }
    }
}
```

The Collections.synchronizedMap method creates a synchronized version of the HashMap, ensuring thread safety, although it entails performance trade-offs due to synchronization overhead.

The HashMap remains a robust and efficient data structure for many applications, offering a versatile solution for managing key-value associations with careful consideration of its unique characteristics and limitations.

5.3 LinkedHashMap: Ordered Key-Value Pairs

The LinkedHashMap is a synchronous implementation of the Map interface, extending HashMap by adding predictable iteration order. This characteristic makes LinkedHashMap particularly useful when we need the retrieval order to be the same as insertion order or to be maintained in a least-recently-used (LRU) order.

LinkedHashMap inherits from HashMap, thus it retains the same basic properties: it permits null values and the null key, and it provides constant-time performance for the basic operations like get and put.

Below is a brief illustration of the creation and use of a LinkedHashMap:

```
import java.util.LinkedHashMap;
import java.util.Map;

public class LinkedHashMapExample {
    public static void main(String[] args) {
        Map<Integer, String> linkedHashMap = new LinkedHashMap<>();

        // Adding elements to LinkedHashMap
        linkedHashMap.put(1, "One");
        linkedHashMap.put(2, "Two");
        linkedHashMap.put(3, "Three");
        // Print elements to observe order
        System.out.println(linkedHashMap);

        // Access an element to observe order preservation
```

```
        linkedHashMap.get(2); // This access does not change the order in insertion-
            order LinkedHashMap
        System.out.println(linkedHashMap);
    }
}
```

Output:
{1=One, 2=Two, 3=Three}
{1=One, 2=Two, 3=Three}

The LinkedHashMap in the above example maintains the order of insertion, as evidenced by the preserved order of elements in its output.

Predictable Order

One of the defining features of LinkedHashMap is that it ensures the order of iteration over keys, values, or entries is predictable. By default, LinkedHashMap maintains insertion-order iteration, which means entries are iterated in the order in which they were inserted.

Alternatively, LinkedHashMap can be configured to maintain access-order iteration, meaning entries are iterated in the order in which they were last accessed, from least-recently accessed to most-recently. This is particularly useful for caching mechanisms, using the access-order pattern to implement an LRU (Least Recently Used) cache. Here is an example illustrating an access-order LinkedHashMap:

```
import java.util.LinkedHashMap;
import java.util.Map;

public class LRUCacheExample {
    public static void main(String[] args) {
        // Setting accessOrder=true for LRU iteration order
        LinkedHashMap<Integer, String> lruCache = new LinkedHashMap<>(16, 0.75f
            , true);

        // Adding elements to LinkedHashMap
        lruCache.put(1, "One");
        lruCache.put(2, "Two");
        lruCache.put(3, "Three");
        System.out.println(lruCache);

        // Access elements
        lruCache.get(2);
        lruCache.get(1);
        System.out.println(lruCache);

        // Adding another element
        lruCache.put(4, "Four");
        System.out.println(lruCache);
    }
}
```

Output:
{1=One, 2=Two, 3=Three}
{3=Three, 2=Two, 1=One}
{3=Three, 2=Two, 1=One, 4=Four}

Accessing elements get(2) and get(1) shifts their positions within the iteration order, demonstrating the LRU characteristics.

Removing the Eldest Entry

The LinkedHashMap class also provides a mechanism to remove the "eldest" entry. The method removeEldestEntry can be overridden to impose a policy for removing old entries. It is invoked by put and putAll operations after inserting a new entry.

Here is an example illustrating how to extend LinkedHashMap with a custom cache size limit:

```
import java.util.LinkedHashMap;
import java.util.Map;

public class LRUCacheWithSizeLimit<K, V> extends LinkedHashMap<K, V> {
    private final int maxSize;

    public LRUCacheWithSizeLimit(int maxSize) {
        super(16, 0.75f, true);
        this.maxSize = maxSize;
    }

    @Override
    protected boolean removeEldestEntry(Map.Entry<K, V> eldest) {
        return size() > maxSize;
    }

    public static void main(String[] args) {
        LRUCacheWithSizeLimit<Integer, String> cache = new
                LRUCacheWithSizeLimit<>(3);

        cache.put(1, "One");
        cache.put(2, "Two");
        cache.put(3, "Three");
        System.out.println(cache);

        cache.get(1);
        cache.get(2);
        cache.put(4, "Four");
        System.out.println(cache);

        cache.put(5, "Five");
        System.out.println(cache);
    }
}
```

Output:
{1=One, 2=Two, 3=Three}
{3=Three, 1=One, 2=Two, 4=Four}
{1=One, 2=Two, 4=Four, 5=Five}

In this implementation, the cache has a maximum size limit of 3. When the fourth entry is added, the oldest entry according to the LRU policy is removed.

Performance Considerations

LinkedHashMap generally performs slightly worse than HashMap due to the added overhead of maintaining the doubly-linked list which preserves order. However, the performance difference is often negligible for many applications. The high predictability of iteration order provides significant advantages that outweigh this minor overhead.

In practice, LinkedHashMap is highly useful for many scenarios requiring predictable iteration order, such as creating caches or constructing sequences where order matters.

5.4 TreeMap: Sorted Key-Value Pairs

A TreeMap is a part of the Java Collections Framework that implements the Map interface. Unlike a HashMap, which stores key-value pairs in an unordered manner, a TreeMap maintains its keys in a sorted order. Internally, TreeMap uses a Red-Black tree, a self-balancing binary search tree, to store data. This ensures that the map remains sorted and allows for log(n) time complexity for insertion, deletion, and lookup.

To illustrate the basic usage of a TreeMap, consider the following example:

```
import java.util.TreeMap;

public class TreeMapExample {
    public static void main(String[] args) {
        TreeMap<String, Integer> map = new TreeMap<>();

        // Adding elements to the TreeMap
        map.put("Apple", 5);
        map.put("Orange", 7);
        map.put("Banana", 3);
        map.put("Pineapple", 8);

        // Displaying elements in the TreeMap
        for (Map.Entry<String, Integer> entry : map.entrySet()) {
            System.out.println("Key: " + entry.getKey() + ", Value: " + entry.getValue
                ());
        }
    }
}
```

In this example, the keys ("Apple", "Orange", "Banana", "Pineapple") are automatically sorted in natural ordering. The output of this program will be:

```
Key: Apple, Value: 5
Key: Banana, Value: 3
Key: Orange, Value: 7
Key: Pineapple, Value: 8
```

It is also possible to sort the TreeMap keys using a custom comparator. This functionality adds flexibility to how entries can be ordered. Consider the following example, which sorts the keys in reverse order:

```
import java.util.TreeMap;
import java.util.Comparator;

public class ReverseOrderTreeMap {
    public static void main(String[] args) {
        // Creating a TreeMap with a custom comparator (reverse order)
        TreeMap<String, Integer> map = new TreeMap<>(Comparator.reverseOrder())
            ;

        // Adding elements to the TreeMap
        map.put("Apple", 5);
        map.put("Orange", 7);
        map.put("Banana", 3);
        map.put("Pineapple", 8);

        // Displaying elements in the TreeMap
        for (Map.Entry<String, Integer> entry : map.entrySet()) {
            System.out.println("Key: " + entry.getKey() + ", Value: " + entry.getValue
                ());
        }
    }
}
```

The output in this case will be:

```
Key: Pineapple, Value: 8
Key: Orange, Value: 7
Key: Banana, Value: 3
Key: Apple, Value: 5
```

TreeMap also provides several methods specific to sorted maps. The headMap, tailMap, and subMap methods allow for the retrieval of a portion of the map based on key ranges. These methods are very useful for range query operations.

```
import java.util.TreeMap;
import java.util.SortedMap;

public class TreeMapRangeQuery {
    public static void main(String[] args) {
        TreeMap<Integer, String> map = new TreeMap<>();

        // Adding elements to the TreeMap
        map.put(1, "One");
        map.put(2, "Two");
        map.put(3, "Three");
        map.put(4, "Four");
        map.put(5, "Five");
```

```
        // Getting a view of the keys from 2 (inclusive) to 4 (exclusive)
        SortedMap<Integer, String> subMap = map.subMap(2, 4);

        // Displaying the subMap
        for (Map.Entry<Integer, String> entry : subMap.entrySet()) {
            System.out.println("Key: " + entry.getKey() + ", Value: " + entry.getValue
                ());
        }

        // Getting a headMap for keys less than 3
        SortedMap<Integer, String> headMap = map.headMap(3);

        // Displaying the headMap
        for (Map.Entry<Integer, String> entry : headMap.entrySet()) {
            System.out.println("Key: " + entry.getKey() + ", Value: " + entry.getValue
                ());
        }

        // Getting a tailMap for keys greater than or equal to 3
        SortedMap<Integer, String> tailMap = map.tailMap(3);

        // Displaying the tailMap
        for (Map.Entry<Integer, String> entry : tailMap.entrySet()) {
            System.out.println("Key: " + entry.getKey() + ", Value: " + entry.getValue
                ());
        }
    }
}
```

The output of this program will be:

```
SubMap:
Key: 2, Value: Two
Key: 3, Value: Three

HeadMap:
Key: 1, Value: One
Key: 2, Value: Two

TailMap:
Key: 3, Value: Three
Key: 4, Value: Four
Key: 5, Value: Five
```

Additionally, TreeMap supports the NavigableMap interface which provides navigation methods such as lowerEntry, floorEntry, ceilingEntry, and higherEntry. These methods can be used to find entries that are closest to a given key.

```
import java.util.TreeMap;
import java.util.Map;

public class NavigableTreeMapExample {
    public static void main(String[] args) {
        TreeMap<String, Integer> map = new TreeMap<>();

        // Adding elements to the TreeMap
        map.put("A", 1);
        map.put("B", 2);
        map.put("C", 3);
```

```
        map.put("D", 4);

        // Finding elements using navigation methods
        Map.Entry<String, Integer> lowerEntry = map.lowerEntry("C"); // Entry with
            key < "C"
        Map.Entry<String, Integer> floorEntry = map.floorEntry("C"); // Entry with
            key <= "C"
        Map.Entry<String, Integer> ceilingEntry = map.ceilingEntry("C"); // Entry
            with key >= "C"
        Map.Entry<String, Integer> higherEntry = map.higherEntry("C"); // Entry
            with key > "C"

        // Displaying navigation results
        System.out.println("Lower Entry: " + lowerEntry);
        System.out.println("Floor Entry: " + floorEntry);
        System.out.println("Ceiling Entry: " + ceilingEntry);
        System.out.println("Higher Entry: " + higherEntry);
    }
}
```

The output of this program will be:

```
Lower Entry: A=1
Floor Entry: C=3
Ceiling Entry: C=3
Higher Entry: D=4
```

Given its properties, TreeMap should be used when a sorted iteration order is needed or when range queries on the keys are required. However, it is important to consider that TreeMap has higher overhead compared to HashMap due to its sorting properties. Thus, if the specific order or range queries are not required, other map implementations may be more efficient.

5.5 ConcurrentHashMap: Thread-Safe Maps

Concurrent programming involves scenarios where multiple threads operate on shared data simultaneously, necessitating the use of data structures that can handle concurrent access to ensure data integrity. ConcurrentHashMap is a part of the java.util.concurrent package, providing a thread-safe alternative to HashMap without the need for explicit synchronization.

ConcurrentHashMap offers high concurrency by segmenting the map into multiple parts (or segments), each governed by its own lock. This segmentation allows multiple threads to read or write to different segments of the map concurrently, significantly improving throughput in multithreaded applications.

```
import java.util.concurrent.ConcurrentHashMap;
```

```
import java.util.concurrent.ExecutorService;
import java.util.concurrent.Executors;

public class ConcurrentHashMapExample {
    public static void main(String[] args) {
        ConcurrentHashMap<Integer, String> map = new ConcurrentHashMap<>();

        ExecutorService executor = Executors.newFixedThreadPool(2);

        Runnable task1 = () -> {
            for (int i = 0; i < 50; i++) {
                map.put(i, "Value" + i);
            }
        };

        Runnable task2 = () -> {
            for (int i = 50; i < 100; i++) {
                map.put(i, "Value" + i);
            }
        };

        executor.submit(task1);
        executor.submit(task2);

        executor.shutdown();

        while (!executor.isTerminated()) {
            // wait for both tasks to complete
        }

        System.out.println(map);
    }
}
```

The above example demonstrates the use of ConcurrentHashMap with multiple threads writing to the map concurrently. The map's internal structure allows these operations without contention, resulting in a map populated with key-value pairs from both tasks without requiring additional locks or synchronization.

Key properties of ConcurrentHashMap ensure thread safety and performance:

- Strong Consistency: Each individual atomic operation, such as put(), get(), remove(), and replace(), guarantees strong consistency.
- Lock-Free Reading: Multiple threads can read from the map concurrently without locking. Iteration over the map's contents uses a "snapshot" method, where it reflects the state at some moment during the iteration without blocking updates.
- High Concurrency: Internally segmented locking (often referred to as lock striping) minimizes contention by allowing concurrent

modifications.

- No Nulls Allowed: ConcurrentHashMap does not permit null keys or values. Attempting to insert a null key or value will result in a NullPointerException.

The segmentation mechanism is crucial to understanding ConcurrentHashMap's design. It effectively reduces contention by isolating individual segments from concurrent modifications. Each segment contains a subset of the hash bins and has its own lock, allowing threads to operate on different segments independently. Here is a deeper insight into its implementation.

Algorithm 3: Basic Operations in ConcurrentHashMap

Input : Key-value pairs (K, V)
Output : Thread-safe ConcurrentHashMap

```
Function put(K, V):
    locate appropriate segment
    acquire segment lock
    compute hash for K
    index into segment's bucket array
    insert new K,V pair
    release segment lock

Function get(K):
    locate appropriate segment
    compute hash for K
    index into segment's bucket array
    return value associated with K

Function remove(K):
    locate appropriate segment
    acquire segment lock
    compute hash for K
    index into segment's bucket array
    remove K and associated value
    release segment lock

Function replace(K, V):
    locate appropriate segment
    acquire segment lock
    compute hash for K
    index into segment's bucket array
    replace existing value with V
    release segment lock
```

One syntactic improvement in Java 8 is the introduction of methods that leverage lambdas for more expressive operations. These methods include computeIfAbsent, merge, and similar functional approaches, facilitating thread-safe computations within the map.

```
public class ConcurrentHashMapLambdaExample {
    public static void main(String[] args) {
        ConcurrentHashMap<String, Integer> map = new ConcurrentHashMap<>();

        map.put("a", 1);
        map.put("b", 2);
```

```
        // computeIfAbsent
        map.computeIfAbsent("c", key -> 3);

        // merge
        map.merge("b", 2, (existingVal, newVal) -> existingVal + newVal);

        // forEach
        map.forEach((key, value) -> System.out.println(key + ": " + value));
    }
}
```

Use-cases for ConcurrentHashMap are prevalent in scenarios requiring high throughput and low latency. For instance, designing a real-time analytics dashboard where multiple threads ingest data and update shared data structures for computation would benefit from the high concurrency guaranteed by ConcurrentHashMap.

5.6 WeakHashMap: Maps with Weak Keys

A WeakHashMap in Java is a specific implementation of the Map interface where the keys are held using java.lang.ref.WeakReference. This allows entries to be removed by the garbage collector when the key is no longer in ordinary use, making WeakHashMap particularly useful for memory-sensitive applications such as caches.

In a HashMap, the keys are strongly referenced, meaning that as long as the map holds a reference to a key, the key cannot be garbage-collected. This can lead to memory leaks if the map holds onto keys that are no longer needed elsewhere in the application. In contrast, WeakHashMap allows for the keys to be garbage-collected when there are no longer any strong references to them. When the garbage collector reclaims a key, the corresponding entry in the WeakHashMap is effectively removed from the map.

```
import java.util.Map;
import java.util.WeakHashMap;

public class WeakHashMapExample {
    public static void main(String[] args) {
        Map<Object, String> weakHashMap = new WeakHashMap<>();

        Object key1 = new Object();
        Object key2 = new Object();

        weakHashMap.put(key1, "value1");
        weakHashMap.put(key2, "value2");

        System.out.println("Before nulling references: " + weakHashMap); // {key1=
              value1, key2=value2}
```

```
        key1 = null; // Eligible for GC
        System.gc();

        System.out.println("After nulling key1 reference and GC: " + weakHashMap);
            // {key2=value2} or {key1=value1, key2=value2}

        key2 = null; // Eligible for GC
        System.gc();

        System.out.println("After nulling key2 reference and GC: " + weakHashMap);
            // {}
    }
}
```

The above example demonstrates a simple use of WeakHashMap. Two keys (key1 and key2) are added to the map. After making key1 null and requesting the garbage collector, key1 and its associated value can be removed from the map. Similarly, making key2 null and forcing garbage collection ensures that key2 and its associated value are also removed.

WeakHashMap is particularly sensible for scenarios such as implementing canonicalizing mappings, where values are stored for as long as the keys are reachable by the application. Canonicalizing mappings are useful for cases where there is no necessity to maintain an entry in the map if the key is no longer reachable by any thread.

A unique attribute of WeakHashMap is its behavior concerning entries where keys become garbage-collected. They are automatically removed from the map, making it unnecessary to manually clean them. However, this also implies that WeakHashMap does not provide predictable iteration behavior since entries can be removed asynchronously due to garbage collection.

```
import java.util.Iterator;
import java.util.Map;
import java.util.WeakHashMap;

public class WeakHashMapIterationExample {
    public static void main(String[] args) {
        Map<Object, String> weakHashMap = new WeakHashMap<>();

        Object key1 = new Object();
        Object key2 = new Object();

        weakHashMap.put(key1, "value1");
        weakHashMap.put(key2, "value2");

        key1 = null; // Eligible for GC
        System.gc();

        Iterator<Map.Entry<Object, String>> iterator = weakHashMap.entrySet().
            iterator();

        while(iterator.hasNext()) {
```

```
            Map.Entry<Object, String> entry = iterator.next();
            if (entry.getValue().equals("value2")) {
                iterator.remove();
            }
        }

        System.out.println("After iteration and removal: " + weakHashMap); // (May
            vary depending on GC timing)
    }
}
```

In the above example, iterating over the WeakHashMap while garbage collection may occur asynchronously can lead to non-deterministic behavior. Notably, entries can be removed during iteration, creating potential inconsistencies in the set of elements being iterated upon at any point in time.

For use cases where predictable behavior is paramount, especially during iteration or when specific map-state guarantees must be maintained, WeakHashMap may not be the optimal choice. Alternatives such as ConcurrentHashMap or traditional HashMap with manual cleanup mechanisms may be preferred.

WeakHashMap keys must have proper equals() and hashCode() implementations, just like other map types. However, due to the weak referencing nature, keys must consider natural identity to avoid unexpected garbage collection or premature entry removal.

Proper usage of WeakHashMap can lead to efficient memory management without sacrificing performance for specific workloads. Understanding the advantages and the inherent caveats ensures that developers can make informed decisions when selecting the appropriate map type for their application requirements.

5.7 IdentityHashMap: Key Comparison by Reference

The IdentityHashMap is a specialized implementation of the Map interface within the Java Collections Framework. Unlike the more commonly used HashMap, which uses the equals() method for comparing keys, the IdentityHashMap relies on reference equality (==) for such comparisons. This unique approach can be particularly beneficial in certain specialized scenarios where the reference comparison of keys is crucial.

IdentityHashMap is defined in the java.util package and extends the abstract class AbstractMap. This map implementation is not designed for general-purpose map operations but rather for cases where you need the reference identity behavior.

```
import java.util.IdentityHashMap;

public class IdentityHashMapExample {
    public static void main(String[] args) {
        IdentityHashMap<String, String> identityMap = new IdentityHashMap<>();

        String key1 = new String("key");
        String key2 = new String("key");

        identityMap.put(key1, "value1");
        identityMap.put(key2, "value2");

        System.out.println(identityMap.get(key1)); // Output: value1
        System.out.println(identityMap.get(key2)); // Output: value2
        System.out.println(identityMap.size()); // Output: 2
    }
}
```

In the above example, the IdentityHashMap stores two entries with "key1" and "key2" even though their equals() method would consider them equal because they contain the same sequence of characters. However, since IdentityHashMap uses reference equality, it treats key1 and key2 as distinct objects.

Implementation Details

IdentityHashMap uses an array-based internal structure to store key-value pairs. The keys and values are stored in adjacent cells within this array. The initial size of the array is 32 elements, providing 16 key-value pair slots, and it grows as more entries are added. Here is a simplified view of the internal representation:

```
Object[] table = new Object[32];
table[0] = key1;
table[1] = value1;
table[2] = key2;
table[3] = value2;
// and so on...
```

This array-based approach, along with identity hashing (System.identityHashCode()), determines the slot for key-value pairs.

Comparing IdentityHashMap with HashMap

The primary distinction between IdentityHashMap and HashMap lies in their key comparison strategy.

- HashMap uses equals() and hashCode() for key comparisons, making it suitable for general-purpose usage.
- IdentityHashMap uses reference equality (==) and the system identity hash code (System.identityHashCode()), making it suitable for specialized use-cases where key comparison by reference is needed.

The code example demonstrated earlier highlights this difference by showcasing how distinct key instances, which are considered equal by equals(), are treated as distinct in IdentityHashMap.

Performance Considerations

IdentityHashMap offers constant-time performance for basic operations (get, put, etc.), assuming a well-distributed hash function. However, it uses more memory compared to HashMap due to its internal array structure and reference-based comparison.

Use Cases

IdentityHashMap is particularly useful in the following scenarios:

- Caching systems where the identity of keys (rather than their logical equality) is important.
- Implementing memoization, where the exact reference of keys needs to be cached.
- Symbol tables in languages where symbol identities should be preserved.
- Tracking object references uniquely during JVM operations like garbage collection or serialization/deserialization processes.

IdentityHashMap supports fast reference-based key comparisons and specific, rare use-cases within applications requiring such characteristics. Understanding its behavior and constraints ensures its effective utilization in optimizing and addressing application-specific requirements.

5.8 EnumMap: Specialized Map for Enums

EnumMap is a specialized implementation for use with enum type keys. As part of the java.util package, EnumMap offers a high-performance alternative to general-purpose map implementations when the keys are enumerated types. An EnumMap is internally represented as an array, which ensures both efficient storage and fast access times.

Declaration and Initialization:

To initialize an EnumMap, you need to specify the key type, which should be an enum. Consider an example where we have an enum called DayOfWeek:

```
public enum DayOfWeek {
    SUNDAY, MONDAY, TUESDAY, WEDNESDAY,
    THURSDAY, FRIDAY, SATURDAY
}
```

An EnumMap can be instantiated as follows:

```
EnumMap<DayOfWeek, String> dayPlan = new EnumMap<>(DayOfWeek.class);
```

Here, dayPlan is an EnumMap where enums of type DayOfWeek are keys, and the value type is String.

Basic Operations:

Like other maps, EnumMap supports all basic operations such as put, get, and remove.

```
dayPlan.put(DayOfWeek.MONDAY, "Go to the gym");
System.out.println(dayPlan.get(DayOfWeek.MONDAY)); // Output: Go to the gym
dayPlan.remove(DayOfWeek.MONDAY);
System.out.println(dayPlan.get(DayOfWeek.MONDAY)); // Output: null
```

Iteration:

Iteration in an EnumMap can be performed using key or entry sets, similar to other maps. However, it is important to note that iteration in EnumMap respects the natural order of the enum constants, i.e., the order in which they are declared.

```
for (DayOfWeek day : dayPlan.keySet()) {
    System.out.println(day + ": " + dayPlan.get(day));
}
```

Efficiency Considerations:

EnumMap is more efficient than HashMap for enum keys due to its predictable key set and array-based implementation. The primary performance benefits include:

- **Speed:** EnumMap provides constant-time performance for put, get, and remove operations.
- **Memory Efficiency:** It uses a very compact representation, allocating space only for the actual enum constants utilized as keys.
- **No Need for Hashing:** Keys are internally represented as ordinal values of enum constants, eliminating the need for costly hash calculations.

Restrictions and Characteristics:

Although EnumMap offers significant advantages, developers should be aware of some limitations:

- EnumMap keys must be of a single enum type.
- Null keys are not supported and attempting to use null as a key will result in a NullPointerException.

- EnumMap is not synchronized, meaning it should not be accessed concurrently by multiple threads without external synchronization.

Use Cases:

EnumMap is ideally suited for scenarios where enum constants naturally map to values. Common use cases include looking up configurations or settings enumerated by type.

```
public enum ConfigOption {
    MAX_THREADS, CONNECTION_TIMEOUT, ENABLE_LOGGING
}

EnumMap<ConfigOption, Object> configurations = new EnumMap<>(ConfigOption.
    class);
configurations.put(ConfigOption.MAX_THREADS, 10);
configurations.put(ConfigOption.CONNECTION_TIMEOUT, 5000);
configurations.put(ConfigOption.ENABLE_LOGGING, true);

System.out.println(configurations.get(ConfigOption.MAX_THREADS)); // Output: 10
System.out.println(configurations.get(ConfigOption.CONNECTION_TIMEOUT)); //
    Output: 5000
System.out.println(configurations.get(ConfigOption.ENABLE_LOGGING)); // Output:
    true
```

Comparison to Other Map Types:

Compared to HashMap, TreeMap, and other map implementations:

- EnumMap has lower memory overhead when dealing with enum keys.
- TreeMap provides sorted map functionality, but at a cost of increased complexity and memory usage.
- HashMap is more versatile, but EnumMap is faster and more space-efficient for enum keys.

The purposeful design of EnumMap for enums ensures that it remains the optimal and recommended choice when the domain of keys is an enumerated type.

5.9 Common Map Operations

In Java, maps are powerful, versatile data structures that allow associations between keys and values. They support numerous operations that facilitate the manipulation and usage of key-value pairs. This section elucidates the most frequently used map operations, providing a fundamental understanding of each and their typical use cases. We will explore put, get, remove, containsKey, containsValue, size, isEmpty, and clear functions with detailed examples.

1. Adding a Key-Value Pair: put

The put method is used to add or update a key-value pair in a map. If the specified key already exists, the corresponding value is updated with the new value passed to the method.

```
import java.util.HashMap;
import java.util.Map;

public class MapPutExample {
    public static void main(String[] args) {
        Map<String, Integer> map = new HashMap<>();
        map.put("apple", 1); // Adds key 'apple' with value 1
        map.put("banana", 2); // Adds key 'banana' with value 2
        map.put("apple", 3); // Updates value of 'apple' to 3

        System.out.println(map);
    }
}
```

Output: {banana=2, apple=3}

2. Retrieving a Value: get

The get method retrieves the value associated with a specified key. If the key does not exist in the map, the method returns null.

```
import java.util.HashMap;
import java.util.Map;

public class MapGetExample {
    public static void main(String[] args) {
        Map<String, Integer> map = new HashMap<>();
        map.put("apple", 1);
        map.put("banana", 2);

        Integer value = map.get("apple"); // Retrieves value for 'apple'
        System.out.println("Value for key 'apple': " + value);

        value = map.get("cherry"); // No entry for 'cherry'
        System.out.println("Value for key 'cherry': " + value);
    }
}
```

Output:
Value for key 'apple': 1
Value for key 'cherry': null

3. Removing a Key-Value Pair: remove

The remove method deletes the key-value pair for a specified key. It returns the value associated with the key, or null if the key was not present.

```
import java.util.HashMap;
import java.util.Map;

public class MapRemoveExample {
    public static void main(String[] args) {
        Map<String, Integer> map = new HashMap<>();
        map.put("apple", 1);
        map.put("banana", 2);

        Integer removedValue = map.remove("apple"); // Removes key 'apple'
        System.out.println("Removed value: " + removedValue);
        System.out.println(map);
    }
}
```

```
Output:
Removed value: 1
{banana=2}
```

4. Checking for a Key: containsKey

The containsKey method checks if the map contains a specific key. It returns true if the key is present, otherwise false.

```
import java.util.HashMap;
import java.util.Map;

public class MapContainsKeyExample {
    public static void main(String[] args) {
        Map<String, Integer> map = new HashMap<>();
        map.put("apple", 1);
        map.put("banana", 2);

        boolean containsApple = map.containsKey("apple");
        System.out.println("Contains key 'apple': " + containsApple);

        boolean containsCherry = map.containsKey("cherry");
        System.out.println("Contains key 'cherry': " + containsCherry);
    }
}
```

```
Output:
Contains key 'apple': true
Contains key 'cherry': false
```

5. Checking for a Value: containsValue

The containsValue method determines if a specified value is associated with any key in the map. It returns true if the value is present, otherwise false.

```
import java.util.HashMap;
import java.util.Map;

public class MapContainsValueExample {
    public static void main(String[] args) {
```

```
        Map<String, Integer> map = new HashMap<>();
        map.put("apple", 1);
        map.put("banana", 2);

        boolean containsValue1 = map.containsValue(1);
        System.out.println("Contains value 1: " + containsValue1);

        boolean containsValue3 = map.containsValue(3);
        System.out.println("Contains value 3: " + containsValue3);
    }
}
```

Output:
Contains value 1: true
Contains value 3: false

6. Obtaining Map Size: size

The size method returns the number of key-value pairs in the map.

```
import java.util.HashMap;
import java.util.Map;

public class MapSizeExample {
    public static void main(String[] args) {
        Map<String, Integer> map = new HashMap<>();
        map.put("apple", 1);
        map.put("banana", 2);

        int size = map.size();
        System.out.println("Size of the map: " + size);
    }
}
```

Output:
Size of the map: 2

7. Checking for Emptiness: isEmpty

The isEmpty method checks if the map contains any key-value pairs. It returns true if the map is empty, otherwise false.

```
import java.util.HashMap;
import java.util.Map;

public class MapIsEmptyExample {
    public static void main(String[] args) {
        Map<String, Integer> map = new HashMap<>();
        System.out.println("Is map empty? " + map.isEmpty());

        map.put("apple", 1);
        System.out.println("Is map empty? " + map.isEmpty());
    }
}
```

Output:
Is map empty? true
Is map empty? false

8. Clearing the Map: clear

The clear method removes all key-value pairs from the map.

```
import java.util.HashMap;
import java.util.Map;

public class MapClearExample {
    public static void main(String[] args) {
        Map<String, Integer> map = new HashMap<>();
        map.put("apple", 1);
        map.put("banana", 2);

        map.clear();
        System.out.println("Map after clear operation: " + map);
    }
}
```

```
Output:
Map after clear operation: {}
```

Understanding these common map operations provides the foundational knowledge required to manipulate maps effectively. Each method serves a specific function, enabling precise control over data stored in key-value associations. Mastery of these operations is essential for leveraging the full capabilities of maps in Java applications.

5.10 Performance Considerations for Maps

Understanding the performance characteristics of different map implementations is crucial for selecting the appropriate map for a given application. The performance of maps in the Java Collections Framework varies based on the underlying data structures and the nature of operations being performed. This section explores the key performance aspects to consider when working with maps, including time complexity, space complexity, and concurrency implications.

Time Complexity

Different map implementations offer varying time complexities for basic operations such as insertion, deletion, and retrieval.

- **HashMap**: HashMap provides average-case O(1) time complexity for get, put, and remove operations, assuming a good hash function that distributes keys uniformly. However, in the worst case, if many keys hash to the same bucket, the time complexity can degrade to O(n).

- **LinkedHashMap**: LinkedHashMap maintains a doubly-linked list running through its entries, adding a small overhead to the operations. Despite this, the average-case time complexities for get, put, and remove operations remain O(1).
- **TreeMap**: TreeMap is implemented as a Red-Black Tree, which guarantees O(log n) time complexity for get, put, and remove operations, providing a predictable performance profile.
- **ConcurrentHashMap**: ConcurrentHashMap aims to provide thread-safe operations with high throughput under concurrent access. Its performance is generally on par with HashMap, with average-case O(1) time complexity. However, some additional overhead exists due to synchronization.
- **WeakHashMap**: Operations on WeakHashMap exhibit similar performance characteristics to HashMap, with average-case O(1) time complexity. The garbage collection overhead, however, might slightly affect performance.
- **IdentityHashMap**: IdentityHashMap has a similar performance to HashMap with average-case O(1) time complexity but uses reference equality rather than object equality.
- **EnumMap**: EnumMap is designed specifically for enumerations and offers very efficient, almost constant time, operations. Its performance is typically better than HashMap or TreeMap for enum keys.

Space Complexity

The amount of memory consumed by different map implementations can also be a critical factor.

- **HashMap** and **LinkedHashMap**: Both implement a hash table-based structure. HashMap requires additional space for storing the bucket array and the entries. LinkedHashMap additionally maintains pointers for maintaining order, incurring slightly higher space complexity.
- **TreeMap**: TreeMap's Red-Black Tree structure has higher space overhead due to the need to store extra pointers and balancing information for each node.

- **ConcurrentHashMap**: ConcurrentHashMap has substantial space overhead because it maintains multiple segments or a more complex data structure to manage concurrent writes.
- **WeakHashMap**: WeakHashMap may use less memory for entries that can be garbage collected when not referenced elsewhere. This can be advantageous in scenarios with large key sets where memory management is a concern.
- **IdentityHashMap**: IdentityHashMap is typically very space-efficient as it avoids object equality checks and only requires a leaner hash table structure.
- **EnumMap**: EnumMap uses an array internally to map enum constants to their corresponding values, which is very space-efficient for the intended use case.

Concurrency and Synchronization

If the application involves concurrent access to maps, considering thread safety and synchronization aspects is crucial.

- **HashMap**: Not thread-safe. Using a HashMap in a multi-threaded environment without external synchronization can lead to data corruption.

```
Map<String, Integer> map = Collections.synchronizedMap(new HashMap<>());
```

- **LinkedHashMap**, **TreeMap**, **WeakHashMap**, and **IdentityHashMap**: Similar to HashMap, these are not thread-safe and require external synchronization for concurrent access.
- **ConcurrentHashMap**: Designed for concurrent use, it employs a sophisticated locking mechanism that allows concurrent reads and a high level of concurrent writes, achieving high throughput.
- **EnumMap**: Not thread-safe. If used in a concurrent setting, external synchronization is required.

Using ConcurrentHashMap enhances access in a multi-threaded environment.

```
ConcurrentHashMap<String, Integer> concurrentMap = new ConcurrentHashMap
    <>();
```

Practical Guidance for Map Selection

Selection of an appropriate map implementation depends on the specific requirements of your application:

- For general-purpose use, where thread safety is not a concern, HashMap is typically the most performant option.
- If preserving insertion order is essential, LinkedHashMap should be considered.
- When there is a need to maintain a sorted order of keys, TreeMap is appropriate despite its higher time complexity.
- In applications involving concurrent access with a need for high throughput, ConcurrentHashMap is the recommended choice.
- For scenarios where issues related to garbage collection of keys arise, WeakHashMap can be beneficial.
- For cases requiring key comparison by reference, IdentityHashMap offers the most efficient solution.
- When using enums as keys, EnumMap provides unmatched efficiency and performance.

Considering these factors ensures optimal performance and resource usage for map-related operations.

5.11 Iterating Over Maps

To proficiently manipulate and traverse maps within the Java Collections Framework, understanding the various techniques to iterate over the entries, keys, and values of a map is paramount.

Using Entry Set: One can iterate over the key-value pairs of a map using its entry set. The entry set provides a Set<Map.Entry<K, V» view of the map which can be traversed using an enhanced for loop or an iterator. This method is efficient and recommended for most use cases.

```
Map<String, Integer> map = new HashMap<>();
map.put("One", 1);
map.put("Two", 2);
map.put("Three", 3);
```

```
for (Map.Entry<String, Integer> entry : map.entrySet()) {
    System.out.println("Key: " + entry.getKey() + ", Value: " + entry.getValue());
}
```

Using Key Set: Another approach is to iterate over the set of keys and then retrieve values corresponding to those keys. This method involves accessing each value by its key, and it is slightly less efficient than using the entry set because it requires an additional lookup.

```
Map<String, Integer> map = new HashMap<>();
map.put("One", 1);
map.put("Two", 2);
map.put("Three", 3);

for (String key : map.keySet()) {
    System.out.println("Key: " + key + ", Value: " + map.get(key));
}
```

Using Values: Iterating over the values contained in the map can be achieved via the values() method. This provides a Collection<V> of all the values present in the map. However, this method is limited as it does not provide access to the keys.

```
Map<String, Integer> map = new HashMap<>();
map.put("One", 1);
map.put("Two", 2);
map.put("Three", 3);

for (Integer value : map.values()) {
    System.out.println("Value: " + value);
}
```

Using Java 8 forEach: Java 8 introduced the forEach method, which allows for a more functional programming approach using lambda expressions.

```
Map<String, Integer> map = new HashMap<>();
map.put("One", 1);
map.put("Two", 2);
map.put("Three", 3);

map.forEach((key, value) -> System.out.println("Key: " + key + ", Value: " + value));
```

Using Stream API: The Stream API in Java 8 can also be utilized to iterate over a map for various tasks, including filtering, mapping, and reducing.

```
Map<String, Integer> map = new HashMap<>();
map.put("One", 1);
map.put("Two", 2);
map.put("Three", 3);

map.entrySet().stream()
```

```
    .forEach(entry -> System.out.println("Key: " + entry.getKey() + ", Value: " +
        entry.getValue()));
```

Concurrent Iteration: When dealing with concurrent maps, such as ConcurrentHashMap, iteration can be safely performed without external synchronization. Iterators returned by the keySet, entrySet, and values views of ConcurrentHashMap are designed to handle concurrent modifications.

```
import java.util.concurrent.ConcurrentHashMap;
import java.util.Map;

ConcurrentHashMap<String, Integer> map = new ConcurrentHashMap<>();
map.put("One", 1);
map.put("Two", 2);
map.put("Three", 3);

for (Map.Entry<String, Integer> entry : map.entrySet()) {
    System.out.println("Key: " + entry.getKey() + ", Value: " + entry.getValue());
}
```

Removing Entries During Iteration: Care must be taken when modifying a map during iteration. Using an iterator, entries can be safely removed; for example, by using the iterator.remove() method.

```
Map<String, Integer> map = new HashMap<>();
map.put("One", 1);
map.put("Two", 2);
map.put("Three", 3);

Iterator<Map.Entry<String, Integer>> iterator = map.entrySet().iterator();
while (iterator.hasNext()) {
    Map.Entry<String, Integer> entry = iterator.next();
    if (entry.getValue() == 2) {
        iterator.remove();
    }
}
```

ConcurrentHashMap allows concurrent modifications, including removals, without throwing a ConcurrentModificationException.

Employing these techniques, developers can efficiently traverse and manipulate maps, selecting the method best suited to their contextual requirements. The approach chosen often depends on the specific needs of the operation being performed and the characteristics of the map implementation in use.

5.12 Custom Map Implementations

Extending the basic functionality of Java's Map interface to suit specific requirements involves creating custom map implementations. While the standard library of maps—such as HashMap, LinkedHashMap, and TreeMap—addresses most needs, there are scenarios requiring unique handling of key-value pairs. Creating a custom map can involve a simple extension of existing maps, or it might necessitate a ground-up implementation of the Map interface.

A custom map is usually preferred when:

- Specific performance characteristics are needed for unusual key access patterns.
- Custom key comparison logic is required.
- Augmented map behavior, such as event-triggered actions on insertion or deletion.

To illustrate the process, we will create a custom map that logs every key-value pair insertion. This map, LoggingHashMap, will be an extension of HashMap, demonstrating straightforward inheritance and method overriding.

```
import java.util.HashMap;
import java.util.Map;

public class LoggingHashMap<K, V> extends HashMap<K, V> {
    @Override
    public V put(K key, V value) {
        System.out.println("Inserting key: " + key + ", value: " + value);
        return super.put(key, value);
    }
}
```

In LoggingHashMap, we override the put method to insert the key-value pair into the HashMap and log the operation. The call to super.put(key, value) ensures that the insertion operation follows the standard behavior defined in HashMap.

When extending from an existing map implementation, it is crucial to understand the behavior of the base class methods. Invoking the super method ensures that the integrity of the map operations is maintained, while adding additional behaviors such as logging.

Ground-Up Implementation

Implementing a custom map from scratch requires adherence to the Map interface. The basic methods a new map class must implement include:

- put(K key, V value): Inserts the specified key-value pair.
- get(Object key): Returns the value associated with the specified key.
- remove(Object key): Removes the mapping for the specified key.
- size(): Returns the number of key-value pairs in the map.
- clear(): Removes all mappings.
- containsKey(Object key): Determines if the map contains a mapping for the specified key.
- containsValue(Object value): Determines if the map contains one or more keys mapping to the specified value.

We will create a minimal example of a custom map that uses an internal list to store entries. This implementation is for educational purposes and does not provide optimal performance for large datasets.

```
import java.util.ArrayList;
import java.util.List;
import java.util.Map;
import java.util.Set;

public class SimpleListMap<K, V> implements Map<K, V> {
    private List<Entry<K, V>> entries = new ArrayList<>();

    @Override
    public V put(K key, V value) {
        for (Entry<K, V> entry : entries) {
            if (entry.getKey().equals(key)) {
                V oldValue = entry.getValue();
                entry.setValue(value);
                return oldValue;
            }
        }
        entries.add(new SimpleEntry<>(key, value));
        return null;
    }

    @Override
    public V get(Object key) {
        for (Entry<K, V> entry : entries) {
            if (entry.getKey().equals(key)) {
                return entry.getValue();
            }
        }
        return null;
```

```
    }

    @Override
    public V remove(Object key) {
        for (Entry<K, V> entry : entries) {
            if (entry.getKey().equals(key)) {
                V value = entry.getValue();
                entries.remove(entry);
                return value;
            }
        }
        return null;
    }

    @Override
    public int size() {
        return entries.size();
    }

    @Override
    public void clear() {
        entries.clear();
    }

    @Override
    public boolean containsKey(Object key) {
        for (Entry<K, V> entry : entries) {
            if (entry.getKey().equals(key)) {
                return true;
            }
        }
        return false;
    }

    @Override
    public boolean containsValue(Object value) {
        for (Entry<K, V> entry : entries) {
            if (entry.getValue().equals(value)) {
                return true;
            }
        }
        return false;
    }

    @Override
    public Set<Entry<K, V>> entrySet() {
        // Method implementation omitted for brevity
        return null;
    }

    // Additional required methods from the Map interface would be implemented here
}
```

Here, we use an internal List to store the map's entries. While this approach is not efficient for large maps, it provides a clear, understandable implementation. The put method searches for an existing key and updates the value if found, otherwise, it adds a new entry. The remove, get, and other methods operate similarly by iterating through the list of entries.

When implementing a map from scratch, several considerations are paramount, including ensuring thread safety if concurrent access is needed, optimizing for performance with appropriate data structures, and adhering to the contract defined by the Map interface documentation.

Custom map implementations can significantly enhance the functionality provided by standard maps, enabling precise control over their behavior. By understanding the underlying principles and carefully planning the implementation, one can tailor map behaviors for specialized use cases.

Chapter 6

Queues and Deques: Handling Ordered Collections

This chapter examines the use of queues and deques in the Java Collections Framework for handling ordered collections. It explains the fundamental operations of the Queue and Deque interfaces and explores various implementations such as PriorityQueue, ArrayBlockingQueue, LinkedBlockingQueue, PriorityBlockingQueue, ArrayDeque, LinkedList as a deque, and ConcurrentLinkedDeque. The chapter also covers common operations, performance considerations, and real-world use cases for these data structures, providing a complete understanding of their roles and applications in Java programming.

6.1 Introduction to Queues and Deques

Queues and deques are essential components within the Java Collections Framework that facilitate the management and manipulation of ordered collections. Understanding the fundamental concepts behind these structures provides the foundation for leveraging their powerful features and optimizing their use in Java programming applications.

A Queue is a collection designed to hold elements prior to processing.

Elements in a queue are typically ordered in a First-In-First-Out (FIFO) manner. This means that the element added first will be the first one to be removed. The Queue interface extends the Collection interface and holds several methods that cater to the typical operations on queues, such as insertion, extraction, and inspection of elements.

A Deque (pronounced as "deck" and standing for Double-Ended Queue) extends the functionality of a queue by allowing elements to be added or removed from both ends. Consequently, a deque can function both as a FIFO queue and as a Last-In-First-Out (LIFO) stack, providing greater flexibility in terms of element processing and manipulation. The Deque interface extends the Queue interface and includes a broader set of methods to support this bi-directional operation.

The following outlines the core operations and characteristics of queues and deques:

- **Enqueue Operation**: Adding an element to the queue. This is typically done at the end (tail) of the queue. In the context of a deque, this operation can also occur at the front (head).
- **Dequeue Operation**: Removing an element from the queue. This is commonly the element at the front (head) of the queue. For deques, elements can be removed from both the head and the tail.
- **Peek Operation**: Retrieving, but not removing, the element at the front (head) of the queue. Deques support peek operations on both ends.
- **Element Ordering**: Queues generally follow FIFO ordering, whereas deques support both FIFO and LIFO ordering.

The Java Collections Framework provides various implementations of the Queue and Deque interfaces, each catering to different scenarios and performance requirements. Below are some common implementations:

- PriorityQueue: This class implements a priority queue, which orders elements based on their natural ordering or by a custom comparator. It does not permit null elements.
- ArrayBlockingQueue: A robust implementation backed by an array, where the capacity is fixed upon the creation of the queue. It supports thread-safe operations.

- LinkedBlockingQueue: Offers a potentially unlimited capacity queue (limited by Integer.MAX_VALUE) backed by linked nodes, providing thread-safe operations.
- ArrayDeque: Implements a resizable-array deque, which provides both FIFO and LIFO operations without thread-safe guarantees.
- LinkedList: Implements a doubly-linked list that can serve as both a queue and a deque. It provides all methods of both the Deque and List interfaces.
- ConcurrentLinkedDeque: Provides a thread-safe deque backed by a linked node implementation, supporting high-performance concurrent access.

By understanding these fundamental concepts and recognizing the different implementations, developers can design and optimize their Java programs more effectively, selecting the most appropriate data structure that meets their specific needs and performance requirements.

In the subsequent sections, we will delve deeper into the operations and particularities of these interfaces, exploring their respective classes in comprehensive detail to provide a profound mastery over the subjects of queues and deques in Java.

6.2 Queue Interface: Basic Operations

The Queue interface in the Java Collections Framework defines a collection designed for holding elements prior to processing. Queues typically, but do not necessarily, order elements in a FIFO (First-In-First-Out) manner. However, there are exceptions, such as PriorityQueue, which orders elements according to their natural ordering or by a specified comparator.

```
public interface Queue<E> extends Collection<E> {
    boolean add(E e);
    boolean offer(E e);
    E remove();
    E poll();
    E element();
    E peek();
}
```

The basic operations of the Queue interface include:

- add(E e): Inserts the specified element into this queue if it is possible to do so immediately without violating capacity restrictions.
- offer(E e): Inserts the specified element into this queue if it is possible to do so immediately without violating capacity restrictions. When using a capacity-restricted queue, this method is generally preferable to the add method.
- remove(): Retrieves and removes the head of this queue.
- poll(): Retrieves and removes the head of this queue, or returns null if this queue is empty.
- element(): Retrieves, but does not remove, the head of this queue.
- peek(): Retrieves, but does not remove, the head of this queue, or returns null if this queue is empty.

Let us explore these operations in greater detail.

add(E e) and offer(E e): While add is the familiar method from the Collection interface, offer is specified specifically for use with capacity-restricted queues. The add method throws an IllegalStateException if the capacity is exceeded, while offer returns false instead.

```
Queue<String> queue = new LinkedList<>();
queue.add("Element1"); // throws IllegalStateException if capacity exceeded
boolean wasAdded = queue.offer("Element2"); // returns false if capacity exceeded
```

remove() and poll(): Both methods retrieve and remove the head of the queue. The remove method throws a NoSuchElementException if the queue is empty, whereas the poll method returns null.

```
Queue<String> queue = new LinkedList<>();
queue.add("Element1");
String head = queue.remove(); // throws NoSuchElementException if queue is empty
String headOrNull = queue.poll(); // returns null if queue is empty
```

element() and peek(): The element method retrieves, but does not remove, the head of the queue. Like remove, it throws a NoSuchElementException if the queue is empty. Conversely, peek retrieves the head or returns null if the queue is empty.

```
Queue<String> queue = new LinkedList<>();
queue.add("Element1");
String head = queue.element(); // throws NoSuchElementException if queue is empty
String headOrNull = queue.peek(); // returns null if queue is empty
```

To understand the behavior of a queue and its interface operations, consider the following example:

```
Queue<Integer> queue = new LinkedList<>();

// Add elements to the queue
queue.offer(10);
queue.offer(20);
queue.offer(30);

// Peek at the head element
System.out.println("Head element: " + queue.peek()); // Output: Head element: 10

// Remove elements from the queue
System.out.println("Removed element: " + queue.poll()); // Output: Removed element:
    10
System.out.println("Removed element: " + queue.poll()); // Output: Removed element:
    20

// Final state of the queue
System.out.println("Queue after removals: " + queue); // Output: Queue after
    removals: [30]
```

The example demonstrates the use of offer, peek, and poll methods to manage queue operations and understand the sequence of elements processed in a FIFO manner.

Awareness and proper utilization of these basic operations form a solid foundation for implementing more complex data structures and algorithms that rely on queues. Understanding the subtle differences between methods that throw exceptions and those that return special values allows developers to write more robust and predictable code.

6.3 PriorityQueue: Natural Order Queues

The PriorityQueue class in Java is a concrete implementation of the Queue interface, designed to handle elements according to their natural ordering or by a specified comparator. This section delves into the structure, operations, and practical applications of PriorityQueue.

To instantiate a PriorityQueue, one can use the following syntax:

```
// Creating a PriorityQueue with natural ordering
PriorityQueue<Integer> pq = new PriorityQueue<>();

// Creating a PriorityQueue with a custom Comparator
Comparator<String> stringLengthComparator = Comparator.comparingInt(String::
    length);
PriorityQueue<String> pqWithComparator = new PriorityQueue<>(
    stringLengthComparator);
```

A PriorityQueue relies on a heap data structure, typically a binary heap, which allows it to efficiently support the priority-ordered operations. Elements in a PriorityQueue are ordered according to their natural ordering (i.e., the compareTo method in Comparable) if no comparator is provided. Otherwise, the elements are ordered according to the supplied comparator.

Operations on PriorityQueue

Common operations associated with PriorityQueue include adding, removing, and inspecting elements. Below, the significant operations and their implications are described:

1. add(E e): Inserts the specified element into this priority queue. Throws ClassCastException if the specified element cannot be compared with elements currently in the queue. 2. offer(E e): Inserts the specified element into this priority queue, returning true upon success and false if the queue's capacity has been exhausted. 3. peek(): Retrieves, but does not remove, the head of this queue, returning null if this queue is empty. 4. poll(): Retrieves and removes the head of this queue, or returns null if this queue is empty. 5. remove(): Retrieves and removes the head of this queue. Throws NoSuchElementException if this queue is empty.

The following code demonstrates basic operations on a PriorityQueue:

```
PriorityQueue<Integer> pq = new PriorityQueue<>();
pq.add(10);
pq.offer(20);
pq.add(15);

// Checking the head of the queue
System.out.println("Head of the queue: " + pq.peek());

// Removing elements
System.out.println("Removed: " + pq.poll()); // 10
System.out.println("Removed: " + pq.poll()); // 15

// Adding another element
pq.add(5);
System.out.println("Head of the queue: " + pq.peek()); // 5
```

```
Head of the queue: 10
Removed: 10
Removed: 15
Head of the queue: 5
```

Internal Structure and Performance

A PriorityQueue is internally implemented using a min-heap, where the smallest element is stored at the root of the heap. This ensures that the retrieval of the minimum element (through peek() or poll()) is both time-efficient and logistically straightforward. The operations to add and remove elements from the PriorityQueue run in $O(log(n))$, where n is the number of elements in the queue.

Here is an example of how the elements might be organized inside a PriorityQueue: - Suppose the PriorityQueue holds the elements: [20, 15, 10, 30, 50]. Internally, the binary heap ensures that the smallest element (10) is always at the root, making it accessible in constant time $O(1)$.

Comparator Example

Using a Comparator allows for custom ordering of elements. This is particularly useful when there is a need to prioritize elements based on criteria other than their natural ordering. Consider the custom comparator for prioritizing strings by their lengths:

```
Comparator<String> stringLengthComparator = Comparator.comparingInt(String::
    length);
PriorityQueue<String> pqWithComparator = new PriorityQueue<>(
    stringLengthComparator);
pqWithComparator.add("apple");
pqWithComparator.add("banana");
pqWithComparator.add("cherry");

System.out.println("Head of the queue: " + pqWithComparator.peek()); // apple
```

```
Head of the queue: apple
```

Potential Use Cases

PriorityQueues are employed in applications that require priority ordering. Examples include:

- **Task Scheduling**: Managing task execution where certain tasks have higher priority.

- **Dijkstra's Algorithm**: For efficiently finding the shortest path in graphs.

- **Event Simulation**: Handling events in a simulation ordered by the time of occurrence.

Understanding and leveraging PriorityQueues allow developers to manage complex ordering of elements in a simple and efficient manner, adhering to either natural or custom-ordered criteria.

6.4 BlockingQueue: Thread-Safe Queues

The BlockingQueue interface in the Java Collections Framework extends the Queue interface to support operations that wait for the queue to become non-empty when retrieving an element, and wait for space to become available in the queue when storing an element. This interface is part of the java.util.concurrent package and is designed to be thread-safe, making it suitable for use in concurrent programming environments.

BlockingQueue does not permit null elements. This is a deliberate design decision because null is used as a sentinel value to indicate the absence of elements in many concurrent data structures and algorithms.

BlockingQueue supports both standard queue operations and additional methods that can block the calling thread until relevant conditions are met.

- put(E e): Inserts the specified element into this queue, waiting if necessary for space to become available.
- take(): Retrieves and removes the head of this queue, waiting if necessary until an element becomes available.
- offer(E e, long timeout, TimeUnit unit): Inserts the specified element into this queue, waiting up to the specified wait time if necessary for space to become available.
- poll(long timeout, TimeUnit unit): Retrieves and removes the head of this queue, waiting up to the specified wait time if necessary for an element to become available.
- remainingCapacity(): Returns the number of additional elements that this queue can ideally accept without blocking.

Example: Using BlockingQueue with Multiple Threads

A common use case for BlockingQueue is to manage a pool of threads that produce or consume data in a multi-threaded producer-consumer scenario. Here is a simple example illustrating this concept:

```
import java.util.concurrent.BlockingQueue;
import java.util.concurrent.LinkedBlockingQueue;

class Producer implements Runnable {
    private final BlockingQueue<Integer> queue;
```

```
    Producer(BlockingQueue<Integer> queue) {
        this.queue = queue;
    }

    @Override
    public void run() {
        try {
            for (int i = 0; i < 10; i++) {
                queue.put(i);
                System.out.println("Produced: " + i);
            }
            queue.put(-1); // Sentinel value to indicate end of production
        } catch (InterruptedException e) {
            Thread.currentThread().interrupt();
        }
    }
}

class Consumer implements Runnable {
    private final BlockingQueue<Integer> queue;

    Consumer(BlockingQueue<Integer> queue) {
        this.queue = queue;
    }

    @Override
    public void run() {
        try {
            int value;
            while ((value = queue.take()) != -1) {
                System.out.println("Consumed: " + value);
            }
        } catch (InterruptedException e) {
            Thread.currentThread().interrupt();
        }
    }
}

public class ProducerConsumerExample {
    public static void main(String[] args) {
        BlockingQueue<Integer> queue = new LinkedBlockingQueue<>();
        Thread producerThread = new Thread(new Producer(queue));
        Thread consumerThread = new Thread(new Consumer(queue));

        producerThread.start();
        consumerThread.start();
    }
}
```

```
Produced: 0
Produced: 1
Produced: 2
Produced: 3
Produced: 4
Produced: 5
Produced: 6
Produced: 7
Produced: 8
Produced: 9
Produced: -1
Consumed: 0
Consumed: 1
Consumed: 2
Consumed: 3
Consumed: 4
Consumed: 5
Consumed: 6
Consumed: 7
Consumed: 8
Consumed: 9
```

BlockingQueue implementations such as ArrayBlockingQueue, LinkedBlockingQueue, and PriorityBlockingQueue each have distinct characteristics and performance implications. The choice of implementation depends on the specific requirements of the application.

ArrayBlockingQueue is a bounded, fixed-size queue backed by an array. It requires the initial capacity of the queue to be specified at the time of creation. This implementation is appropriate when the maximum size of the queue is known and fixed:

```
import java.util.concurrent.ArrayBlockingQueue;
import java.util.concurrent.BlockingQueue;

BlockingQueue<Integer> queue = new ArrayBlockingQueue<>(10);

// Producer thread
new Thread(() -> {
    try {
        for (int i = 0; i < 10; i++) {
            queue.put(i);
            System.out.println("Produced: " + i);
        }
    } catch (InterruptedException e) {
        Thread.currentThread().interrupt();
    }
}).start();

// Consumer thread
new Thread(() -> {
    try {
        while (true) {
            Integer value = queue.take();
            System.out.println("Consumed: " + value);
        }
    } catch (InterruptedException e) {
        Thread.currentThread().interrupt();
    }
}).start();
```

LinkedBlockingQueue is an optionally-bounded queue based on linked nodes. It can be created with a defined capacity or without a specified bound, in which case it will be constrained only by available memory. This implementation offers higher throughput under less contention compared to ArrayBlockingQueue:

```
import java.util.concurrent.BlockingQueue;
import java.util.concurrent.LinkedBlockingQueue;

BlockingQueue<Integer> queue = new LinkedBlockingQueue<>(10);

// Producer thread
new Thread(() -> {
    try {
        for (int i = 0; i < 10; i++) {
            queue.put(i);
            System.out.println("Produced: " + i);
        }
    } catch (InterruptedException e) {
        Thread.currentThread().interrupt();
    }
}).start();

// Consumer thread
new Thread(() -> {
    try {
        while (true) {
            Integer value = queue.take();
            System.out.println("Consumed: " + value);
        }
    } catch (InterruptedException e) {
        Thread.currentThread().interrupt();
    }
}).start();
```

PriorityBlockingQueue is an unbounded queue that orders elements according to their natural ordering, or by a comparator provided at the queue construction time. Unlike PriorityQueue, a PriorityBlockingQueue does not permit null elements:

```
import java.util.concurrent.BlockingQueue;
import java.util.concurrent.PriorityBlockingQueue;

BlockingQueue<Integer> queue = new PriorityBlockingQueue<>();

// Producer thread
new Thread(() -> {
    try {
        for (int i = 10; i > 0; i--) {
            queue.put(i);
            System.out.println("Produced: " + i);
        }
    } catch (InterruptedException e) {
        Thread.currentThread().interrupt();
    }
}).start();

// Consumer thread
```

```
new Thread(() -> {
    try {
        while (true) {
            Integer value = queue.take();
            System.out.println("Consumed: " + value);
        }
    } catch (InterruptedException e) {
        Thread.currentThread().interrupt();
    }
}).start();
```

The BlockingQueue interface and its implementations are essential tools for building robust and efficient concurrent applications. Proper understanding and usage of these queues can substantially enhance the performance and reliability of multi-threaded Java programs.

6.5 ArrayBlockingQueue: Fixed Size Queues

The ArrayBlockingQueue class is a part of the java.util.concurrent package and is an implementation of the BlockingQueue interface. As its name implies, ArrayBlockingQueue is a blocking queue backed by an array. This implementation permits a fixed-sized queue, meaning that it has a specific capacity to hold elements, beyond which no further insertions are possible until space is made available by removing elements. A distinguishing feature of ArrayBlockingQueue is its ability to support operations that block when the queue is full or empty, making it particularly useful in concurrent programming where thread management is essential.

Constructors

ArrayBlockingQueue supports several constructors that control different aspects of its behavior. Here are the primary ones:

- ArrayBlockingQueue(int capacity): Creates an ArrayBlockingQueue with the specified capacity and non-fair access policy.
- ArrayBlockingQueue(int capacity, boolean fair): Creates an ArrayBlockingQueue with the specified capacity and fairness setting. If fair is true, waiting threads are granted access in the order they came; otherwise, the access order is unspecified.
- ArrayBlockingQueue(int capacity, boolean fair, Collection<? ex-

tends E> c): Creates an ArrayBlockingQueue with the specified capacity, fairness setting, and elements initialized from the specified collection c.

Important Methods

Understanding the key methods of ArrayBlockingQueue is crucial for effectively utilizing this data structure. These methods broadly fall into categories for insertion, removal, and inspection operations, each available in different forms: blocking, timed, and non-blocking.

- boolean add(E e): Inserts the specified element into this queue if it is possible to do so immediately without exceeding the queue's capacity, returning true upon success. If the queue is full, throws an IllegalStateException.
- boolean offer(E e): Inserts the specified element into this queue if it is possible to do so immediately without exceeding the queue's capacity. When the queue is full, it returns false.
- void put(E e): Inserts the specified element into this queue, waiting for space to become available if the queue is full.
- boolean offer(E e, long timeout, TimeUnit unit): Inserts the specified element into this queue, waiting up to the specified wait time if necessary for space to become available.
- E take(): Retrieves and removes the head of this queue, waiting if necessary until an element becomes available.
- E poll(): Retrieves and removes the head of this queue, or returns null if this queue is empty.
- E poll(long timeout, TimeUnit unit): Retrieves and removes the head of this queue, waiting up to the specified wait time if necessary for an element to become available.
- E peek(): Retrieves, but does not remove, the head of this queue, or returns null if this queue is empty.

Example Usage

Consider the following example to illustrate the basic operations of ArrayBlockingQueue:

```
import java.util.concurrent.ArrayBlockingQueue;
import java.util.concurrent.TimeUnit;

public class ArrayBlockingQueueExample {
    public static void main(String[] args) {
        ArrayBlockingQueue<Integer> queue = new ArrayBlockingQueue<>(3);

        try {
            // Inserting elements
            queue.put(1);
            queue.put(2);
            queue.put(3);
            System.out.println("Queue after putting 3 elements: " + queue);

            // Trying to offer an element with timeout
            if(!queue.offer(4, 2, TimeUnit.SECONDS)) {
                System.out.println("Unable to add element, the queue is full.");
            }

            // Polling elements
            System.out.println("Removed element: " + queue.poll());
            System.out.println("Queue after polling: " + queue);
        } catch (InterruptedException e) {
            e.printStackTrace();
        }
    }
}
```

The output of the above program would be:

```
Queue after putting 3 elements: [1, 2, 3]
Unable to add element, the queue is full.
Removed element: 1
Queue after polling: [2, 3]
```

Fairness Policy

The fairness policy in ArrayBlockingQueue is controlled by the fair parameter in its constructor. When instantiated with fairness set to true, the queue follows a first-come-first-served order, ensuring that the longest-waiting thread is given priority access to the queue. This can help to prevent thread starvation, but it may come at the cost of reduced throughput compared to a non-fair policy, where thread access is less predictable but potentially more efficient.

Performance Considerations

ArrayBlockingQueue is designed to be efficient and has a lower memory footprint compared to blocking queues backed by linked nodes, such as LinkedBlockingQueue. However, the contention for accessing the shared array can generate a performance bottleneck under high concurrency because all threads must coordinate through a single, fixed-sized structure. The implementation uses locks to ensure thread safety, which can impact performance in highly competitive environments. Tuning the size of the queue and considering the fairness policy are critical factors in optimizing performance for specific use cases.

Practical Applications

ArrayBlockingQueue is highly useful in scenarios where you need a bounded queue to prevent resource exhaustion. Common applications include:

- **Producer-Consumer Patterns**: Where producers and consumers share a bounded buffer.
- **Rate Limiting**: To control the rate at which resources are processed or tasks are executed.
- **Pipelining Tasks**: In multi-threaded applications to manage tasks between different stages of a pipeline.

Employing ArrayBlockingQueue where appropriate ensures robust, manageable, and consistent behavior in concurrent applications, providing a predictable fixed-size buffer for regulatory task handling.

6.6 LinkedBlockingQueue: Linked List Queues

LinkedBlockingQueue is a thread-safe implementation of a blocking queue that is backed by linked nodes. Unlike ArrayBlockingQueue, which has a fixed capacity, LinkedBlockingQueue can be optionally bounded, providing more flexibility and scalability. This section delves into the characteristics, operations, and uses of LinkedBlockingQueue in the Java Collections Framework, offering detailed insight into its underlying mechanics and advantages for concurrent programming.

LinkedBlockingQueue implements both the BlockingQueue and Queue interfaces, making it part of the broader category of queues that support operations waiting for space to become available or elements to be present.

To initialize a LinkedBlockingQueue, you can either set a capacity limit or allow it to be unbounded:

```
// Creating an unbounded LinkedBlockingQueue
LinkedBlockingQueue<Integer> unboundedQueue = new LinkedBlockingQueue<>();
```

```
// Creating a bounded LinkedBlockingQueue with a capacity of 100
LinkedBlockingQueue<Integer> boundedQueue = new LinkedBlockingQueue<>(100);
```

The design leverages the benefits of linked structure for dynamic memory usage. When the queue is bounded, it maintains the specified upper limit, ensuring that attempts to exceed this limit will cause operations such as put to block until space becomes available.

The primary methods and their blocking/non-blocking variants that form the core of LinkedBlockingQueue operations include:

- add(E e) - Inserts the specified element if it is possible to do so immediately without violating capacity restrictions, returning true upon success. Throws IllegalStateException if the queue is full.
- offer(E e) - Inserts the specified element if it is possible to do so immediately without violating capacity restrictions. Returns true upon success, false otherwise.
- put(E e) - Inserts the specified element, waiting if necessary for space to become available.
- poll() - Retrieves and removes the head of the queue, or returns null if the queue is empty.
- take() - Retrieves and removes the head of the queue, waiting if necessary until an element becomes available.
- peek() - Retrieves, but does not remove, the head of the queue, or returns null if the queue is empty.
- size() - Returns the number of elements in the queue.
- remainingCapacity() - Returns the number of additional elements that the queue can ideally (in the absence of memory or resource constraints) accept without blocking.

The blocking methods such as put(E e) and take() enable the LinkedBlockingQueue to function effectively in producer-consumer constructs. For instance:

```
class Producer implements Runnable {
    private final LinkedBlockingQueue<Integer> queue;

    Producer(LinkedBlockingQueue<Integer> queue) {
        this.queue = queue;
    }
```

```
    @Override
    public void run() {
        try {
            for (int i = 0; i < 50; i++) {
                queue.put(i);
                System.out.println("Produced: " + i);
            }
        } catch (InterruptedException e) {
            Thread.currentThread().interrupt();
        }
    }
}
```

```
class Consumer implements Runnable {
    private final LinkedBlockingQueue<Integer> queue;

    Consumer(LinkedBlockingQueue<Integer> queue) {
        this.queue = queue;
    }

    @Override
    public void run() {
        try {
            while (true) {
                Integer item = queue.take();
                System.out.println("Consumed: " + item);
            }
        } catch (InterruptedException e) {
            Thread.currentThread().interrupt();
        }
    }
}
```

The usage patterns seen here accurately depict how a LinkedBlockingQueue can allow for robust and efficient management of concurrent tasks.

A closer examination of LinkedBlockingQueue's implementation reveals critical details about its construction and behavior. Internally, it utilizes a linked-list structure with nodes containing the elements. The nodes are represented as instances of a nested static class, Node<E>. Each node contains a reference to the element and a reference to the next node, forming the foundation for its deque operations.

The following operations provide illustrative examples of the blocking queue's capabilities and facilitate understanding of its use cases:

```
// Producer adding elements to the queue
Producer producer = new Producer(boundedQueue);
new Thread(producer).start();

// Consumer to remove elements from the queue
Consumer consumer = new Consumer(boundedQueue);
new Thread(consumer).start();
```

```
Produced: 0
Produced: 1
Consumed: 0
Consumed: 1
// and so on...
```

LinkedBlockingQueue is specifically designed to maximize throughput and efficiency under concurrent producer-consumer workloads. It achieves this by leveraging separate locks for put and take operations, reducing contention and achieving higher throughput levels in multi-threaded environments.

This linked structure's dynamic capacity and its ability to block producers when the queue is full or consumers when empty ensure that LinkedBlockingQueue serves as an invaluable tool in concurrent programming scenarios. By utilizing this class, developers can manage complex multitasking operations efficiently and effectively, ensuring robust data processing and task coordination in applications.

6.7 PriorityBlockingQueue: Thread-Safe Priority Queues

The PriorityBlockingQueue is part of the java.util.concurrent package, providing a thread-safe implementation of a priority queue. A priority queue, as discussed previously, orders elements based on their natural ordering or via a specified Comparator at the time of queue construction. The PriorityBlockingQueue enhances this concept by ensuring thread safety, making it an ideal choice for concurrent applications.

To instantiate a PriorityBlockingQueue, one can use one of its constructors. The default constructor creates a priority queue with an initial capacity of 11, ordered according to the natural ordering of its elements. Alternatively, constructors allowing for initial capacity specification and custom comparator definitions are available.

```
// Default constructor with natural ordering
PriorityBlockingQueue<Integer> pbq1 = new PriorityBlockingQueue<>();

// Initial capacity of 20
PriorityBlockingQueue<Integer> pbq2 = new PriorityBlockingQueue<>(20);

// Custom comparator
PriorityBlockingQueue<String> pbq3 = new PriorityBlockingQueue<>(20,
    Comparator.reverseOrder());
```

PriorityBlockingQueue supports all the standard operations defined by the Queue interface. Notably, it does not permit null elements and does not guarantee that elements with equal priority will be ordered consistently. This is an essential consideration for edge cases in concurrent processing where object equality may affect result predictability.

```
// Adding elements to the PriorityBlockingQueue
pbq1.add(10);
pbq1.add(30);
pbq1.add(20);

// Polling items based on their natural order
Integer head = pbq1.poll(); // returns 10
```

At its core, PriorityBlockingQueue leverages an array-based implementation of the binary heap to maintain order. This internal structure facilitates efficient priority access. However, it does not enforce capacity restrictions, as the queue dynamically grows to accommodate additional elements. Despite the lack of a capacity limit, users should be diligent of the potential for out-of-memory errors in environments with uncontrolled workloads.

Thread safety in PriorityBlockingQueue is achieved through internal locking mechanisms. These provide atomicity for methods such as put, take, and offer, crucial for multi-threaded producer-consumer scenarios. Below is an example of using PriorityBlockingQueue with multiple threads:

```
PriorityBlockingQueue<Integer> queue = new PriorityBlockingQueue<>();

Runnable producer = () -> {
    for (int i = 0; i < 100; i++) {
        queue.put(i);
    }
};

Runnable consumer = () -> {
    try {
        while (true) {
            Integer item = queue.take();
            System.out.println("Consumed: " + item);
        }
    } catch (InterruptedException e) {
        Thread.currentThread().interrupt();
    }
};

Thread producerThread = new Thread(producer);
Thread consumerThread = new Thread(consumer);

producerThread.start();
consumerThread.start();
```

The put method is particularly important because it blocks the producer if the queue is full until space is available, ensuring proper flow control. Meanwhile, the take method blocks the consumer if the queue is empty until an element becomes available.

For a more nuanced use case, consider employing custom comparators to define priority criteria beyond natural ordering. This is exemplified by the following implementation of a task scheduler, where tasks of different types are ordered by their priority levels.

```
class Task implements Comparable<Task> {
    private final String name;
    private final int priority;

    public Task(String name, int priority) {
        this.name = name;
        this.priority = priority;
    }

    @Override
    public int compareTo(Task other) {
        return Integer.compare(this.priority, other.priority);
    }

    @Override
    public String toString() {
        return "Task{" + "name='" + name + '\'' + ", priority=" + priority + '}';
    }
}

PriorityBlockingQueue<Task> taskQueue = new PriorityBlockingQueue<>();
taskQueue.put(new Task("LowPriorityTask", 10));
taskQueue.put(new Task("HighPriorityTask", 1));
taskQueue.put(new Task("MediumPriorityTask", 5));

while (!taskQueue.isEmpty()) {
    System.out.println(taskQueue.poll());
}
```

The output from the above scheduler will display tasks ordered by their priority levels:

```
Task{name='HighPriorityTask', priority=1}
Task{name='MediumPriorityTask', priority=5}
Task{name='LowPriorityTask', priority=10}
```

PriorityBlockingQueue integrates seamlessly with the ScheduledThreadPoolExecutor, which leverages priority queues for task scheduling. It is crucial to remember that while thread-safe, net operations on PriorityBlockingQueue are not guaranteed to be fair or ordered, a relevant factor in highly concurrent systems. Effective utilization of PriorityBlockingQueue requires deep comprehension of priority queue mechanics, concurrency principles and thorough testing under concurrent conditions.

Understanding PriorityBlockingQueue within the broader ecosystem of Java's queue implementations enriches the programmer's toolkit for tackling complex, concurrent data processing challenges effectively.

6.8 Deque Interface: Double-Ended Queues

The Deque interface in Java, which stands for double-ended queue, extends the functionalities of Queue interface to support element insertion, removal, and inspection at both ends of the deque. A deque can act both as a queue and as a stack, providing flexibility and a wide range of applications in software design.

Core Methods of the Deque Interface

The Deque interface introduces several methods that facilitate operations at both ends of the collection. Below are key methods grouped by their functionality:

- **Insertion**
  - void addFirst(E e)
  - void addLast(E e)
  - boolean offerFirst(E e)
  - boolean offerLast(E e)
- **Removal**
  - E removeFirst()
  - E removeLast()
  - E pollFirst()
  - E pollLast()
- **Examination**
  - E getFirst()
  - E getLast()
  - E peekFirst()
  - E peekLast()

Usage and Characteristics

The Deque interface provides equal efficiency for operations at both ends. Here's an example of how a deque can be used:

```
Deque<String> deque = new ArrayDeque<>();
deque.addFirst("Element 1 (First)");
deque.addLast("Element 2 (Last)");
System.out.println(deque.getFirst()); // Outputs: Element 1 (First)
System.out.println(deque.getLast()); // Outputs: Element 2 (Last)
```

In this example, ArrayDeque is used as the concrete implementation of the Deque interface. ArrayDeque does not have capacity restrictions and grows as needed.

Comparison with Queue and Stack

The Deque interface plays a hybrid role by integrating the characteristics of both queues and stacks:

- When used as a queue, elements can be added at the back and removed from the front. This behavior is illustrated using addLast and removeFirst methods.
- When used as a stack, elements are added and removed from the same end of the deque. The stack operations are similar to using push and pop methods, wherein addFirst and removeFirst can be employed.

Fail-Fast Behavior

Similar to other collections, implementations of the Deque interface such as ArrayDeque and LinkedList exhibit fail-fast behavior. This means that if the deque is structurally modified at any time after the iterator is created, the iterator will throw a ConcurrentModificationException. This fail-fast behavior ensures that concurrent modification bugs are detected early during development.

Example Scenario: Task Scheduling

The Deque interface is suitable for scenarios where operations are needed at both ends of the collection. One such scenario is task scheduling in a multi-threaded environment:

```
public class TaskScheduler {
    private Deque<Runnable> taskQueue = new LinkedList<>();

    public void addTaskFirst(Runnable task) {
```

```
        taskQueue.addFirst(task);
    }

    public void addTaskLast(Runnable task) {
        taskQueue.addLast(task);
    }

    public Runnable getNextTask() {
        return taskQueue.pollFirst();
    }

    public Runnable getLastTask() {
        return taskQueue.pollLast();
    }
}
```

In this example, tasks can be added to the front or back of the queue, thereby enabling flexible priority management. The scheduler can retrieve tasks from the front or back, which can be useful for balancing immediate and deferred task execution.

Implementation Considerations

When choosing an implementation of the Deque interface, consider the following:

- ArrayDeque: Provides efficient implementations of Deque interface methods without the overhead of synchronization.
- LinkedList: Offers a simple implementation that also implements other interfaces such as List.
- ConcurrentLinkedDeque: Provides a thread-safe variant, suitable for concurrent access scenarios.

Understanding the correct application of Deque and choosing the appropriate implementation is crucial for efficient resource management and performance optimization in Java applications.

6.9 ArrayDeque: Resizable-Array Implementation

The ArrayDeque class in Java is a resizable array implementation of the Deque interface. It provides a highly efficient implementation of a double-ended queue, allowing elements to be added or removed from both ends.

ArrayDeque is part of the java.util package and is defined as follows:

```
public class ArrayDeque<E> extends AbstractCollection<E>
                            implements Deque<E>, Cloneable, Serializable {
    // Class implementation
}
```

ArrayDeque does not have a capacity limit; it grows dynamically as needed to accommodate elements. This resizable nature gives it flexibility over traditional fixed-size array implementations.

Key characteristics and operations provided by ArrayDeque include the following:

1. **Capacity Handling**: ArrayDeque dynamically resizes when necessary using the System.arraycopy method for efficient data copying. The initial default capacity is 16, doubling in size when required.

```
private void ensureCapacity(int newSize) {
    int oldCapacity = elements.length;
    if (newSize > oldCapacity) {
        int newCapacity = oldCapacity * 2;
        if (newCapacity < newSize) {
            newCapacity = newSize;
        }
        elements = Arrays.copyOf(elements, newCapacity);
    }
}
```

2. **Adding Elements**: Methods like addFirst(E e), addLast(E e), offerFirst(E e), and offerLast(E e) allow insertion at either end of the deque. offerFirst and offerLast are preferable for potentially failing insertions as they return false if the operation fails while addFirst and addLast throw exceptions in such cases.

```
public void addFirst(E e) {
    if (e == null) throw new NullPointerException();
    elements[head = (head - 1) & (elements.length - 1)] = e;
    if (head == tail) ensureCapacity(elements.length + 1);
}

public boolean offerFirst(E e) {
    if (e == null) return false;
    addFirst(e);
    return true;
}
```

3. **Removing Elements**: Methods like removeFirst(), removeLast(), pollFirst(), and pollLast() facilitate element removal from both ends. pollFirst() and pollLast() are safer alternatives that return null rather

than throwing exceptions if the deque is empty.

```
public E pollFirst() {
    E x = elements[head];
    if (x == null)
        return null;
    elements[head] = null;
    head = (head + 1) & (elements.length - 1);
    return x;
}

public E removeFirst() {
    E x = pollFirst();
    if (x == null)
        throw new NoSuchElementException();
    return x;
}
```

4. **Accessing Elements**: Methods such as getFirst() and getLast() for accessing elements without removing them, providing quicker insight without dequeue manipulation.

```
public E getFirst() {
    E x = elements[head];
    if (x == null)
        throw new NoSuchElementException();
    return x;
}
```

5. **Iteration**: ArrayDeque implements the Iterable interface, allowing traversal using an iterator. The iterator returned by this class's iterator() method traverses the elements in the order they were added.

```
public Iterator<E> iterator() {
    return new DeqIterator();
}

private class DeqIterator implements Iterator<E> {
    private int cursor = head;

    public boolean hasNext() {
        return cursor != tail;
    }

    public E next() {
        if (cursor == tail)
            throw new NoSuchElementException();
        E result = elements[cursor];
        cursor = (cursor + 1) & (elements.length - 1);
        return result;
    }
}
```

6. **Thread Safety**: ArrayDeque is not synchronized. If multiple threads access a ArrayDeque concurrently, and at least one of the threads modifies the deque structurally, it must be synchronized ex-

ternally.

```
Deque<Integer> deque = new ArrayDeque<>();
Collections.synchronizedCollection(deque);
```

7. **Performance**: ArrayDeque exhibits constant-time performance for operations at both the head and tail, making it a robust choice for implementing deques.

```
Execution time of add, remove, get operations: O(1)
Memory footprint: Dynamic, based on element quantity.
```

8. **Memory Management**: Removing elements from the deque helps in aiding garbage collection since the slots are explicitly set to null post-removal.

```
public E pollFirst() {
    E x = elements[head];
    if (x == null)
        return null;
    elements[head] = null;
    head = (head + 1) & (elements.length - 1);
    return x;
}
```

The ArrayDeque class offers a highly efficient and dynamically resizable deque suited to scenarios requiring frequent insertions and deletions from both ends. Its performance characteristics make it preferable for implementing bounded queues, performing backtracking algorithms, or serving as a double-ended stack in numerous applications.

6.10 LinkedList as a Deque

The LinkedList implementation in the Java Collections Framework is a versatile data structure that can be used both as a list and as a deque. In this section, we will focus exclusively on its role as a deque, delving into its operations, performance characteristics, and typical use cases.

LinkedList implements the Deque interface, which means it provides all the functionalities of a double-ended queue. This allows for elements to be added or removed from both ends of the list efficiently.

Basic Operations

The basic operations available in a LinkedList when used as a deque revolve around insertion, deletion, and access of elements. These operations mirror those outlined in the Deque interface.

- addFirst(E e): Inserts the specified element at the beginning of this deque.
- addLast(E e): Inserts the specified element at the end of this deque.
- offerFirst(E e): Inserts the specified element at the front of this deque, or returns false if the deque is full.
- offerLast(E e): Inserts the specified element at the end of this deque, or returns false if the deque is full.
- removeFirst(): Retrieves and removes the first element of this deque.
- removeLast(): Retrieves and removes the last element of this deque.
- pollFirst(): Retrieves and removes the first element of this deque, or returns null if this deque is empty.
- pollLast(): Retrieves and removes the last element of this deque, or returns null if this deque is empty.
- getFirst(): Retrieves, but does not remove, the first element of this deque.
- getLast(): Retrieves, but does not remove, the last element of this deque.
- peekFirst(): Retrieves, but does not remove, the first element of this deque, or returns null if this deque is empty.
- peekLast(): Retrieves, but does not remove, the last element of this deque, or returns null if this deque is empty.

Code Example

Below is an example illustrating how a LinkedList can be utilized as a deque. This example demonstrates basic operations such as adding, removing, and accessing elements from both ends of the deque.

```
import java.util.LinkedList;
import java.util.Deque;

public class LinkedListDequeExample {
    public static void main(String[] args) {
        Deque<String> deque = new LinkedList<>();
```

```
        // Adding elements to the deque
        deque.addFirst("Element 1 (First)");
        deque.addLast("Element 2 (Last)");

        // Printing elements
        System.out.println("Initial Deque: " + deque);

        // Accessing elements
        String firstElement = deque.peekFirst();
        System.out.println("First Element: " + firstElement);

        String lastElement = deque.peekLast();
        System.out.println("Last Element: " + lastElement);

        // Removing elements
        deque.removeFirst();
        deque.removeLast();

        // Final state of the deque
        System.out.println("Final Deque: " + deque);
    }
}
```

The output of this program will be:

```
Initial Deque: [Element 1 (First), Element 2 (Last)]
First Element: Element 1 (First)
Last Element: Element 2 (Last)
Final Deque: []
```

Performance Considerations

LinkedList provides constant-time complexity for insertion and deletion operations, both at the beginning and the end of the deque. This is because LinkedList nodes are doubly-linked, allowing direct access to each end of the list. Hence, operations like addFirst(E e), addLast(E e), removeFirst(), and removeLast() perform optimally irrespective of the list size.

However, it's important to note that accessing elements at random positions is not as efficient. Since LinkedList does not provide indexed sequential access, operations such as get(int index) or set(int index, E element) result in linear time complexity, necessitating traversal of the list from a known end.

Compared to other deque implementations like ArrayDeque, LinkedList might incur a higher memory overhead due to the storage of node pointers alongside the actual data. This aspect is worth considering based on the application's memory constraints and performance requirements.

Use Cases

LinkedList is particularly suitable for applications demanding frequent addition and removal of elements at both ends of the deque. Common scenarios include:

- **Buffer Implementation**: LinkedList can be used as a buffer where data is written to and read from both ends. Its efficient insertion and deletion capabilities make it ideal for such use cases.
- **Undo/Redo Functionality**: In applications requiring undo/redo functionality, actions can be stored in a LinkedList, allowing for efficient retrieval and execution from either end.
- **Task Scheduling**: A deque can manage tasks that need to be processed in the order they arrive (FIFO) or in reverse order (LIFO), making LinkedList suitable for such task scheduling systems.

When deciding whether to use LinkedList as a deque, it's crucial to weigh its operational advantages against its memory overhead and access time complexities. This consideration ensures the chosen data structure best suits the application's specific needs, balancing performance and resource usage effectively.

6.11 ConcurrentLinkedDeque: Thread-Safe Double-Ended Queues

The ConcurrentLinkedDeque is a member of the Java Collections Framework and provides a scalable, thread-safe, double-ended queue (deque) implementation. It is part of the java.util.concurrent package, which offers high-performance, concurrent data structures.

ConcurrentLinkedDeque is an appropriate choice for scenarios requiring high throughput and reliable concurrent behavior. As a lock-free, thread-safe implementation, it supports both non-blocking insertions and removals at both ends, making it particularly suitable for producer-consumer patterns and other concurrent workflows. The implementation details of ConcurrentLinkedDeque are based on a variant of the Michael-Scott lock-free queue algorithm, extended to support operations at both ends.

A ConcurrentLinkedDeque does not have capacity restrictions, and it typically performs better than alternatives like BlockingDeque when the application does not require explicit blocking capabilities.

To utilize ConcurrentLinkedDeque, one must import the necessary package and instantiate the deque object. Here we demonstrate the primary operations using practical code examples.

```
import java.util.concurrent.ConcurrentLinkedDeque;

public class ConcurrentLinkedDequeExample {
    public static void main(String[] args) {
        ConcurrentLinkedDeque<Integer> deque = new ConcurrentLinkedDeque<>();

        // Adding elements (offer and add methods)
        deque.offerFirst(1);
        deque.offerLast(2);
        deque.addFirst(0);
        deque.addLast(3);

        // Removing elements (poll and remove methods)
        int first = deque.pollFirst(); // Retrieves and removes the first element
        int last = deque.pollLast(); // Retrieves and removes the last element
        System.out.println("First element removed: " + first);
        System.out.println("Last element removed: " + last);

        // Element retrieval without removal (peek and get methods)
        int peekFirst = deque.peekFirst(); // Retrieves the first element without
            removing
        int peekLast = deque.peekLast(); // Retrieves the last element without
            removing
        System.out.println("First element: " + peekFirst);
        System.out.println("Last element: " + peekLast);
    }
}
```

```
First element removed: 0
Last element removed: 3
First element: 1
Last element: 2
```

In the example above, we demonstrate standard deque operations such as offer, add, poll, remove, and peek. These operations are atomic and thread-safe, ensuring consistency and reliability in concurrent access scenarios.

The ConcurrentLinkedDeque employs several methods to accommodate both ends of the deque:

- offerFirst(E e): Inserts the specified element at the front of the deque.
- offerLast(E e): Inserts the specified element at the end of the deque.
- addFirst(E e): Inserts the specified element at the front of the deque.
- addLast(E e): Inserts the specified element at the end of the

deque.

- pollFirst(): Retrieves and removes the first element of the deque, or returns null if the deque is empty.
- pollLast(): Retrieves and removes the last element of the deque, or returns null if the deque is empty.
- peekFirst(): Retrieves but does not remove the first element of the deque, or returns null if the deque is empty.
- peekLast(): Retrieves but does not remove the last element of the deque, or returns null if the deque is empty.

Next, consider a real-world use case: a multi-threaded application where tasks need to be processed in the order they are added, but with the flexibility to insert urgent tasks at the front of the queue.

```
import java.util.concurrent.ConcurrentLinkedDeque;

public class TaskProcessor {
    private final ConcurrentLinkedDeque<Runnable> taskQueue = new
         ConcurrentLinkedDeque<>();

    public void addTask(Runnable task) {
        taskQueue.addLast(task);
    }

    public void addUrgentTask(Runnable task) {
        taskQueue.addFirst(task);
    }

    public void processTasks() {
        while (!taskQueue.isEmpty()) {
            Runnable task = taskQueue.pollFirst();
            if (task != null) {
                task.run();
            }
        }
    }

    public static void main(String[] args) {
        TaskProcessor processor = new TaskProcessor();
        processor.addTask(() -> System.out.println("Regular Task 1"));
        processor.addUrgentTask(() -> System.out.println("Urgent Task 1"));
        processor.addTask(() -> System.out.println("Regular Task 2"));

        Thread workerThread = new Thread(processor::processTasks);
        workerThread.start();
    }
}
```

```
Urgent Task 1
Regular Task 1
Regular Task 2
```

This example illustrates the use of ConcurrentLinkedDeque for a task scheduling system. Regular tasks are added to the end of the deque, while urgent tasks can be added to the front, ensuring they are processed first. The processTasks method continuously fetches and executes tasks from the front of the deque until it is empty.

Key performance characteristics and considerations when using ConcurrentLinkedDeque include:

- **Lock-Free and Wait-Free Operations**: The implementation ensures that operations do not block and can proceed concurrently, providing high throughput under heavy contention.
- **Memory Overhead**: While providing excellent concurrency characteristics, ConcurrentLinkedDeque may incur additional memory overhead due to the underlying linked node structure.
- **Fairness**: Operations on ConcurrentLinkedDeque are not guaranteed to be strictly fair, meaning that under high contention, some threads may consistently win the race to access the deque.
- **Garbage Collection**: Dangling nodes (nodes removed from the deque) may linger until garbage collection occurs, which could introduce latency in memory reclamation under certain workloads.

Designers of concurrent applications must weigh these characteristics to determine the suitability of ConcurrentLinkedDeque for their specific needs. Proper understanding and careful application of these concepts can lead to highly efficient and robust concurrent systems.

6.12 Common Queue and Deque Operations

In Java, the Queue and Deque interfaces provide a variety of methods for manipulating the elements in these ordered collections. Understanding these operations is crucial for making the most of these data structures in your applications. While Queue primarily supports operations for handling a single-ended collection, the Deque interface extends these capabilities to support double-ended operations. This section delves into the most common and useful operations provided by these interfaces, offering detailed insights into their behavior and usage.

Queue Operations

The Queue interface specifies fundamental operations that allow elements to be inserted, removed, and inspected.

- add(E e): Inserts the specified element into the queue if it is possible to do so immediately without violating capacity restrictions. Returns true upon success and throws an IllegalStateException if no space is currently available.
- offer(E e): Inserts the specified element into the queue, returning true upon success and false if no space is currently available.
- remove(): Retrieves and removes the head of the queue. Throws a NoSuchElementException if the queue is empty.
- poll(): Retrieves and removes the head of the queue, or returns null if the queue is empty.
- element(): Retrieves, but does not remove, the head of the queue. Throws a NoSuchElementException if the queue is empty.
- peek(): Retrieves, but does not remove, the head of the queue, or returns null if the queue is empty.

Below is a sample Java code demonstrating these operations:

```
// Create a Queue instance using LinkedList
Queue<Integer> queue = new LinkedList<>();

// Add elements to the queue
queue.add(1);
queue.offer(2);

// Retrieve and remove the head of the queue
int removedElement = queue.remove(); // returns 1

// Retrieve the head without removing it
int headElement = queue.element(); // returns 2
headElement = queue.peek(); // returns 2

// Remove the head
queue.poll(); // queue is now empty

// Attempt to remove an element from an empty queue
try {
    queue.remove(); // throws NoSuchElementException
} catch (NoSuchElementException e) {
```

```
    // Handle exception
}
```

Deque Operations

The Deque interface extends Queue operations to both ends of the collection, enabling insertion, removal, and inspection from both the head (or front) and the tail (or back) of the deque.

- addFirst(E e): Inserts the specified element at the front of the deque.
- addLast(E e): Inserts the specified element at the end of the deque.
- offerFirst(E e): Inserts the specified element at the front of the deque, returning true upon success and false if no space is available.
- offerLast(E e): Inserts the specified element at the end of the deque, returning true upon success and false if no space is available.
- removeFirst(): Retrieves and removes the first element of the deque. Throws a NoSuchElementException if the deque is empty.
- removeLast(): Retrieves and removes the last element of the deque. Throws a NoSuchElementException if the deque is empty.
- pollFirst(): Retrieves and removes the first element of the deque, or returns null if the deque is empty.
- pollLast(): Retrieves and removes the last element of the deque, or returns null if the deque is empty.
- getFirst(): Retrieves, but does not remove, the first element of the deque. Throws a NoSuchElementException if the deque is empty.
- getLast(): Retrieves, but does not remove, the last element of the deque. Throws a NoSuchElementException if the deque is empty.
- peekFirst(): Retrieves, but does not remove, the first element of the deque, or returns null if the deque is empty.

- peekLast(): Retrieves, but does not remove, the last element of the deque, or returns null if the deque is empty.

Below is a sample Java code demonstrating these operations:

```
// Create a Deque instance using LinkedList
Deque<Integer> deque = new LinkedList<>();

// Add elements to both ends of the deque
deque.addFirst(1);
deque.addLast(2);

// Retrieve and remove elements from both ends
int firstElement = deque.removeFirst(); // returns 1
int lastElement = deque.removeLast(); // returns 2

// Add elements back to the deque
deque.offerFirst(3);
deque.offerLast(4);

// Retrieve elements without removing them
int headElement = deque.peekFirst(); // returns 3
int tailElement = deque.peekLast(); // returns 4

// Remove elements using poll methods
deque.pollFirst(); // returns 3
deque.pollLast(); // returns 4, deque is now empty

// Attempt to remove elements from an empty deque
try {
    deque.removeFirst(); // throws NoSuchElementException
} catch (NoSuchElementException e) {
    // Handle exception
}
```

Additional methods provided by the Deque interface allow for element examination, manipulation, and retrieval without strict adherence to a single order of operation. These include methods for insertion, removal, and inspection at both ends of the deque, enhancing the versatility of the Deque in complex data structure management scenarios. Understanding and employing these operations accurately ensures efficient and effective utilization of Java's Queue and Deque interfaces.

6.13 Use Cases and Scenarios for Queues and Deques

Queues and deques are pivotal data structures in a multitude of scenarios due to their inherent characteristics of ordered collection handling. Their wide range of applications extends from simple buffering mechanisms to complex task scheduling systems. The following detailed analysis provides examples and justifications for their use in various real-world contexts.

1. Task Scheduling and Processing

Queues are integral to task scheduling systems where tasks are managed in a first-in, first-out (FIFO) manner. This is particularly useful in an environment where tasks arrive in a sequential order and need to be processed in the same sequence. Java's java.util.concurrent package provides robust implementations such as LinkedBlockingQueue and ArrayBlockingQueue for such purposes.

```
import java.util.concurrent.LinkedBlockingQueue;

public class TaskScheduler {
    private LinkedBlockingQueue<Runnable> taskQueue = new LinkedBlockingQueue
        <>();

    public void addTask(Runnable task) {
        taskQueue.add(task);
    }

    public void executeTasks() throws InterruptedException {
        while (!taskQueue.isEmpty()) {
            Runnable task = taskQueue.take();
            new Thread(task).start();
        }
    }
}
```

In this example, tasks are added to the taskQueue and executed in the order they are received. This ensures task synchronization and orderly processing.

2. Order Processing Systems

Online retail platforms often use queues to manage order processing. Orders generated by customers are placed in a queue and processed one at a time by the system. Using a PriorityQueue, orders with higher priority can be processed faster. For example, premium customer orders might be given higher priority.

```
import java.util.PriorityQueue;

public class OrderProcessor {
    private PriorityQueue<Order> orderQueue = new PriorityQueue<>();

    public void addOrder(Order order) {
        orderQueue.add(order);
    }

    public void processOrders() {
        while (!orderQueue.isEmpty()) {
            Order order = orderQueue.poll();
```

```
            processOrder(order);
        }
    }

    private void processOrder(Order order) {
        // Order processing logic here
    }
}
```

Here, Order objects are stored in a PriorityQueue, which processes orders based on their priority.

3. Breadth-First Search in Graphs

Queues are also instrumental in graph traversal algorithms such as Breadth-First Search (BFS). In BFS, nodes are explored in layers; all vertices of a certain depth are processed before moving on to the next depth level.

```
import java.util.LinkedList;
import java.util.Queue;

public class Graph {
    private int numVertices;
    private LinkedList<Integer> adjList[];

    public Graph(int vertices) {
        numVertices = vertices;
        adjList = new LinkedList[vertices];
        for (int i = 0; i < vertices; ++i)
            adjList[i] = new LinkedList<>();
    }

    public void addEdge(int src, int dest) {
        adjList[src].add(dest);
    }

    public void BFS(int start) {
        boolean visited[] = new boolean[numVertices];
        Queue<Integer> queue = new LinkedList<>();

        visited[start] = true;
        queue.add(start);

        while (!queue.isEmpty()) {
            int vertex = queue.poll();
            System.out.print(vertex + " ");

            for (int next : adjList[vertex]) {
                if (!visited[next]) {
                    visited[next] = true;
                    queue.add(next);
                }
            }
        }
    }
}
```

In this case, a LinkedList queue is employed to store nodes that need to be visited in the BFS algorithm.

4. Messaging Systems

In messaging systems, queues are utilized to handle message traffic between producers and consumers. The BlockingQueue interface supports this use case by providing thread-safe operations necessary for inter-thread communication.

```
import java.util.concurrent.ArrayBlockingQueue;
import java.util.concurrent.BlockingQueue;

public class MessageQueue {
    private BlockingQueue<String> queue = new ArrayBlockingQueue<>(10);

    public void sendMessage(String message) throws InterruptedException {
        queue.put(message);
    }

    public String receiveMessage() throws InterruptedException {
        return queue.take();
    }
}
```

This implementation ensures that the sendMessage and receiveMessage operations are safely handled even in a multi-threaded environment.

5. Undo Mechanism in Text Editors

Deques are useful for implementing undo functionalities. By maintaining a Deque of user actions, both undo and redo can be efficiently managed using push, pop, and removeLast operations.

```
import java.util.ArrayDeque;
import java.util.Deque;

public class TextEditor {
    private Deque<String> undoStack = new ArrayDeque<>();
    private Deque<String> redoStack = new ArrayDeque<>();

    public void type(String text) {
        undoStack.push(text);
        redoStack.clear();
    }

    public void undo() {
        if (!undoStack.isEmpty()) {
            String lastAction = undoStack.pop();
            redoStack.push(lastAction);
        }
    }

    public void redo() {
        if (!redoStack.isEmpty()) {
            String lastUndo = redoStack.pop();
            undoStack.push(lastUndo);
        }
```

```
    }
}
```

This code demonstrates how a text editor can maintain a history of actions for undo and redo operations.

6. Palindrome Checking

Deques facilitate palindrome checking by allowing comparisons from both ends of a sequence. Utilizing methods such as addFirst, addLast, removeFirst, and removeLast, a word or phrase can be inspected for palindromic properties.

```
import java.util.ArrayDeque;
import java.util.Deque;

public class PalindromeChecker {
    public boolean isPalindrome(String s) {
        Deque<Character> deque = new ArrayDeque<>();

        for (char c : s.toCharArray()) {
            if (Character.isLetterOrDigit(c)) {
                deque.addLast(Character.toLowerCase(c));
            }
        }

        while (deque.size() > 1) {
            if (deque.removeFirst() != deque.removeLast()) {
                return false;
            }
        }

        return true;
    }
}
```

In this implementation, characters from the input string are added to the Deque and then compared from both ends to check for palindromic structure.

These examples illustrate the versatility and efficacy of queues and deques in handling ordered collections across various domains, emphasizing the significance of selecting the appropriate implementation to optimize performance and maintain thread-safety when necessary.

Chapter 7

Navigating through Sorted Collections

This chapter delves into the concept of sorted collections within the Java Collections Framework, focusing on natural and custom orderings. It covers key implementations such as TreeSet and TreeMap, along with the NavigableSet and NavigableMap interfaces. The chapter also explores thread-safe sorted collections like ConcurrentSkipListSet and ConcurrentSkipListMap. Additionally, it discusses common operations, performance considerations, and practical use cases, equipping readers with a comprehensive understanding of how to navigate and utilize sorted collections in Java.

7.1 Introduction to Sorted Collections

In Java programming, the manipulation and storage of data in a systematic manner can greatly influence the efficiency and elegance of the code. Sorted collections, a pivotal part of the Java Collections Framework, play a crucial role in this regard by maintaining elements in a specific sequence based on their natural ordering or through a defined comparator. This provides significant advantages in terms of performance, data integrity, and access simplicity.

The term "sorted collections" refers to data structures that maintain their elements in a consistent and predictable order. These collections offer various methods to retrieve and manipulate data based on this ordering. Java provides several implementations such as TreeSet and TreeMap, each designed to offer a unique set of features and efficiencies.

Natural Ordering and Custom Ordering

A fundamental concept in sorted collections is *natural ordering*. Java's Comparable interface enables objects to define their default ordering mechanism. Implementing the compareTo method in a class allows you to specify how instances of that class should be ordered relative to each other. This ordering is referred to as the natural order of objects.

```
import java.util.*;

class Person implements Comparable<Person> {
    private String name;
    private int age;

    public Person(String name, int age) {
        this.name = name;
        this.age = age;
    }

    @Override
    public int compareTo(Person other) {
        return Integer.compare(this.age, other.age);
    }

    @Override
    public String toString() {
        return name + " (" + age + ")";
    }
}

public class NaturalOrderingExample {
    public static void main(String[] args) {
        Set<Person> people = new TreeSet<>();
        people.add(new Person("Alice", 30));
        people.add(new Person("Bob", 25));
        people.add(new Person("Charlie", 35));
        for (Person person : people) {
            System.out.println(person);
        }
    }
}
```

Execution of the above code will produce the following output:

```
Bob (25)
Alice (30)
Charlie (35)
```

It is important to recognize that natural ordering may not always be sufficient. When a custom ordering is required, the Comparator interface can be utilized. This interface allows the definition of multiple sorting strategies independent of the class whose instances are being sorted.

```
import java.util.*;

class Person {
    private String name;
    private int age;

    public Person(String name, int age) {
        this.name = name;
        this.age = age;
    }

    public String getName() {
        return name;
    }

    public int getAge() {
        return age;
    }

    @Override
    public String toString() {
        return name + " (" + age + ")";
    }
}

public class CustomOrderingExample {
    public static void main(String[] args) {
        Set<Person> peopleByName = new TreeSet<>(Comparator.comparing(Person::
                getName));
        Set<Person> peopleByAge = new TreeSet<>(Comparator.comparingInt(Person
                ::getAge));

        List<Person> persons = Arrays.asList(
            new Person("Alice", 30),
            new Person("Bob", 25),
            new Person("Charlie", 35)
        );

        peopleByName.addAll(persons);
        peopleByAge.addAll(persons);

        System.out.println("Sorted by name:");
        for (Person person : peopleByName) {
            System.out.println(person);
        }

        System.out.println("Sorted by age:");
        for (Person person : peopleByAge) {
            System.out.println(person);
        }
    }
}
```

The execution of this code will result in:

```
Sorted by name:
Alice (30)
Bob (25)
Charlie (35)

Sorted by age:
Bob (25)
Alice (30)
Charlie (35)
```

Key Implementations of Sorted Collections

TreeSet and TreeMap are the primary implementations of sorted collections. Both are part of the java.util package and utilize a red-black tree internally to maintain elements in sorted order.

TreeSet: TreeSet implements the NavigableSet interface, which extends SortedSet. This structure stores elements in a sorted sequence, providing methods for operations such as:

- first - Returns the first (lowest) element.
- last - Returns the last (highest) element.
- ceiling - Returns the smallest element greater than or equal to the given element.
- floor - Returns the greatest element less than or equal to the given element.
- higher - Returns the smallest element strictly greater than the given element.
- lower - Returns the greatest element strictly less than the given element.

```
import java.util.*;

public class TreeSetExample {
    public static void main(String[] args) {
        TreeSet<String> treeSet = new TreeSet<>();
        treeSet.add("Banana");
        treeSet.add("Apple");
        treeSet.add("Pineapple");

        System.out.println("First element: " + treeSet.first());
        System.out.println("Last element: " + treeSet.last());
        System.out.println("Element greater than Banana: " + treeSet.higher("Banana")
            );
    }
}
```

Expected output:

```
First element: Apple
Last element: Pineapple
Element greater than Banana: Pineapple
```

TreeMap: TreeMap implements the NavigableMap interface, which extends SortedMap. This structure maps keys to values, maintaining keys in a sorted order. Key operations include:

- firstKey - Returns the first (lowest) key.
- lastKey - Returns the last (highest) key.
- ceilingKey - Returns the least key greater than or equal to the given key.
- floorKey - Returns the greatest key less than or equal to the given key.
- higherKey - Returns the least key strictly greater than the given key.
- lowerKey - Returns the greatest key strictly less than the given key.

```
import java.util.*;

public class TreeMapExample {
    public static void main(String[] args) {
        TreeMap<Integer, String> treeMap = new TreeMap<>();
        treeMap.put(3, "Three");
        treeMap.put(1, "One");
        treeMap.put(2, "Two");

        System.out.println("First key: " + treeMap.firstKey());
        System.out.println("Last key: " + treeMap.lastKey());
        System.out.println("Key greater than 1: " + treeMap.higherKey(1));
    }
}
```

Expected output:

```
First key: 1
Last key: 3
Key greater than 1: 2
```

Understanding the core concepts and basic operations of sorted collections is critical as it forms the foundation for navigating and utilizing these data structures effectively. By mastering the use of TreeSet and TreeMap, one can harness the power of order and predictability to create efficient and robust Java applications.

7.2 Understanding Natural Ordering

Natural ordering in Java refers to the implicit or inherent sequence of elements that adheres to their natural sequence as dictated by the Comparable interface. This ordering is commonly employed in sorted collections like TreeSet and TreeMap, where elements must implement the Comparable interface to be sorted naturally. The Comparable interface requires the implementation of the compareTo method, which defines how instances of a class compare with each other.

The Comparable<T> interface is a generic interface containing a single method:

```
public int compareTo(T o);
```

This method returns an integer that determines the order between the current object and the specified object o. The return values are interpreted as follows:

- A negative integer if the current object is less than o.
- Zero if the current object is equal to o.
- A positive integer if the current object is greater than o.

Consider the following example where Comparable is implemented in a Person class, which is sorted based on the name field:

```
public class Person implements Comparable<Person> {
    private String name;
    private int age;

    public Person(String name, int age) {
        this.name = name;
        this.age = age;
    }

    public String getName() {
        return name;
    }

    public int getAge() {
        return age;
    }

    @Override
    public int compareTo(Person other) {
        return this.name.compareTo(other.name);
    }

    @Override
```

```
    public String toString() {
        return "Person{name='" + name + "', age=" + age + "}";
    }
}
```

In this code, the compareTo method is implemented to compare Person objects based on their name attributes. This ensures that if a collection of Person objects is sorted, it will be ordered lexicographically by the name.

To illustrate how natural ordering works with the TreeSet class, consider the following example:

```
import java.util.TreeSet;

public class NaturalOrderingExample {
    public static void main(String[] args) {
        TreeSet<Person> people = new TreeSet<>();
        people.add(new Person("Alice", 30));
        people.add(new Person("Bob", 25));
        people.add(new Person("Charlie", 35));

        for (Person person : people) {
            System.out.println(person);
        }
    }
}
```

When executed, this code produces the following output:

```
Person{name='Alice', age=30}
Person{name='Bob', age=25}
Person{name='Charlie', age=35}
```

This output demonstrates that the TreeSet uses the natural ordering defined by the compareTo method in the Person class to sort its elements.

Natural ordering is not limited to custom classes, but also applies to Java's built-in classes such as String, Integer, Double, and others. Each of these classes implements the Comparable interface to provide a natural ordering. For example, the natural ordering of Integer and Double is numerical, while String is ordered lexicographically.

It is essential that the compareTo method is consistent with equals. That is, compareTo should return zero if and only if equals returns true for the same pair of objects. Failure to comply with this consistency can result in erroneous behavior in collections that rely on natural ordering.

Here is an example demonstrating the importance of the consistency between compareTo and equals:

```
public class InconsistentPerson implements Comparable<InconsistentPerson> {
    private String name;
    private int age;
```

```
    public InconsistentPerson(String name, int age) {
        this.name = name;
        this.age = age;
    }

    public String getName() {
        return name;
    }

    public int getAge() {
        return age;
    }

    @Override
    public int compareTo(InconsistentPerson other) {
        return this.name.compareTo(other.name);
    }

    @Override
    public boolean equals(Object obj) {
        if (this == obj) return true;
        if (obj == null || getClass() != obj.getClass()) return false;
        InconsistentPerson that = (InconsistentPerson) obj;
        return age == that.age && name.equals(that.name);
    }

    @Override
    public int hashCode() {
        return Objects.hash(name, age);
    }

    @Override
    public String toString() {
        return "InconsistentPerson{name='" + name + "', age=" + age + "}";
    }
}
```

Even though compareTo only considers the name attribute, the equals method compares both the name and age attributes, leading to potential inconsistencies when used in sorted collections.

To summarize these core principles, remember: 1. Implement Comparable by overriding compareTo. 2. Ensure compareTo is consistent with equals. 3. Use natural ordering for built-in classes and ensure custom classes like Person are naturally ordered.

Understanding these fundamentals enables more effective utilization of sorted collections such as TreeSet and TreeMap within the Java Collections Framework, ensuring accurate and predictable orderings of elements.

7.3 Comparator Interface: Custom Ordering

The Comparator interface in Java provides a powerful mechanism for defining custom orderings of objects, apart from their natural ordering defined by the Comparable interface. A class that implements the Comparator interface must override the compare method, enabling it to order instances of the class in any desired manner.

Signature of the Comparator Interface

The Comparator interface is a generic interface defined as follows:

```
public interface Comparator<T> {
    int compare(T o1, T o2);
    boolean equals(Object obj);
}
```

The primary method is compare(T o1, T o2), which compares its two arguments and returns:

- a negative integer if the first argument is smaller than the second;
- zero if the first argument is equal to the second;
- a positive integer if the first argument is greater than the second.

The equals(Object obj) method is used to compare the Comparator itself with another object, which is less commonly overridden.

Implementing a Comparator

The following example demonstrates a custom Comparator to sort strings by their length, rather than their natural lexicographical order:

```
import java.util.Comparator;

public class LengthComparator implements Comparator<String> {
    @Override
    public int compare(String str1, String str2) {
        return Integer.compare(str1.length(), str2.length());
    }
}
```

In this instance, the compare method compares the lengths of the two strings using Integer.compare(int x, int y), ensuring that:

- If str1.length() is less than str2.length(), compare returns a negative integer.

- If str1.length() is equal to str2.length(), compare returns zero.
- If str1.length() is greater than str2.length(), compare returns a positive integer.

Using the Comparator

To utilize the Comparator, it can be passed to any of the sorted collections or algorithms that support custom ordering. For example, applying the LengthComparator to a TreeSet:

```
import java.util.TreeSet;

public class ComparatorExample {
    public static void main(String[] args) {
        Comparator<String> comparator = new LengthComparator();
        TreeSet<String> treeSet = new TreeSet<>(comparator);

        treeSet.add("banana");
        treeSet.add("apple");
        treeSet.add("kiwi");
        treeSet.add("strawberry");

        for (String fruit : treeSet) {
            System.out.println(fruit);
        }
    }
}
```

The console output would be:

```
kiwi
apple
banana
strawberry
```

This output demonstrates that the strings within the TreeSet are ordered by their lengths rather than the default lexicographical order.

Comparators Using Lambda Expressions

In Java 8 and newer, Comparator interfaces can be conveniently implemented using lambda expressions. An equivalent LengthComparator using a lambda expression is shown below:

```
import java.util.TreeSet;

public class LambdaComparatorExample {
    public static void main(String[] args) {
        Comparator<String> lengthComparator = (str1, str2) -> Integer.compare(str1.
            length(), str2.length());
        TreeSet<String> treeSet = new TreeSet<>(lengthComparator);

        treeSet.add("banana");
        treeSet.add("apple");
        treeSet.add("kiwi");
        treeSet.add("strawberry");
```

```
        for (String fruit : treeSet) {
            System.out.println(fruit);
        }
    }
}
```

Compound Comparators

Comparators can be compounded by combining multiple comparator instances. For instance, to sort an array of Person objects first by their age, and then by their name in case of ties, compound comparators can be utilized as follows:

```
import java.util.Comparator;

public class Person {
    private String name;
    private int age;

    public Person(String name, int age) {
        this.name = name;
        this.age = age;
    }

    public String getName() {
        return name;
    }

    public int getAge() {
        return age;
    }
}

Comparator<Person> ageComparator = Comparator.comparingInt(Person::getAge);
Comparator<Person> nameComparator = Comparator.comparing(Person::getName);
Comparator<Person> compoundComparator = ageComparator.thenComparing(
    nameComparator);
```

In this code, Comparator.comparingInt(Person::getAge) creates a comparator that orders Person instances by their age, while Comparator.comparing(Person::getName) sorts by name. The method thenComparing chains these comparators, allowing primary sorting by age and secondary sorting by name.

This approach ensures that developers can create intricate sorting logics tailored to specific requirements, all through a streamlined and expressive interface provided by the Comparator.

7.4 TreeSet: Naturally Sorted Sets

Java's TreeSet class implements the NavigableSet interface and provides a collection that ensures that the elements are sorted in their natural order or by a specified comparator at instantiation time. The natural ordering is defined by the Comparable interface, which means elements are sorted based on their compare-to method. For a practical exploration, consider the following key aspects of TreeSet.

Creating a TreeSet The TreeSet can be initialized in multiple ways. Here is an instance of its basic instantiation where the natural ordering is leveraged:

```
import java.util.TreeSet;

public class TreeSetExample {
    public static void main(String[] args) {
        TreeSet<Integer> numbers = new TreeSet<>();
        numbers.add(5);
        numbers.add(1);
        numbers.add(3);
        numbers.add(9);
        numbers.add(7);
        System.out.println("TreeSet: " + numbers);
    }
}
```

The expected output, which demonstrates the natural ordering (ascending order for Integer objects), would be:

```
TreeSet: [1, 3, 5, 7, 9]
```

Custom Ordering with Comparator The TreeSet can also be initialized with a custom comparator to define alternative orderings. Consider a scenario where we need the reverse order of natural integers:

```
import java.util.TreeSet;
import java.util.Comparator;

public class TreeSetCustomOrder {
    public static void main(String[] args) {
        Comparator<Integer> reverseOrder = (a, b) -> b - a;
        TreeSet<Integer> numbers = new TreeSet<>(reverseOrder);
        numbers.add(5);
        numbers.add(1);
        numbers.add(3);
        numbers.add(9);
        numbers.add(7);
        System.out.println("TreeSet with custom comparator: " + numbers);
    }
}
```

The output for this program will be:

```
TreeSet with custom comparator: [9, 7, 5, 3, 1]
```

Key Operations and Performance Operations like adding, removing, and searching for elements are fundamental in any collection. In a TreeSet, these operations have logarithmic time complexity, O(log n), due to the underlying Red-Black tree structure. Here is a summary of key operations and their respective code examples:

- add(E e): Adds the specified element if it is not already present.
- remove(Object o): Removes the specified element if it is present.
- contains(Object o): Returns true if this set contains the specified element.
- isEmpty(): Checks if the set is empty.
- size(): Returns the number of elements in the set.

```
public class TreeSetOperations {
    public static void main(String[] args) {
        TreeSet<String> set = new TreeSet<>();

        // Adding elements
        set.add("apple");
        set.add("banana");
        set.add("cherry");

        // Checking if an element exists
        System.out.println("Contains 'apple': " + set.contains("apple"));

        // Displaying the number of elements
        System.out.println("Size of TreeSet: " + set.size());

        // Removing an element
        set.remove("banana");
        System.out.println("After removal of 'banana': " + set);

        // Checking if the set is empty
        System.out.println("Is the TreeSet empty?: " + set.isEmpty());
    }
}
```

Expected output:

```
Contains 'apple': true
Size of TreeSet: 3
After removal of 'banana': [apple, cherry]
Is the TreeSet empty?: false
```

NavigableSet Interface The TreeSet class additionally implements the NavigableSet interface, which provides methods to navigate through the set. Some of these methods include:

- lower(E e): Returns the greatest element less than the given element, or null if no such element exists.
- floor(E e): Returns the greatest element less than or equal to the given element, or null if no such element exists.
- ceiling(E e): Returns the least element greater than or equal to the given element, or null if no such element exists.
- higher(E e): Returns the least element greater than the given element, or null if no such element exists.

```
public class TreeSetNavigable {
    public static void main(String[] args) {
        TreeSet<Integer> numbers = new TreeSet<>();
        numbers.add(1);
        numbers.add(2);
        numbers.add(3);
        numbers.add(4);
        numbers.add(5);

        System.out.println("Lower than 3: " + numbers.lower(3));
        System.out.println("Floor of 3: " + numbers.floor(3));
        System.out.println("Ceiling of 3: " + numbers.ceiling(3));
        System.out.println("Higher than 3: " + numbers.higher(3));
    }
}
```

Expected output:

```
Lower than 3: 2
Floor of 3: 3
Ceiling of 3: 3
Higher than 3: 4
```

These methods provide a more nuanced control over the data structure, enabling programmers to effectively query the set based on particular needs and ensure precise data retrieval.

Iteration Iterating over a TreeSet is straightforward and can be done with enhanced for-loops or iterators:

```
public class TreeSetIteration {
    public static void main(String[] args) {
        TreeSet<String> fruits = new TreeSet<>();
        fruits.add("apple");
        fruits.add("banana");
        fruits.add("cherry");
```

```
        // Enhanced for-loop
        for (String fruit : fruits) {
            System.out.println(fruit);
        }

        // Iterator
        Iterator<String> iterator = fruits.iterator();
        while (iterator.hasNext()) {
            System.out.println(iterator.next());
        }
    }
}
```

Expected output:

```
apple
banana
cherry
apple
banana
cherry
```

Understanding TreeSet is crucial for mastering sorted collections in Java. From leveraging the natural ordering to customizing it with comparators, as well as using the navigable methods, TreeSet offers powerful and flexible functionalities for sorted data management.

7.5 TreeMap: Naturally Sorted Maps

The TreeMap class in the Java Collections Framework represents a naturally sorted map. This class implements the NavigableMap interface, which is a sub-interface of the SortedMap interface, and it provides a way to store key-value pairs in a sorted order. The sorting of keys is determined either by their natural ordering or by a custom Comparator provided at the time of the map's creation.

TreeMap is implemented using a Red-Black tree, a self-balancing binary search tree that guarantees $O(\log n)$ time complexity for basic operations like get, put, remove, and containsKey.

During initialization, if no Comparator is provided, the keys must be mutually comparable—that is, they must implement the Comparable interface or a ClassCastException will be thrown. Below is an example of how to create a TreeMap with natural ordering and custom ordering using a Comparator:

```
import java.util.TreeMap;
import java.util.Comparator;
```

```
// Natural ordering
TreeMap<Integer, String> naturalOrderMap = new TreeMap<>();

// Custom ordering
Comparator<String> customComparator = (s1, s2) -> s1.length() - s2.length();
TreeMap<String, String> customOrderMap = new TreeMap<>(customComparator);
```

Key properties of the TreeMap are that it maintains a sorted order of the keys, and all operations that query or modify the map and depend on the order are expected to run in $O(\log n)$ time.

TreeMap offers several methods that leverage its sorted nature:

- firstKey: Returns the first (lowest) key currently in the map.
- lastKey: Returns the last (highest) key currently in the map.
- higherKey(K key): Returns the least key strictly greater than the given key, or null if there is no such key.
- lowerKey(K key): Returns the greatest key strictly less than the given key, or null if there is no such key.
- ceilingKey(K key): Returns the least key greater than or equal to the given key, or null if there is no such key.
- floorKey(K key): Returns the greatest key less than or equal to the given key, or null if there is no such key.
- putIfAbsent(K key, V value): If the specified key is not already associated with a value, associate it with the given value.

Here are some examples demonstrating these methods:

```
import java.util.TreeMap;

public class TreeMapExample {
    public static void main(String[] args) {
        TreeMap<Integer, String> treeMap = new TreeMap<>();

        // Adding elements
        treeMap.put(1, "one");
        treeMap.put(3, "three");
        treeMap.put(2, "two");

        // Getting the first and last keys
        System.out.println("First Key: " + treeMap.firstKey()); // Output: 1
        System.out.println("Last Key: " + treeMap.lastKey()); // Output: 3

        // Getting higher and lower keys
        System.out.println("Higher Key than 2: " + treeMap.higherKey(2)); // Output:
            3
        System.out.println("Lower Key than 2: " + treeMap.lowerKey(2)); // Output: 1
```

```
        // Getting ceiling and floor keys
        System.out.println("Ceiling Key for 2: " + treeMap.ceilingKey(2)); // Output: 2
        System.out.println("Floor Key for 2: " + treeMap.floorKey(2)); // Output: 2

        // Using putIfAbsent
        treeMap.putIfAbsent(2, "two-two");
        System.out.println("Value for key 2: " + treeMap.get(2)); // Output: two
    }
}
```

Another important feature of TreeMap is the subMap method, which allows for creating a view of a portion of the map. This view is defined by a range of keys, which provides a convenient way to perform range queries. The range may be specified as either open, closed, or a mix of both.

The following example demonstrates how to use subMap:

```
import java.util.SortedMap;
import java.util.TreeMap;

public class TreeMapSubMapExample {
    public static void main(String[] args) {
        TreeMap<Integer, String> treeMap = new TreeMap<>();
        treeMap.put(1, "one");
        treeMap.put(3, "three");
        treeMap.put(2, "two");
        treeMap.put(5, "five");
        treeMap.put(4, "four");

        // subMap from key 2 (inclusive) to key 4 (exclusive)
        SortedMap<Integer, String> subMap = treeMap.subMap(2, 4);
        System.out.println("SubMap: " + subMap);
        // Output: {2=two, 3=three}
    }
}
```

A key characteristic of TreeMap is its adherence to a strict natural ordering or provided Comparator. This ensures all keys are stored in a manner that allows fast access and manipulation. This property is particularly advantageous in scenarios that require ordering and range queries.

Understanding the efficient usage of TreeMap, including its methods and properties, enhances one's ability to manage and manipulate sorted key-value pairs effectively. The application of this class spans various domains, such as tasks requiring consistent ordering, natural key progression, and range-based queries.

7.6 NavigableSet Interface: Enhanced TreeSet Operations

The NavigableSet interface in the java.util package extends the capabilities of a SortedSet. By implementing the NavigableSet interface, TreeSet gains access to a comprehensive set of methods that provide a greater level of control over set navigation, retrieval, and manipulation, thereby offering enhanced operations beyond the basic ordered set functionalities.

The key methods of the NavigableSet interface include: lower, floor, ceiling, higher, pollFirst, pollLast, and sub-set views like descendingSet. These methods facilitate intricate maneuvers on the elements within a TreeSet, making the TreeSet a powerful tool for managing sorted data.

Key Methods Overview

- lower(E e): Returns the greatest element in this set strictly less than the given element, or null if there is no such element.
- floor(E e): Returns the greatest element in this set less than or equal to the given element, or null if there is no such element.
- ceiling(E e): Returns the least element in this set greater than or equal to the given element, or null if there is no such element.
- higher(E e): Returns the least element in this set strictly greater than the given element, or null if there is no such element.
- pollFirst(): Retrieves and removes the first (lowest) element, or returns null if this set is empty.
- pollLast(): Retrieves and removes the last (highest) element, or returns null if this set is empty.
- descendingSet(): Returns a reverse order view of the elements contained in this set.

Example Implementation of Traversing a TreeSet using NavigableSet

```
import java.util.NavigableSet;
import java.util.TreeSet;

public class NavigableSetExample {
    public static void main(String[] args) {
        NavigableSet<Integer> navigableSet = new TreeSet<>();
```

```
        // Adding elements
        navigableSet.add(15);
        navigableSet.add(10);
        navigableSet.add(20);
        navigableSet.add(25);
        navigableSet.add(5);

        // Using lower() method
        System.out.println("Element lower than 15: " + navigableSet.lower(15)); //
             Output: 10

        // Using floor() method
        System.out.println("Element floor 15: " + navigableSet.floor(15)); // Output: 15

        // Using ceiling() method
        System.out.println("Element ceiling 15: " + navigableSet.ceiling(15)); // Output
             : 15

        // Using higher() method
        System.out.println("Element higher than 15: " + navigableSet.higher(15)); //
             Output: 20

        // Polling first and last elements
        System.out.println("First element: " + navigableSet.pollFirst()); // Output: 5
        System.out.println("Last element: " + navigableSet.pollLast()); // Output: 25

        // Iterating over the remaining elements in descending order
        NavigableSet<Integer> descendingSet = navigableSet.descendingSet();
        System.out.println("Elements in descending order:");
        for (Integer elem : descendingSet) {
            System.out.println(elem);
        }
    }
}
```

The NavigableSet interface augments the traditional TreeSet with methods specifically designed for navigation. Logical scenarios prompt specific methods:

- - lower(E e) and higher(E e) methods effectively answer questions concerning nearest neighbors of an element.
- - floor(E e) and ceiling(E e) functions extend this capacity by including possible element matches.
- - The pollFirst() and pollLast() methods allow for the incremental extraction of elements, which is particularly beneficial in persistent processing streams or queued data contexts.
- - The descendingSet() method is conducive for scenarios demanding reverse ordered traversals.

The adept use of these NavigableSet methods facilitates precise control over sorted sets, culminating in refined data handling strategies evident in complex computational tasks.

7.7 NavigableMap Interface: Enhanced TreeMap Operations

The NavigableMap interface extends the SortedMap interface, introducing navigation methods to conduct search and mapping operations more efficiently within a map structure. This interface is a part of the java.util package, and it refines many of the operations provided by SortedMap by adding methods that return the nearest matches for given keys.

To better understand the capabilities of the NavigableMap interface, it is essential to analyze some of the most commonly used methods:

- ceilingEntry(K key): Returns a key-value mapping associated with the least key greater than or equal to the given key, or null if no such key exists.
- floorEntry(K key): Returns a key-value mapping associated with the greatest key less than or equal to the given key, or null if no such key exists.
- higherEntry(K key): Returns a key-value mapping associated with the least key strictly greater than the given key, or null if no such key exists.
- lowerEntry(K key): Returns a key-value mapping associated with the greatest key strictly less than the given key, or null if no such key exists.
- pollFirstEntry(): Removes and returns a key-value mapping associated with the least key in the map, or returns null if the map is empty.
- pollLastEntry(): Removes and returns a key-value mapping associated with the greatest key in the map, or returns null if the map is empty.

```
import java.util.NavigableMap;
import java.util.TreeMap;
```

```
public class NavigableMapExample {
    public static void main(String[] args) {
        NavigableMap<Integer, String> navMap = new TreeMap<>();
        navMap.put(1, "one");
        navMap.put(3, "three");
        navMap.put(5, "five");
        navMap.put(7, "seven");

        // Finding entries based on the key
        System.out.println("Ceiling Entry for 4: " + navMap.ceilingEntry(4));
        System.out.println("Floor Entry for 4: " + navMap.floorEntry(4));
        System.out.println("Higher Entry for 4: " + navMap.higherEntry(4));
        System.out.println("Lower Entry for 4: " + navMap.lowerEntry(4));

        // Polling entries
        System.out.println("Poll First Entry: " + navMap.pollFirstEntry());
        System.out.println("Poll Last Entry: " + navMap.pollLastEntry());

        // Demonstrating remaining map entries
        System.out.println("Remaining Map: " + navMap);
    }
}
```

```
Ceiling Entry for 4: 5=five
Floor Entry for 4: 3=three
Higher Entry for 4: 5=five
Lower Entry for 4: 3=three
Poll First Entry: 1=one
Poll Last Entry: 7=seven
Remaining Map: {3=three, 5=five}
```

The NavigableMap also allows for retrieval operations in a reverse-ordered view. Utilizing descendingMap(), one can procure a view of the mappings contained in this map in reverse key order:

```
NavigableMap<Integer, String> descendingMap = navMap.descendingMap();
System.out.println("Descending Map: " + descendingMap);
```

```
Descending Map: {5=five, 3=three}
```

The NavigableMap interface's sub-map views, such as headMap(K toKey, boolean inclusive) and tailMap(K fromKey, boolean inclusive), allow for slicing the map based on specified key ranges, providing developers with more control over view subsets:

```
NavigableMap<Integer, String> headMap = navMap.headMap(5, true);
System.out.println("Head Map (inclusive): " + headMap);

NavigableMap<Integer, String> tailMap = navMap.tailMap(3, false);
System.out.println("Tail Map (exclusive): " + tailMap);
```

```
Head Map (inclusive): {3=three, 5=five}
Tail Map (exclusive): {5=five}
```

The NavigableMap interface enriches the basic SortedMap operations with fine-grained navigation capabilities. When applying these methods, it is critical to handle null responses to avoid NullPointerException, as these methods return null when there are no suitable entries for a specified key. Leveraging the extended functionalities provided by NavigableMap is advantageous in scenarios demanding precise control over sorted data structures in Java. Proper utilization of these methods can lead to better performance and more readable code for complex data handling tasks.

7.8 ConcurrentSkipListSet: Thread-Safe Sorted Sets

The ConcurrentSkipListSet is a member of the Java Collections Framework introduced with Java 6, providing a high-performance, scalable, and thread-safe implementation of a NavigableSet. This section will delve into the principles, characteristics, and applications of ConcurrentSkipListSet, enhancing your understanding of how to utilize this sorted collection in a multi-threaded environment.

The ConcurrentSkipListSet class is part of the java.util.concurrent package. It implements the NavigableSet interface and is backed by a ConcurrentSkipListMap. The ConcurrentSkipListMap provides concurrent access and maintains the elements in a naturally ordered manner or according to a specified Comparator.

```
import java.util.concurrent.ConcurrentSkipListSet;

public class Example {
    public static void main(String[] args) {
        ConcurrentSkipListSet<Integer> skipListSet = new ConcurrentSkipListSet<>()
            ;
        skipListSet.add(3);
        skipListSet.add(1);
        skipListSet.add(2);

        System.out.println(skipListSet);
    }
}
```

```
Output:
[1, 2, 3]
```

Characteristics of ConcurrentSkipListSet

- *Thread-Safe*: ConcurrentSkipListSet is designed to be safely used by multiple threads without explicit synchronization. It employs fine-grained locking to ensure thread safety and improve concurrency.

- *Non-Blocking Algorithms*: Unlike blocking algorithms that rely on locking mechanisms, ConcurrentSkipListSet utilizes a non-blocking algorithm, ensuring better performance and responsiveness in concurrent applications.
- *Sorted Order*: The elements in a ConcurrentSkipListSet are sorted either by their natural ordering or by a custom Comparator provided at set creation time.
- *NavigableSet Features*: As it implements NavigableSet, it includes methods such as lower(), floor(), ceiling(), and higher() to navigate through the set.
- *Bounded Collections*: Methods like subSet(), headSet(), and tailSet() allow for the creation of viewsets representing subsets of the original collection.

Creating and Using ConcurrentSkipListSet

In the following example, we illustrate the creation of a ConcurrentSkipListSet with custom ordering using a Comparator:

```
import java.util.Comparator;
import java.util.concurrent.ConcurrentSkipListSet;

public class CustomComparatorExample {
    public static void main(String[] args) {
        Comparator<String> comparator = (s1, s2) -> s2.compareTo(s1);
        ConcurrentSkipListSet<String> reverseOrderSet = new ConcurrentSkipListSet
            <>(comparator);

        reverseOrderSet.add("apple");
        reverseOrderSet.add("banana");
        reverseOrderSet.add("cherry");

        System.out.println(reverseOrderSet);
    }
}
```

```
Output:
[cherry, banana, apple]
```

Handling Concurrent Access

ConcurrentSkipListSet's non-blocking properties make it highly suitable for use in concurrent applications where performance and responsiveness are critical. The following example demonstrates its usage in a multi-threaded scenario where multiple threads are adding elements to the set:

```
import java.util.concurrent.ConcurrentSkipListSet;

public class MultiThreadedExample {
    public static void main(String[] args) throws InterruptedException {
        ConcurrentSkipListSet<Integer> skipListSet = new ConcurrentSkipListSet<>()
            ;

        Runnable task = () -> {
            for (int i = 0; i < 10; i++) {
                skipListSet.add(i);
            }
        };

        Thread thread1 = new Thread(task);
        Thread thread2 = new Thread(task);
        thread1.start();
        thread2.start();
        thread1.join();
        thread2.join();

        System.out.println(skipListSet);
    }
}
```

```
Output:
[0, 1, 2, 3, 4, 5, 6, 7, 8, 9]
```

Performance and Use Cases

ConcurrentSkipListSet is particularly beneficial in scenarios requiring a combination of sorted and concurrent access. It is commonly used in:

- *Real-time Data Processing*: Suitable for applications that process data in real-time and require consistent and predictable navigation through elements.
- *Event-Driven Systems*: Ideal for systems that need to manage events in a sorted order and require concurrent handling to meet high throughput demands.
- *Cache Implementations*: Works well for implementing caches where elements need to be evicted based on time or access patterns and concurrency control is essential.

Given these properties, the ConcurrentSkipListSet is a powerful utility for developers needing a sorted set that performs efficiently under concurrent modifications. It balances complexity and performance, making it an excellent choice for building scalable, multithreaded applications.

7.9 ConcurrentSkipListMap: Thread-Safe Sorted Maps

The ConcurrentSkipListMap is a member of the Java Collections Framework, belonging to the group of concurrent collections. It is designed to manage large volumes of data in a multi-threaded environment while ensuring that the data remains in a sorted state. The ConcurrentSkipListMap implements both the NavigableMap and ConcurrentNavigableMap interfaces, combining navigability and concurrent safety features.

The underpinnings of ConcurrentSkipListMap leverage the skip list data structure, which allows for log(n) time complexity for most common operations such as insertions, deletions, and lookups. Unlike TreeMap, which relies on a balanced tree structure, skip lists use multiple layers of linked lists to maintain order and allow for efficient navigation.

A ConcurrentSkipListMap is crucial for applications that require a sorted map accessible by multiple threads without external synchronization. This collection is typically used in scenarios such as maintaining a real-time leaderboard, managing time-sequenced data, and in cache implementations that benefit from sorted order retrieval.

```
import java.util.concurrent.ConcurrentSkipListMap;

public class ConcurrentSkipListMapExample {
    public static void main(String[] args) {
        ConcurrentSkipListMap<Integer, String> map = new ConcurrentSkipListMap
            <>();

        map.put(3, "three");
        map.put(1, "one");
        map.put(2, "two");

        map.forEach((key, value) -> System.out.println(key + " => " + value));

        System.out.println("First Key: " + map.firstKey());
        System.out.println("Last Key: " + map.lastKey());

        System.out.println("Head Map: " + map.headMap(2));
        System.out.println("Tail Map: " + map.tailMap(2));
        System.out.println("Sub Map: " + map.subMap(1, 3));
    }
}
```

```
1 => one
2 => two
3 => three
First Key: 1
Last Key: 3
Head Map: {1=one}
Tail Map: {2=two, 3=three}
Sub Map: {1=one, 2=two}
```

The example illustrates instantiating a ConcurrentSkipListMap and performing fundamental operations. The put method efficiently inserts entries while maintaining the sorted order. As shown, iteration over the map entries produces naturally sorted output based on the keys. Methods, such as firstKey(), lastKey(), headMap(), tailMap(), and subMap() demonstrate key navigational capabilities.

One of the significant advantages offered by ConcurrentSkipListMap is its thread-safe nature without wrapping it in synchronized blocks. It employs fine-grained locking mechanisms to achieve concurrency, which results in better throughput under high contention compared to global-locking strategies.

The following algorithm highlights the concurrent insertion and retrieval process managed by ConcurrentSkipListMap:

Algorithm 4: Concurrent Operations in ConcurrentSkipListMap

```
Data: ConcurrentSkipListMap map
Result: Thread-safe operations for insertion and retrieval
while true do
    if new entry to be inserted then
        map.put(entryKey, entryValue);
    end
    if entry to be retrieved then
        result = map.get(entryKey);
        if result == null then
            handle absence of entry;
        end
    end
    if entry to be removed then
        map.remove(entryKey);
    end
end
```

This algorithm ensures that concurrent threads can perform insertion, retrieval, and removal operations safely. The underlying mechanics handle synchronization internally, freeing developers from managing thread coordination themselves.

Given its design, ConcurrentSkipListMap is particularly suitable for scenarios where read and write operations occur frequently and concurrently. Its skip list structure lends itself well to applications needing fast, ordered access with the added benefit of thread safety.

Performance considerations are also notable for ConcurrentSkipListMap. While it generally provides efficient performance, certain operations can incur higher costs compared to non-concurrent collections due to the overhead of maintaining thread safety. However, the trade-off is justified in multi-threaded environments where consistency, order, and concurrent access must be maintained.

A critical point to remember when using ConcurrentSkipListMap is the nuances around its concurrent nature. Iterators of the ConcurrentSkipListMap are weakly consistent, which means that they reflect a state of the map at some point when the iterator was created and may not show changes done during iteration, except for the results of structural modifications (insertions/deletions) reflected after the iterator's creation.

By mastering ConcurrentSkipListMap, developers can exploit its robust framework to build highly reliable, thread-safe applications that require ordered data management in high-concurrency contexts.

7.10 Common Operations on Sorted Collections

Sorted collections in Java ensure that the elements are maintained in a specific order. This section elaborates on the common operations applicable to these collections, with a primary focus on TreeSet, TreeMap, NavigableSet, and NavigableMap.

Adding Elements Adding elements to a sorted collection such as TreeSet or TreeMap is a fundamental operation. In TreeSet, the add method inserts the specified element, ensuring the set remains sorted.

```
TreeSet<String> treeSet = new TreeSet<>();
treeSet.add("banana");
treeSet.add("apple");
treeSet.add("cherry");
```

For TreeMap, elements are added using the put method, with key-value pairs ensuring the map remains sorted by keys.

```
TreeMap<Integer, String> treeMap = new TreeMap<>();
treeMap.put(3, "three");
treeMap.put(1, "one");
treeMap.put(2, "two");
```

Removing Elements Removing elements from a TreeSet or TreeMap is accomplished using the remove method. For TreeSet, this method removes the specified element.

```
treeSet.remove("banana");
```

In TreeMap, the remove method can remove the mapping for a specific key.

```
treeMap.remove(2);
```

Retrieving Elements Retrieving elements in sorted collections can be achieved using methods such as first, last, ceiling, floor, higher, and lower.

```
String firstElement = treeSet.first();
String lastElement = treeSet.last();
Integer ceilingKey = treeMap.ceilingKey(2);
Integer floorKey = treeMap.floorKey(2);
Integer higherKey = treeMap.higherKey(1);
Integer lowerKey = treeMap.lowerKey(3);
```

These methods in NavigableSet and NavigableMap facilitate locating specific elements, enhancing the utility of sorted collections.

Navigating and Subsetting Navigable collections provide methods to create subsets, which are particularly useful for operations over ranges of elements. TreeSet offers subSet, headSet, and tailSet methods.

```
NavigableSet<String> subSet = treeSet.subSet("apple", true, "cherry", true);
NavigableSet<String> headSet = treeSet.headSet("cherry", true);
NavigableSet<String> tailSet = treeSet.tailSet("banana", false);
```

Similarly, methods in TreeMap enable the creation of submaps.

```
NavigableMap<Integer, String> subMap = treeMap.subMap(1, true, 3, true);
NavigableMap<Integer, String> headMap = treeMap.headMap(3, true);
NavigableMap<Integer, String> tailMap = treeMap.tailMap(2, false);
```

These methods extract portions of the collections while preserving their sorted nature. For example, subSet creates a subset with elements ranging from "apple" to "cherry", inclusive.

Iterating Over Elements Iteration over sorted collections can be done in natural order using iterators.

```
Iterator<String> iterator = treeSet.iterator();
while (iterator.hasNext()) {
    String element = iterator.next();
    System.out.println(element);
}
```

Using descending iterators, one can iterate in reverse order.

```
Iterator<String> descIterator = treeSet.descendingIterator();
while (descIterator.hasNext()) {
    String element = descIterator.next();
    System.out.println(element);
}
```

Iterators in TreeMap can be employed to traverse key-value pairs.

```
Iterator<Map.Entry<Integer, String>> mapIterator = treeMap.entrySet().iterator();
while (mapIterator.hasNext()) {
    Map.Entry<Integer, String> entry = mapIterator.next();
    System.out.println(entry.getKey() + " => " + entry.getValue());
}
```

Bulk Operations Bulk operations are provided in sorted collections to add or remove multiple elements. For instance, addAll and removeAll methods enable such operations.

```
TreeSet<String> newSet = new TreeSet<>();
newSet.add("date");
newSet.add("elderberry");

treeSet.addAll(newSet);
treeSet.removeAll(newSet);
```

Similarly, TreeMap supports putAll to add all mappings from another map.

```
TreeMap<Integer, String> newMap = new TreeMap<>();
newMap.put(4, "four");
newMap.put(5, "five");

treeMap.putAll(newMap);
```

Comparing and Checking Elements Basic operations such as contains to verify the presence of an element and size to determine the number of elements are crucial for many algorithms.

```
boolean containsApple = treeSet.contains("apple");
int setSize = treeSet.size();
```

Similarly, for TreeMap:

```
boolean containsKey2 = treeMap.containsKey(2);
boolean containsValueTwo = treeMap.containsValue("two");
int mapSize = treeMap.size();
```

Each operation ensures the collection adheres to its sorting properties while maintaining efficiency. Efficient control over the size and membership of sorted collections is often critical for applications needing organized data management.

Combining Sorted Collections Combining two sorted collections while keeping them sorted is a frequently required operation. Using the addAll method in TreeSet can combine two sets.

```
TreeSet<String> anotherSet = new TreeSet<>(Arrays.asList("fig", "grape"));
treeSet.addAll(anotherSet);
```

For TreeMap, the putAll method achieves a similar outcome for maps.

```
TreeMap<Integer, String> anotherMap = new TreeMap<>();
anotherMap.put(6, "six");
anotherMap.put(7, "seven");
treeMap.putAll(anotherMap);
```

Understanding and mastering these operations empower developers to efficiently leverage sorted collections ensuring optimal performance and correctness in data handling tasks.

7.11 Use Cases for Sorted Collections

Sorted collections within the Java Collections Framework offer various use cases across multiple domains. Their ability to maintain elements in a specified order—either natural or custom defined—makes them crucial for many algorithmic and real-world problems. This section outlines detailed scenarios and application areas where sorted collections such as TreeSet, TreeMap, NavigableSet, NavigableMap, ConcurrentSkipListSet, and ConcurrentSkipListMap can be effectively utilized.

1. Managing Ordered Data: Sorted collections are ideal for maintaining ordered datasets. For instance, in an application requiring chronological ordering of events, TreeMap can be used. Assume a logging service where log entries must be ordered by their timestamp:

```
TreeMap<Long, String> logEntries = new TreeMap<>();
logEntries.put(1627815623L, "User A logged in");
logEntries.put(1627815723L, "User B logged in");
logEntries.put(1627815823L, "User A logged out");
```

In this example, log entries are automatically sorted by their timestamps (keys), facilitating efficient retrieval, insertion, and deletion operations.

2. Implementing Priority Queues: Although PriorityQueue is often used, TreeSet can serve as an alternative to ensure elements are processed based on priority or custom orderings. For instance, in a job scheduling system, tasks can be prioritized:

```
TreeSet<Job> jobQueue = new TreeSet<>(Comparator.comparingInt(Job::getPriority)
    );
jobQueue.add(new Job("Job1", 2));
jobQueue.add(new Job("Job2", 1));
jobQueue.add(new Job("Job3", 3));
```

Here, a TreeSet ensures that jobs with higher priority are processed first based on their priority values.

3. Financial Applications: In financial systems, sorted collections are used extensively for managing market data, tracking orders, and handling trades. NavigableMap can assist in maintaining ranges of values, such as price bands in a stock market application:

```
NavigableMap<Double, Order> orderBook = new TreeMap<>();
orderBook.put(100.50, new Order("Buy", 100));
orderBook.put(101.00, new Order("Sell", 50));
orderBook.put(99.75, new Order("Buy", 150));
```

Financial operations often require querying ranges of prices or navigating through them, which NavigableMap handles effectively, supporting operations like subMap, headMap, and tailMap.

4. Geographic Information Systems (GIS): For GIS applications, sorting spatial data by coordinates or other attributes is crucial. TreeMap and TreeSet can be used to store and query geographic locations efficiently:

```
TreeMap<Coordinate, LocationData> locationMap = new TreeMap<>();
locationMap.put(new Coordinate(40.7128, -74.0060), new LocationData("New York"));
locationMap.put(new Coordinate(34.0522, -118.2437), new LocationData("Los Angeles"
    ));
```

This sorted data enables efficient lookups and can be particularly useful for nearest-neighbor searches or range queries based on geographic regions.

5. Autocomplete Systems: Autocomplete and typeahead suggestions often rely on sorted collections to manage and retrieve potential matches quickly. Utilizing a TreeSet allows efficient management of prefix searches:

```
NavigableSet<String> dictionary = new TreeSet<>();
dictionary.add("apple");
dictionary.add("application");
dictionary.add("banana");
```

Users can quickly find and retrieve autocomplete suggestions based on typed prefixes, using methods like tailSet.

6. Session and Token Management: In web applications, managing user sessions or tokens often requires tracking expiration times in a sorted manner. Using ConcurrentSkipListMap can maintain session expirations in a thread-safe environment:

```
ConcurrentSkipListMap<Long, Session> sessionExpiryMap = new
    ConcurrentSkipListMap<>();
sessionExpiryMap.put(System.currentTimeMillis() + 300000, new Session("User1"));
sessionExpiryMap.put(System.currentTimeMillis() + 150000, new Session("User2"));
```

This ensures that expired sessions are efficiently removed or processed based on their expiration times without concurrency issues.

7. Data Deduplication: Sorted collections can effectively eliminate duplicates while maintaining order. For example, compressing sorted logs or events where duplicates are common:

```
SortedSet<Event> uniqueEvents = new TreeSet<>();
uniqueEvents.addAll(eventList);
```

Employing TreeSet ensures efficient maintenance of unique elements in a naturally sorted order.

8. Range Queries and Sub-collections: Handling range-based queries is another prominent use case. In educational systems, storing and querying student scores efficiently can be managed with NavigableMap:

```
NavigableMap<Integer, String> studentScores = new TreeMap<>();
studentScores.put(85, "Alice");
studentScores.put(90, "Bob");
studentScores.put(78, "Charlie");
```

Methods like headMap(90) or subMap(80, 95) make it straightforward to extract and analyze scores within specific intervals.

Implementing sorted collections across various applications facilitates efficient data management, ensures orderliness, and enhances performance. Their flexibility and the rich set of operations provided by the Java Collections Framework make them indispensable tools for developers tackling complex datasets and real-time challenges.

7.12 Performance Considerations for Sorted Collections

The performance characteristics of sorted collections in Java are crucial for selecting the appropriate collection type based on specific application requirements. Analyzing the time and space complexity of key operations—such as insertion, deletion, and lookup—can guide the decision-making process and optimize the efficiency of Java applications.

Time Complexity Analysis

1. **TreeSet and TreeMap**: Both $\mathrm{TreeSet}$ and $\mathrm{TreeMap}$ are typically implemented using Red-Black trees, which are a type of self-balancing binary search tree. The primary operations (insertion, deletion, and lookup) have a worst-case time complexity of $O(\log n)$, where n is the number of elements in the collection. Red-Black trees balance themselves after each modification, ensuring that the tree's height remains logarithmic relative to the number of elements.

2. **ConcurrentSkipListSet and ConcurrentSkipListMap**: These collections utilize skip lists, which provide an alternative to balanced trees for maintaining element order. The expected time complexity for insertion, deletion, and lookup operations is $O(\log n)$, assuming that the probabilistic balancing mechanism of skip lists works effectively in practice. Although the worst-case time complexity can degrade to $O(n)$ in extremely rare cases, this scenario is highly improbable.

Space Complexity Analysis

1. **TreeSet and TreeMap**: The memory footprint for $\mathrm{TreeSet}$ and $\mathrm{TreeMap}$ primarily depends on the storage required for the nodes in the Red-Black tree. Each node stores references to its parent, left child, right child, and the key-value pair (for $\mathrm{TreeMap}$). Consequently, the space complexity for these collections is $O(n)$.

2. **ConcurrentSkipListSet and ConcurrentSkipListMap**: Skip lists manage multiple levels of linked lists to facilitate logarithmic time operations. Each element in a skip list potentially participates in several lists, which can increase the space overhead. Nevertheless, on average, the space complexity remains $O(n)$ due to the probabilistic level selection.

Thread Safety and Concurrency

1. **Non-thread-safe Collections**: TreeSet and TreeMap are not thread-safe, which means that they cannot be safely accessed or modified by multiple threads without external synchronization. The use of synchronized blocks or locks can ensure thread safety but introduces additional computational overhead due to context switching and contention.

2. **Thread-safe Collections**: ConcurrentSkipListSet and ConcurrentSkipListMap are designed for concurrent access and modifications. These collections provide thread safety without necessitating external synchronization. Internal algorithms manage concurrent modifications, minimizing contention and leveraging fine-grained lock-free techniques. However, this increased complexity might incur a slight performance penalty in single-threaded scenarios.

Garbage Collection and Memory Management

1. **Tree-Based Collections**: The node-heavy structure of Red-Black trees implies that garbage collection must manage numerous short-lived node objects, especially if many elements are frequently inserted and removed. Efficient garbage collection becomes critical in applications with high insertion and deletion rates to prevent memory-related bottlenecks.

2. **Skip List-Based Collections**: Skip lists' reliance on multiple linked lists means that elements link to several nodes. As a result, garbage collection must handle potentially many such connections. The more frequent allocation and deallocation of nodes can create memory churn, requiring high-performance garbage collectors to avoid latency spikes.

Performance Optimizations

1. **Bulk Operations**: Interfaces such as NavigableSet and NavigableMap offer methods like bulk remove and headSet that can be used to optimize operations by working on sections of the data. These operations can offer performance improvements by reducing the overhead of managing individual elements separately.

```
// Example of bulk operation on NavigableSet
NavigableSet<Integer> set = new TreeSet<>();
set.addAll(Arrays.asList(1, 2, 3, 4, 5, 6, 7));
// Remove a range of elements
set.subSet(3, true, 6, true).clear();
```

Output: [1, 2, 7]

2. **Load Factor and Rehashing**: Although rehashing is more relevant for hash-based collections, understanding the underlying mechan-

ics of load factor adjustments can help in managing expansions and the resultant performance spikes in sorted collections when auxiliary structures, such as hashmaps within skip lists, are employed.

Real-World Application Scenarios

1. **Low-latency Applications**: In systems requiring low-latency operations, such as high-frequency trading platforms, the choice between Red-Black trees and skip lists can be influenced by the predictability of operations. The consistent $O(\log n)$ performance of $\mathrm{TreeSet}$ and $\mathrm{TreeMap}$ might be preferable.

2. **Concurrent Environments**: Applications requiring concurrent access to sorted collections, like web servers managing session data, would benefit from the non-blocking nature of $\mathrm{ConcurrentSkipListSet}$ and $\mathrm{ConcurrentSkipListMap}$.

Selecting the appropriate sorted collection requires a nuanced understanding of both the theoretical performance metrics and practical implications on system behavior.

Chapter 8

Customizing Collections with Comparators and Sorting

This chapter focuses on customizing collections through the use of comparators and sorting techniques in Java. It covers the implementation of the Comparator interface, utilizing lambda expressions and method references, and discusses sorting lists, sets, and maps by keys and values. The chapter also explores chaining comparators, reverse ordering, and differentiates between Comparator and Comparable. Practical use cases for custom sorting are examined to provide a deep understanding of how to tailor collection orderings to specific needs.

8.1 Introduction to Comparators and Sorting

In the Java programming language, the need to manage collections effectively is paramount. One of the primary mechanisms to achieve this is through sorting. Sorting involves arranging items in a collection in a specific order based on defined criteria. The Comparator interface is central to customizing the order of elements in a collection. Understanding the Comparator interface and its role in sorting is critical for mastering Java collections.

A Comparator in Java is an object that imposes a total ordering on some collection of objects. Comparators can be passed to a sort method (such as Collections.sort or Arrays.sort) to allow precise control over the sort order. The Comparator interface defines a single method:

```
int compare(T o1, T o2);
```

This method compares its two arguments for order. It returns a negative integer, zero, or a positive integer if the first argument is less than, equal to, or greater than the second. This contrasts with the Comparable interface, where each object is only capable of comparing itself with another object.

Java's built-in implementation provides a robust framework for sorting but does not fit every use case. Customizing the sorting order using Comparator makes it possible to handle complex requirements.

Utilizing Comparators

To utilize a Comparator, one must implement the compare method. This can be done using either traditional anonymous inner classes or modern lambda expressions and method references. For instance, here is an example of sorting a list of strings by their lengths using an anonymous inner class:

```
List<String> words = Arrays.asList("apple", "banana", "cherry");

Collections.sort(words, new Comparator<String>() {
    @Override
    public int compare(String s1, String s2) {
        return Integer.compare(s1.length(), s2.length());
    }
});
```

In this example, the compare method is implemented to sort strings based on their lengths. The Collections.sort method accepts the list and the Comparator.

Lambda Expressions and Method References

Java 8 introduced lambda expressions, a more concise and readable way to create instances of Comparator. The previous example can be rewritten using a lambda expression:

```
Collections.sort(words, (s1, s2) -> Integer.compare(s1.length(), s2.length()));
```

Lambdas can further streamline the code, improving readability and reducing verbosity. Method references, another feature of Java 8, can make the code even cleaner in certain scenarios. For example:

```
Collections.sort(words, Comparator.comparingInt(String::length));
```

This method reference String::length points to the method that gets the length of a string, which is passed to Comparator.comparingInt, creating a Comparator based on string lengths.

Intrinsic Sorting Mechanisms in Java

Java offers intrinsic sorting mechanisms in both utilities such as Collections and Arrays. They provide powerful, flexible tools for sorting:

- Collections.sort(List<T> list, Comparator<? super T> c)
- Arrays.sort(T[] a, Comparator<? super T> c)

Both methods leverage the Comparator to define the order of sorting.

Additionally, inherently ordered collections implement the SortedSet and SortedMap interfaces. Classes such as TreeSet and TreeMap automatically maintain their elements in a sorted order determined either by their natural ordering or a specified Comparator.

Understanding how comparators integrate into these collections and sorting methods allows for customizing collection orderings to fit any specific need.

Conclusion

Comprehending the core mechanisms and tools provided by Java for comparators and sorting forms the foundation for more advanced topics. By utilizing both traditional and modern syntaxes, developers can achieve efficient and tailored collection orderings. The integration between Comparator and different Java collections enables intricate and highly specific sorting capabilities. The ability to sort not just lists but also sets and maps based on arbitrarily complex criteria greatly enhances the flexibility and power of Java programming in the context of collections.

8.2 Implementing Comparator Interface

The Comparator interface in Java is used to order the objects of a user-defined class. This interface is found in the java.util package and contains two methods: compare(T o1, T o2) and equals(Object obj).

However, it is important to note that in most cases, we only need to implement the compare method to establish custom ordering.

Comparator is a functional interface, which means you can implement it using a lambda expression or a method reference, making the code more concise and readable. Nevertheless, understanding the fundamental approach of implementing the Comparator interface directly is crucial for grasping how custom sorting mechanisms work internally.

A typical implementation involves creating a custom class that implements the Comparator interface and overrides the compare method to define the order logic. This method takes two objects of the same type and returns a negative integer, zero, or a positive integer if the first argument is less than, equal to, or greater than the second, respectively.

Let us consider a class Person with attributes name and age:

```
public class Person {
    private String name;
    private int age;

    public Person(String name, int age) {
        this.name = name;
        this.age = age;
    }

    public String getName() {
        return name;
    }

    public int getAge() {
        return age;
    }
}
```

To implement a Comparator for Person objects based on their age, we create a PersonAgeComparator class as follows:

```
import java.util.Comparator;

public class PersonAgeComparator implements Comparator<Person> {

    @Override
    public int compare(Person p1, Person p2) {
        return Integer.compare(p1.getAge(), p2.getAge());
    }
}
```

In this example, the compare method compares the ages of two Person objects. The Integer.compare method is used to handle the comparison, ensuring that the resulting value is correctly interpreted (-1 if the first age is less than the second, 0 if they are equal, and 1 if the first is greater).

We can now use this Comparator to sort a collection of Person objects. Consider the following code snippet that demonstrates using the PersonAgeComparator to sort a list:

```
import java.util.ArrayList;
import java.util.Collections;
import java.util.List;

public class Main {
    public static void main(String[] args) {
        List<Person> people = new ArrayList<>();
        people.add(new Person("Alice", 30));
        people.add(new Person("Bob", 25));
        people.add(new Person("Charlie", 35));

        Collections.sort(people, new PersonAgeComparator());

        for (Person person : people) {
            System.out.println(person.getName() + ": " + person.getAge());
        }
    }
}
```

The output of the above code will be:

```
Bob: 25
Alice: 30
Charlie: 35
```

This demonstrates the sorting of Person objects by age in ascending order using our custom Comparator.

Additionally, we may implement multiple comparators for various sorting criteria. For instance, to sort persons by their names lexicographically, we define another Comparator:

```
public class PersonNameComparator implements Comparator<Person> {

    @Override
    public int compare(Person p1, Person p2) {
        return p1.getName().compareTo(p2.getName());
    }
}
```

This Comparator can be used similarly to sort the list of Person objects by name:

```
Collections.sort(people, new PersonNameComparator());
```

Understanding the implementation of multiple Comparators for a single class, as well as the capability to switch between different sorting strategies, provides flexibility in how collections of objects are ordered. This is essential for efficiently managing and displaying data in various applications and scenarios.

8.3 Using Comparator with Collections

The Comparator interface plays an integral role in Java's collection framework, facilitating custom sort orderings for collection elements. When used within Java's java.util.Collections utility class, Comparator can be leveraged to define and apply a specific order across various types of collections such as List, Set, and Map.

Sorting a List with Comparator

Sorting a List using a Comparator can be achieved with the Collections.sort() method, which accepts a List and a Comparator as parameters. Consider the following example where we sort a list of Person objects by their age.

First, define the Person class:

```
public class Person {
    private String name;
    private int age;

    public Person(String name, int age) {
        this.name = name;
        this.age = age;
    }

    public String getName() {
        return name;
    }

    public int getAge() {
        return age;
    }
}
```

Next, define a Comparator for Person by age:

```
import java.util.Comparator;

public class AgeComparator implements Comparator<Person> {
    @Override
    public int compare(Person p1, Person p2) {
        return Integer.compare(p1.getAge(), p2.getAge());
    }
}
```

Now, apply this Comparator to sort a List of Person objects:

```
import java.util.*;

public class Main {
    public static void main(String[] args) {
```

```
        List<Person> people = new ArrayList<>();
        people.add(new Person("Alice", 28));
        people.add(new Person("Bob", 22));
        people.add(new Person("Charlie", 33));

        Collections.sort(people, new AgeComparator());

        for (Person person : people) {
            System.out.println(person.getName() + ": " + person.getAge());
        }
    }
}
```

```
Bob: 22
Alice: 28
Charlie: 33
```

Sorting a Set with Comparator

For sorting a Set, you would typically use a SortedSet (like TreeSet), which takes a Comparator upon construction. Consider the following example for sorting a set of Person objects by their age:

```
import java.util.*;

public class Main {
    public static void main(String[] args) {
        Set<Person> people = new TreeSet<>(new AgeComparator());

        people.add(new Person("Alice", 28));
        people.add(new Person("Bob", 22));
        people.add(new Person("Charlie", 33));

        for (Person person : people) {
            System.out.println(person.getName() + ": " + person.getAge());
        }
    }
}
```

```
Bob: 22
Alice: 28
Charlie: 33
```

The TreeSet maintains the natural order defined by the Comparator provided at construction time, ensuring the set elements are always sorted by age.

Sorting a Map by Values with Comparator

When sorting a Map, it is important to note that a map itself does not support sorting by values directly. You can, however, extract the entries into a List, sort that list with a Comparator, and then construct a new map based on the sorted entries. Following is an example:

Consider a map where the keys are String names and the values are Integer ages:

```
import java.util.*;

public class Main {
    public static void main(String[] args) {
        Map<String, Integer> nameToAge = new HashMap<>();
        nameToAge.put("Alice", 28);
        nameToAge.put("Bob", 22);
        nameToAge.put("Charlie", 33);

        List<Map.Entry<String, Integer>> entryList = new ArrayList<>(nameToAge.
            entrySet());

        Collections.sort(entryList, new Comparator<Map.Entry<String, Integer>>() {
            @Override
            public int compare(Map.Entry<String, Integer> e1, Map.Entry<String,
                Integer> e2) {
                return e1.getValue().compareTo(e2.getValue());
            }
        });

        for (Map.Entry<String, Integer> entry : entryList) {
            System.out.println(entry.getKey() + ": " + entry.getValue());
        }
    }
}
```

```
Bob: 22
Alice: 28
Charlie: 33
```

This approach utilizes a list to hold the map entries. The Comparator sorts based on the values, and iterating over the sorted entries displays them in the desired order.

Each of the examples illustrated demonstrates how Comparator provides a flexible mechanism to establish custom orderings for collections in Java. Understanding and employing Comparator aptly ensures the ability to order collections to fit any specified criteria.

8.4 Lambda Expressions and Comparators

Lambda expressions, introduced in Java 8, provide a clear and concise way to represent functional interfaces, including the Comparator interface, which represents a function that takes two arguments and compares them. Utilizing lambda expressions can significantly simplify the syntax for creating comparators compared to anonymous inner classes.

A comparator implemented using a lambda expression can be written succinctly by specifying the arguments, the arrow token (->), and the expression body that defines the comparison logic. Consider a basic example where we have a List of String objects that we want to sort by their lengths:

```
List<String> strings = Arrays.asList("apple", "banana", "cherry", "date");
Collections.sort(strings, (s1, s2) -> Integer.compare(s1.length(), s2.length()));
```

In this example, (s1, s2) -> Integer.compare(s1.length(), s2.length()) is a lambda expression that implements the Comparator<String> interface by comparing the lengths of two strings.

Using lambda expressions with comparators offers several advantages:

- **Conciseness:** The syntax is more compact and readable compared to anonymous inner class implementations.
- **Clarity:** The intent of the comparison logic is more immediately apparent.
- **Higher-order functions:** Lambda expressions can more easily be combined with other functional programming constructs, such as method references and default methods on interfaces.

Example: Sorting by Multiple Criteria

In practice, sorting often involves multiple criteria. For instance, consider a scenario where we have a list of Person objects, each with a name and age, and we want to sort first by name and then by age:

```
List<Person> people = Arrays.asList(
    new Person("Alice", 30),
    new Person("Bob", 25),
    new Person("Alice", 25),
    new Person("Charlie", 30)
);

Collections.sort(people,
    (p1, p2) -> {
        int nameCompare = p1.getName().compareTo(p2.getName());
        if (nameCompare != 0) {
            return nameCompare;
        } else {
            return Integer.compare(p1.getAge(), p2.getAge());
        }
    }
);
```

In this example, the lambda expression within Collections.sort implements a comparator that first compares by the name field. If the names are different (nameCompare != 0), it returns the result of the name comparison. If the names are the same, it falls back to comparing the age field.

Simplifying with Comparator Composers

Java provides a more streamlined approach to multi-criteria comparisons using the Comparator interface's default methods, such as thenComparing. The above example can be rewritten as follows:

```
Collections.sort(people,
    Comparator.comparing(Person::getName)
              .thenComparing(Person::getAge)
);
```

This approach leverages method references (Person::getName and Person::getAge) and the Comparator utility methods to produce a more readable and maintainable comparison chain.

Practical Considerations

When using lambda expressions with comparators, consider the following practical tips:

- Ensure that your comparison logic handles null values appropriately if they may be present in your collections.
- Use Comparator.nullsFirst or Comparator.nullsLast to specify how null values should be treated, for example:

  ```
  Comparator<String> comparator = Comparator.nullsFirst(
      Comparator.comparingInt(String::length)
  );
  ```

  This comparator handles null values by placing them before non-null values and then sorting by string length.
- Be cautious with the performance of comparison logic, especially when dealing with large collections or complex comparison chains.

Mastering lambda expressions opens up a suite of functional programming techniques within Java, allowing for more elegant and flexible code. Combining lambda expressions with comparators strengthens your ability to customize the ordering of collections effectively.

8.5 Method References in Comparators

Method references provide a shorthand notation for invoking methods and can be used to enhance the readability and conciseness of comparator implementations in Java. They allow us to create comparators using a more declarative style, which becomes especially powerful when combined with the features of the Comparator interface.

The syntax for method references is ClassName::methodName. There are four types of method references:

- Static method references: ClassName::staticMethodName
- Instance method references of a particular object: instance::instanceMethodName
- Instance method references of an arbitrary object of a particular type: ClassName::instanceMethodName
- Constructor references: ClassName::new

Each of these can be used to implement comparators in different contexts. Let's explore how each type of method reference can be utilized in the context of comparators.

Static Method References

Static method references are suitable when you have a static method that can be used to compare two instances. Suppose we have a Person class shown below:

```
public class Person {
    private String name;
    private int age;

    // Getters and constructors omitted for brevity

    public static int compareByAge(Person p1, Person p2) {
        return Integer.compare(p1.getAge(), p2.getAge());
    }
}
```

To create a comparator using a static method reference, you can use the following syntax:

```
Comparator<Person> ageComparator = Person::compareByAge;
```

When sorting a list of Person objects by age, the static method reference is leveraged as follows:

```
List<Person> people = ... // assume this is populated
people.sort(Person::compareByAge);
```

Instance Method References of a Particular Object

Consider a scenario where an instance method of a particular object is relevant for comparison. For example, if we have a comparator based on string length, and an instance of the Comparator class.

```
Comparator<String> lengthComparator = (s1, s2) -> Integer.compare(s1.length(), s2.
    length());
```

This can be simplified using an instance method reference:

```
import java.util.Comparator;

public class StringLengthComparator {
    public int compare(String s1, String s2) {
        return Integer.compare(s1.length(), s2.length());
    }
}

StringLengthComparator comp = new StringLengthComparator();
Comparator<String> lengthComparator = comp::compare;
```

Instance Method References of an Arbitrary Object of a Particular Type

In cases where we need to call an instance method on each element being compared, this form becomes practical. For instance, to compare strings by their length:

```
Comparator<String> lengthComparator = Comparator.comparingInt(String::length);
```

This method reference indicates that the length() method of any String instance should be used to perform the comparison.

Constructor References

Constructor references allow for creating comparators that instantiate objects for comparison purposes. However, their use is less common in the context of comparators. They are more often utilized for creating factory methods in streams and collectors configurations.

For a practical example, consider the following:

```
import java.util.function.Supplier;

Supplier<Person> personSupplier = Person::new;
```

While this does not directly relate to comparators, it illustrates the use of constructor references in Java.

Overall, seamless integration of method references in comparators brings clarity and reduces verbosity, resulting in more maintainable and understandable code.

8.6 Sorting Lists with Comparator

Sorting lists is a fundamental operation in software development. Java provides powerful mechanisms to sort lists using the Comparator interface. Understanding how to leverage these mechanisms effectively is key to mastering custom sorting.

The Comparator interface consists of a single method, compare, that can be implemented to define custom sorting logic. Here is a simple example illustrating how to sort a list of String objects in ascending order based on their length:

```
import java.util.*;

public class SortStringsByLength {
    public static void main(String[] args) {
        List<String> strings = Arrays.asList("banana", "apple", "pear", "grape");

        Comparator<String> lengthComparator = new Comparator<String>() {
            @Override
            public int compare(String s1, String s2) {
                return Integer.compare(s1.length(), s2.length());
            }
        };

        Collections.sort(strings, lengthComparator);

        for (String string : strings) {
            System.out.println(string);
        }
    }
}
```

The output of the above program will be:

```
pear
apple
grape
banana
```

In this example, the compare method compares the lengths of two String objects using Integer.compare, which returns a negative integer, zero, or a positive integer as the first argument is less than, equal to, or greater than the second.

Java 8 introduced lambdas, providing a more concise way to express the same logic:

```
import java.util.*;

public class SortStringsByLengthLambda {
    public static void main(String[] args) {
        List<String> strings = Arrays.asList("banana", "apple", "pear", "grape");

        Comparator<String> lengthComparator = (s1, s2) -> Integer.compare(s1.
            length(), s2.length());

        Collections.sort(strings, lengthComparator);

        strings.forEach(System.out::println);
    }
}
```

With the lambda expression, the syntax is cleaner and easier to read.

Java also provides the Comparator.comparing method, which is useful for creating comparators using method references. For example, the previous comparator can be further simplified using Comparator.comparing:

```
import java.util.*;

public class SortStringsByLengthComparing {
    public static void main(String[] args) {
        List<String> strings = Arrays.asList("banana", "apple", "pear", "grape");

        Collections.sort(strings, Comparator.comparing(String::length));

        strings.forEach(System.out::println);
    }
}
```

Using Comparator.comparing, the code becomes even more concise and intuitive.

Sometimes, you may need to sort in descending order. The Comparator interface provides a reversed method to reverse the order. Below is an example demonstrating how to sort a list of integers in descending order:

```
import java.util.*;

public class SortIntegersDescending {
    public static void main(String[] args) {
        List<Integer> numbers = Arrays.asList(4, 1, 3, 6, 2, 5);

        Collections.sort(numbers, Comparator.naturalOrder().reversed());

        numbers.forEach(System.out::println);
    }
}
```

The output will be:

```
6
5
4
3
2
1
```

The Comparator.naturalOrder method returns a comparator that compares Comparable objects in their natural order. The reversed method is then used to sort the list in reverse order.

One powerful feature of the Comparator interface is its ability to chain multiple comparators. Consider a scenario where you have a list of Person objects and you want to sort them first by last name, and then by first name. This can be achieved by combining multiple comparators.

```
import java.util.*;

public class SortPersons {
    static class Person {
        String firstName;
        String lastName;

        public Person(String firstName, String lastName) {
            this.firstName = firstName;
            this.lastName = lastName;
        }

        @Override
        public String toString() {
            return firstName + " " + lastName;
        }
    }

    public static void main(String[] args) {
        List<Person> people = Arrays.asList(
            new Person("John", "Doe"),
            new Person("Jane", "Doe"),
            new Person("Alice", "Smith"),
            new Person("Bob", "Smith")
        );

        Comparator<Person> lastNameComparator = Comparator.comparing(person ->
              person.lastName);
        Comparator<Person> firstNameComparator = Comparator.comparing(person
             -> person.firstName);

        Collections.sort(people, lastNameComparator.thenComparing(
             firstNameComparator));

        people.forEach(System.out::println);
    }
}
```

The output will be:

```
John Doe
Jane Doe
Bob Smith
Alice Smith
```

First, the list is sorted by last name. When last names are equal, the thenComparing method is used to sort by first name, ensuring a thorough and precise ordering.

Correctly applying comparators to sort lists involves understanding and utilizing the Comparator interface, lambda expressions, method references, and chaining comparators. This flexibility allows for robust, customized sorting that fits specific needs and ensures optimal list management.

8.7 Sorting Sets with Comparator

Unlike lists, sets in Java do not maintain the order of elements as they are primarily designed to ensure the uniqueness of their elements. However, sorted versions of sets can be achieved using SortedSet interface and its implementation, TreeSet. In this section, we will explore how to sort sets using comparators by employing TreeSet.

The TreeSet class in Java provides a natural ordering mechanism for its elements. To sort the elements according to custom criteria, we can provide a custom comparator at the time of TreeSet creation. The Comparator interface is a functional interface in Java that defines a single method, compare(T o1, T o2). This method can be implemented to define a custom comparison logic. Here's how to go about this:

```
import java.util.Comparator;
import java.util.SortedSet;
import java.util.TreeSet;

public class CustomTreeSetSorting {
    public static void main(String[] args) {
        Comparator<String> lengthComparator = new Comparator<String>() {
            @Override
            public int compare(String s1, String s2) {
                return Integer.compare(s1.length(), s2.length());
            }
        };

        SortedSet<String> sortedSet = new TreeSet<>(lengthComparator);
        sortedSet.add("pear");
        sortedSet.add("banana");
        sortedSet.add("apple");
        sortedSet.add("cherry");

        for (String element : sortedSet) {
            System.out.println(element);
```

```
        }
    }
}
```

Upon executing the above code, the output will be:

pear
apple
banana
cherry

In this example, a TreeSet is created with a custom comparator lengthComparator which sorts strings based on their lengths. The TreeSet constructor accepts the comparator, ensuring that all elements added to the set are ordered according to the provided comparator.

Flexibility Through Lambdas

Lambda expressions can be used to make the comparator creation more concise and readable. The same example can be refactored using lambda expressions as follows:

```
import java.util.Comparator;
import java.util.SortedSet;
import java.util.TreeSet;

public class CustomTreeSetSortingWithLambda {
    public static void main(String[] args) {
        Comparator<String> lengthComparator = (s1, s2) -> Integer.compare(s1.
            length(), s2.length());

        SortedSet<String> sortedSet = new TreeSet<>(lengthComparator);
        sortedSet.add("pear");
        sortedSet.add("banana");
        sortedSet.add("apple");
        sortedSet.add("cherry");

        for (String element : sortedSet) {
            System.out.println(element);
        }
    }
}
```

The comparator is defined using a lambda expression, making the code more compact while maintaining the same functionality.

Employing Method References

Method references can be used if an existing method matches the functional interface method. For numeric comparison, Integer.compare can be directly referenced:

```
import java.util.Comparator;
import java.util.SortedSet;
import java.util.TreeSet;

public class CustomTreeSetSortingWithMethodReference {
```

```
    public static void main(String[] args) {
        Comparator<String> lengthComparator = Comparator.comparingInt(String::
            length);

        SortedSet<String> sortedSet = new TreeSet<>(lengthComparator);
        sortedSet.add("pear");
        sortedSet.add("banana");
        sortedSet.add("apple");
        sortedSet.add("cherry");

        for (String element : sortedSet) {
            System.out.println(element);
        }
    }
}
```

This utilizes the Comparator.comparingInt method which is a convenient approach to create comparators for the comparison of integer values based on the length of the strings.

Practical Applications

Sorting sets with custom comparators is especially useful in scenarios where elements need to be evaluated based on criteria other than their natural ordering. For instance, sorting complex objects:

```
import java.util.Comparator;
import java.util.SortedSet;
import java.util.TreeSet;

class Person {
    private String name;
    private int age;

    public Person(String name, int age) {
        this.name = name;
        this.age = age;
    }

    public String getName() {
        return name;
    }

    public int getAge() {
        return age;
    }

    @Override
    public String toString() {
        return name + " : " + age;
    }
}

public class PersonTreeSetSorting {
    public static void main(String[] args) {
        Comparator<Person> ageComparator = Comparator.comparingInt(Person::
            getAge);

        SortedSet<Person> sortedSet = new TreeSet<>(ageComparator);
```

```
        sortedSet.add(new Person("John", 25));
        sortedSet.add(new Person("Alice", 30));
        sortedSet.add(new Person("Bob", 20));
        sortedSet.add(new Person("Diana", 35));

        for (Person person : sortedSet) {
            System.out.println(person);
        }
    }
}
```

Output:

```
Bob : 20
John : 25
Alice : 30
Diana : 35
```

In this practical example, a set of Person objects is sorted by age using a Comparator defined with method references.

By utilizing Comparator, TreeSet, lambda expressions, and method references, Java developers can effectively control the ordering of elements in a set according to complex, dynamic criteria. This approach provides essential flexibility for various real-world applications where custom sorting logic is required.

8.8 Sorting Maps by Keys and Values

In Java, Map interfaces such as HashMap, LinkedHashMap, and TreeMap are extensively used in applications where key-value associations are required. However, sorting these maps based on keys and values can sometimes be non-trivial. While TreeMap explicitly maintains a sorted order of keys, other implementations like HashMap do not maintain any order. This section will delve into methods for sorting maps by their keys or values, employing the Comparator interface to facilitate custom sorting routines.

To illustrate sorting maps, we will use both HashMap and TreeMap, and demonstrate sorting by keys as well as by values.

Sorting by Keys

The simplest way to sort a map by its keys is to use a TreeMap. The TreeMap automatically sorts its keys in their natural order or by a specified Comparator at map creation time. However, for educational purposes, we will create an example illustrating how to sort a HashMap by its keys using a Comparator.

Let us consider the following HashMap:

```
import java.util.*;

public class MapSortingExample {
    public static void main(String[] args) {
        Map<String, Integer> map = new HashMap<>();
        map.put("apple", 3);
        map.put("banana", 2);
        map.put("cherry", 1);

        System.out.println("Original HashMap: " + map);

        Map<String, Integer> sortedMap = new TreeMap<>(map);
        System.out.println("Sorted by Keys (TreeMap): " + sortedMap);

        // Sorting HashMap by keys using a Comparator
        List<Map.Entry<String, Integer>> entryList = new ArrayList<>(map.
            entrySet());
        entryList.sort(Map.Entry.comparingByKey());
        System.out.println("Sorted by Keys (HashMap): " + entryList);
    }
}
```

Output:

```
Original HashMap: {banana=2, apple=3, cherry=1}
Sorted by Keys (TreeMap): {apple=3, banana=2, cherry=1}
Sorted by Keys (HashMap): [apple=3, banana=2, cherry=1]
```

In this example, the TreeMap constructor initializes with the entries of the HashMap, inherently sorting the keys. For the HashMap, we convert the map entries into a list, sort the list using Map.Entry.comparingByKey(), and subsequently display the sorted entries.

Sorting by Values

Sorting a map by its values is slightly more complex since Map does not provide direct methods for this. We need to extract the entries, sort them, and construct a new map or simply display the sorted entries. Using the same HashMap as before, we'll sort by values:

```
import java.util.*;

public class MapSortingExampleByValue {
    public static void main(String[] args) {
        Map<String, Integer> map = new HashMap<>();
        map.put("apple", 3);
        map.put("banana", 2);
        map.put("cherry", 1);

        // Sorting HashMap by values using a Comparator
        List<Map.Entry<String, Integer>> entryList = new ArrayList<>(map.
            entrySet());
        entryList.sort(Map.Entry.comparingByValue());
        System.out.println("Sorted by Values: " + entryList);
```

```
        // Converting sorted entries back to a LinkedHashMap to maintain order
        Map<String, Integer> sortedByValueMap = new LinkedHashMap<>();
        for (Map.Entry<String, Integer> entry : entryList) {
            sortedByValueMap.put(entry.getKey(), entry.getValue());
        }
        System.out.println("Sorted by Values (HashMap form): " + sortedByValueMap);
    }
}
```

Output:

```
Sorted by Values: [cherry=1, banana=2, apple=3]
Sorted by Values (HashMap form): {cherry=1, banana=2, apple=3}
```

In this example, we sorted the entries of the HashMap using Map.Entry.comparingByValue() and then converted the sorted list of entries back into a LinkedHashMap to maintain the order determined by sorting.

Method References and Lambdas

Java 8 introduced method references and lambda expressions, significantly simplifying comparator creation. For instance:

```
import java.util.*;

public class MapSortWithLambda {
    public static void main(String[] args) {
        Map<String, Integer> map = new HashMap<>();
        map.put("apple", 3);
        map.put("banana", 2);
        map.put("cherry", 1);

        // Using lambda expressions to sort by key
        List<Map.Entry<String, Integer>> entryListByKey = new ArrayList<>(map.
            entrySet());
        entryListByKey.sort((e1, e2) -> e1.getKey().compareTo(e2.getKey()));
        System.out.println("Sorted by Keys with Lambda: " + entryListByKey);

        // Using lambda expressions to sort by value
        List<Map.Entry<String, Integer>> entryListByValue = new ArrayList<>(map.
            entrySet());
        entryListByValue.sort((e1, e2) -> e1.getValue().compareTo(e2.getValue()));
        System.out.println("Sorted by Values with Lambda: " + entryListByValue);
    }
}
```

Output:

```
Sorted by Keys with Lambda: [apple=3, banana=2, cherry=1]
Sorted by Values with Lambda: [cherry=1, banana=2, apple=3]
```

These examples use lambda expressions to succinctly express the sorting mechanisms. Instead of explicit Comparator implementations, lambdas provide a more readable and maintainable approach.

By understanding and utilizing these methods, one can efficiently manage and sort maps, allowing for tailored data processing and representation in various Java applications. This flexibility in sorting maps by keys and values is fundamental for scenarios demanding ordered data structures.

8.9 Chaining Comparators

Chaining comparators is a powerful technique allowing multiple comparison criteria to be applied sequentially. This becomes particularly useful when objects need to be sorted by more than one attribute, ensuring a fine-grained and flexible sorting mechanism. The idea is straightforward: if the first comparison results in equality, the second comparator is invoked, and this process continues until a non-zero result is produced or all comparators are exhausted.

In Java, chaining comparators can be achieved by combining multiple comparators using the thenComparing method, which is part of the Comparator interface. This method can be used to specify a sequence of comparators that are applied one after the other.

```
import java.util.Comparator;
import java.util.List;
import java.util.ArrayList;
import java.util.Collections;

class Student {
    String firstName;
    String lastName;
    double grade;

    Student(String firstName, String lastName, double grade) {
        this.firstName = firstName;
        this.lastName = lastName;
        this.grade = grade;
    }

    @Override
    public String toString() {
        return firstName + " " + lastName + ": " + grade;
    }
}

public class ComparatorChainingExample {
    public static void main(String[] args) {
        List<Student> students = new ArrayList<>();
        students.add(new Student("John", "Doe", 88.5));
        students.add(new Student("Jane", "Smith", 92.3));
        students.add(new Student("John", "Smith", 85.9));
        students.add(new Student("Jane", "Doe", 90.1));

        Comparator<Student> byFirstName = Comparator.comparing(student ->
                student.firstName);
```

```
        Comparator<Student> byLastName = Comparator.comparing(student ->
            student.lastName);
        Comparator<Student> byGrade = Comparator.comparingDouble(student ->
            student.grade);

        Comparator<Student> chainedComparator = byFirstName
                                                .thenComparing(byLastName)
                                                .thenComparing(byGrade);

        Collections.sort(students, chainedComparator);

        for (Student student : students) {
            System.out.println(student);
        }
    }
}
```

```
Jane Doe: 90.1
Jane Smith: 92.3
John Doe: 88.5
John Smith: 85.9
```

In this example, comparing and thenComparing methods are used to create a chain of comparators:

- byFirstName: Compares Student objects based on their firstName.
- byLastName: Compares Student objects based on their lastName.
- byGrade: Compares Student objects based on their grade.

These comparators are chained together in chainedComparator. First, students are compared by their first name. If two students have the same first name, they are then compared by their last name. If both names are the same, the students are compared by their grades. This results in a comprehensive sorting mechanism, ensuring that students are ordered accurately according to the specified criteria.

Advanced Chaining with Lambda Expressions

Lambda expressions can be used to simplify the chaining process further, providing a concise and readable syntax. Consider the following example:

```
Comparator<Student> chainedComparatorLambda = Comparator
    .comparing((Student student) -> student.firstName)
    .thenComparing(student -> student.lastName)
    .thenComparing(student -> student.grade);

Collections.sort(students, chainedComparatorLambda);

students.forEach(System.out::println);
```

In this revised approach, lambda expressions are directly embedded within the comparing and thenComparing methods. This bypasses the need to define separate comparators (byFirstName, byLastName, byGrade), streamlining the code without sacrificing readability or functionality.

Consistency and Natural Ordering

When chaining comparators, it is crucial to ensure the combined comparator remains consistent with the natural ordering, if applicable. For instance, if the objects being sorted implement the Comparable interface, the comparator sequence must honor this ordering requirement to avoid unpredictable behaviors.

Assuming Student implements Comparable and defines a natural ordering based on grades:

```
class Student implements Comparable<Student> {
    // existing fields and methods

    @Override
    public int compareTo(Student other) {
        return Double.compare(this.grade, other.grade);
    }
}

Comparator<Student> chainedComparatorWithNaturalOrder = Comparator
    .comparing((Student student) -> student.firstName)
    .thenComparing(student -> student.lastName)
    .thenComparingDouble(Student::getGrade);
```

In this approach, the final comparator in the chain explicitly respects the natural ordering of Student, which is based on grades according to the compareTo method.

Practical Considerations

When designing chained comparators, certain practical aspects warrant consideration:

- Comparator Reusability: Design comparators as standalone, reusable components where feasible. While lambda expressions provide compact chaining, named comparators improve modularity.
- Null Handling: Include null checks if attributes may be null, ensuring robust comparison logic. The static methods Comparator.nullsFirst and Comparator.nullsLast facilitate this.
- Performance: Analyze performance implications, especially for

large datasets. Chained comparators that traverse multiple attributes might impact the sorting efficiency.

By attentively addressing these details, effective and efficient chained comparators can be constructed, enhancing custom sorting operations and yielding precise, context-aware orderings.

8.10 Reverse Ordering with Comparator

In certain scenarios, there may be a need to sort collections in descending order rather than the default ascending order. The Comparator interface in Java provides straightforward means to achieve reverse ordering, thereby giving developers greater flexibility in tailoring the sorting behavior of collections.

To reverse the order of elements using a Comparator, Java offers the reversed() method. This method is particularly useful when an existing comparator is already defined, and you need the exact opposite order. Let us examine the functionality and usage of Comparator.reversed() in detail.

Consider a list of integers that we want to sort in descending order. We can accomplish this using a comparator that sorts the integers in natural order first and then applying the reversed() method.

```
import java.util.*;

public class ReverseOrderExample {
    public static void main(String[] args) {
        List<Integer> numbers = Arrays.asList(5, 3, 8, 1, 9);

        // Comparator for natural order
        Comparator<Integer> comparator = Comparator.naturalOrder();

        // Reverse the order
        numbers.sort(comparator.reversed());

        // Print the sorted list
        System.out.println(numbers);
    }
}
```

```
[9, 8, 5, 3, 1]
```

In this code, the Comparator.naturalOrder() method is used to obtain a comparator that sorts integers in their natural (ascending) order. The reversed() method is then called on this comparator to reverse the sort order. Consequently, the numbers list is sorted in descending order, and the result is displayed.

Reverse ordering is equally applicable to custom sorting of complex objects. For instance, suppose we have a list of Person objects, and each Person has a name and age attribute. If we want to sort this list based on age in descending order, we can utilize a custom comparator.

```
import java.util.*;

class Person {
    String name;
    int age;

    Person(String name, int age) {
        this.name = name;
        this.age = age;
    }

    @Override
    public String toString() {
        return name + ": " + age;
    }
}

public class ReverseOrderCustomObjects {
    public static void main(String[] args) {
        List<Person> people = Arrays.asList(
            new Person("Alice", 30),
            new Person("Bob", 25),
            new Person("Charlie", 35)
        );

        // Comparator to sort by age in ascending order
        Comparator<Person> ageComparator = Comparator.comparingInt(person ->
            person.age);

        // Reverse the comparator
        people.sort(ageComparator.reversed());

        // Print the sorted list
        people.forEach(System.out::println);
    }
}
```

```
Charlie: 35
Alice: 30
Bob: 25
```

Here, a Comparator is created to compare Person objects by their age attribute in ascending order. The ageComparator.reversed() method is then used to reverse the ordering to descending. The resulting sorted list is printed, with the objects sorted by age in descending order.

The reversed() method can also be combined with more complex comparator chains to achieve nuanced sorting orders. For example, consider sorting a list of Person objects first by age in descending order and then by name in ascending order as a tie-breaker.

```
import java.util.*;

class Person {
    String name;
    int age;

    Person(String name, int age) {
        this.name = name;
        this.age = age;
    }

    @Override
    public String toString() {
        return name + ": " + age;
    }
}

public class CombinedReverseOrder {
    public static void main(String[] args) {
        List<Person> people = Arrays.asList(
            new Person("Alice", 30),
            new Person("Bob", 25),
            new Person("Charlie", 35),
            new Person("Alice", 35)
        );

        // Composite comparator: first by age (descending), then by name (ascending)
        Comparator<Person> compositeComparator =
            Comparator.comparingInt((Person person) -> person.age).reversed()
                    .thenComparing(person -> person.name);

        people.sort(compositeComparator);

        // Print the sorted list
        people.forEach(System.out::println);
    }
}
```

```
Alice: 35
Charlie: 35
Alice: 30
Bob: 25
```

This example illustrates how a composite comparator can be created by chaining comparators using Comparator.thenComparing(). The compositeComparator first sorts by age in descending order, and for persons with the same age, it sorts by name in ascending order. This powerful mechanism allows fine-grained control over the sorting logic.

Reverse ordering with comparators enhances the versatility of collection sorting in Java, enabling a broad range of custom ordering requirements to be met with minimal effort. Incorporating reverse ordering in multi-stage comparator chains is particularly useful for complex sorting needs.

8.11 Comparator vs Comparable

Java provides two interfaces, Comparator and Comparable, for sorting collections of objects. While both interfaces serve this fundamental purpose, their mechanisms differ significantly and offer different flexibilities and constraints. Understanding these differences is critical to effectively leveraging their capabilities in custom sorting scenarios.

The Comparable interface is typically used to define a natural ordering for a class. For example, numerical classes like Integer or Double implement Comparable to provide ordering based on numerical value. Likewise, a String class implements Comparable to provide lexicographic ordering. When a class implements the Comparable interface, it must override the compareTo method. The compareTo method's contract states:

- A negative integer should be returned if the current object is less than the specified object.
- Zero should be returned if the current object is equal to the specified object.
- A positive integer should be returned if the current object is greater than the specified object.

Here's an example of a class implementing the Comparable interface:

```
public class Student implements Comparable<Student> {
    private String name;
    private int rollNumber;

    public Student(String name, int rollNumber) {
        this.name = name;
        this.rollNumber = rollNumber;
    }

    @Override
    public int compareTo(Student other) {
        return Integer.compare(this.rollNumber, other.rollNumber);
    }
}
```

This Student class orders instances based on the rollNumber field. The primary advantage of Comparable is its simplicity and the intuitive integration into the class definition. However, a significant disadvantage is that it restricts the class to a single sort order, limiting flexibility.

The Comparator interface provides external comparison logic, which affords greater flexibility by allowing multiple different comparisons to be implemented for a single class. The Comparator interface also requires the implementation of a single method, compare. This method has a similar contract to compareTo:

- A negative integer should be returned if the first argument is less than the second argument.
- A positive integer should be returned if the first argument is greater than the second argument.
- Zero should be returned if the first argument is equal to the second argument.

Here is a straightforward example of a Comparator for the Student class:

```
import java.util.Comparator;

public class StudentNameComparator implements Comparator<Student> {
    @Override
    public int compare(Student s1, Student s2) {
        return s1.getName().compareTo(s2.getName());
    }
}
```

In this instance, the StudentNameComparator class enables sorting Student objects based on their name attribute. The key benefit of using a Comparator is the ability to define multiple comparators for different sorting criteria without modifying the original class definition. This avoids cluttering the class with various sorting logic and maintains separation of concerns.

A practical implementation often involves using both Comparable and Comparator:

```
public class Student implements Comparable<Student> {
    private String name;
    private int rollNumber;

    // Constructor, getters, and setters

    @Override
    public int compareTo(Student other) {
        return Integer.compare(this.rollNumber, other.rollNumber);
    }

    public static final Comparator<Student> BY_NAME = new Comparator<Student
        >() {
        @Override
        public int compare(Student s1, Student s2) {
            return s1.getName().compareTo(s2.getName());
        }
```

```
    };
}
```

In the example above, Student implements Comparable for roll number-based ordering and provides a static Comparator for name-based ordering. This hybrid approach leverages the simplicity of Comparable for a primary natural order and the flexibility of Comparator for alternative orderings.

To demonstrate usage, consider the following code to sort a list of Student objects:

```
import java.util.ArrayList;
import java.util.Collections;
import java.util.List;

public class Main {
    public static void main(String[] args) {
        List<Student> students = new ArrayList<>();
        students.add(new Student("Alice", 3));
        students.add(new Student("Bob", 1));
        students.add(new Student("Charlie", 2));

        // Sorting by roll number (Comparable)
        Collections.sort(students);
        for (Student s : students) {
            System.out.println(s.getName() + " " + s.getRollNumber());
        }

        // Sorting by name (Comparator)
        students.sort(Student.BY_NAME);
        for (Student s : students) {
            System.out.println(s.getName() + " " + s.getRollNumber());
        }
    }
}
```

The resulting output demonstrates the dual sorting criteria:

```
Bob 1
Charlie 2
Alice 3
Alice 3
Bob 1
Charlie 2
```

The first sorting operation arranges the students according to roll number, as defined by the Comparable interface, whereas the subsequent sorting operation arranges them by name, using the Comparator.

Determining when to use Comparable versus Comparator depends on the specific application requirements. If a class has a single predominant natural sorting order that rarely changes, implementing Comparable is appropriate. However, for complex sorting scenarios requiring multiple different orderings, Comparator provides a more flexible and modular approach.

8.12 Custom Sorting Use Cases

Understanding how to customize the sorting of different Java collections is an essential skill for developing efficient and effective Java applications. Custom sorting allows developers to control the order of elements based on various attributes, providing the ability to tailor the behavior of collections for specific requirements. This section illustrates practical use cases where custom sorting can be advantageous, highlighting real-world scenarios and demonstrating the application of comparators in these contexts.

One common use case for custom sorting involves sorting a list of employee objects by their attributes. Consider a Employee class with attributes name, age, and salary. Sorting employees by their salary can be performed using a custom comparator. Below is a sample implementation:

```
import java.util.*;

class Employee {
    String name;
    int age;
    double salary;

    Employee(String name, int age, double salary) {
        this.name = name;
        this.age = age;
        this.salary = salary;
    }

    // Getters and toString method omitted for brevity
}

class SalaryComparator implements Comparator<Employee> {
    public int compare(Employee e1, Employee e2) {
        return Double.compare(e1.salary, e2.salary);
    }
}
```

To apply the SalaryComparator and sort a list of employees:

```
public class CustomSortingExample {
    public static void main(String[] args) {
        List<Employee> employees = new ArrayList<>();
        employees.add(new Employee("Alice", 30, 70000.00));
        employees.add(new Employee("Bob", 25, 50000.00));
        employees.add(new Employee("Charlie", 28, 60000.00));

        Collections.sort(employees, new SalaryComparator());
```

```
        for (Employee employee : employees) {
            System.out.println(employee);
        }
    }
}
```

```
Employee{name='Bob', age=25, salary=50000.0}
Employee{name='Charlie', age=28, salary=60000.0}
Employee{name='Alice', age=30, salary=70000.0}
```

Another notable use case is sorting data structures in a more complex configuration. For instance, in a scenario where an online store keeps track of products and wishes to sort these products by multiple fields, such as category first and then price within each category, chaining comparators becomes beneficial. Assume the Product class has category and price attributes:

```
class Product {
    String category;
    double price;

    Product(String category, double price) {
        this.category = category;
        this.price = price;
    }

    // Getters and toString method omitted for brevity
}

class CategoryComparator implements Comparator<Product> {
    public int compare(Product p1, Product p2) {
        return p1.category.compareTo(p2.category);
    }
}

class PriceComparator implements Comparator<Product> {
    public int compare(Product p1, Product p2) {
        return Double.compare(p1.price, p2.price);
    }
}
```

In this example, the products are first sorted by category, and within each category, they are subsequently sorted by price:

```
public class CustomChainingExample {
    public static void main(String[] args) {
        List<Product> products = new ArrayList<>();
        products.add(new Product("Electronics", 999.99));
        products.add(new Product("Groceries", 2.99));
        products.add(new Product("Electronics", 199.99));
        products.add(new Product("Groceries", 1.99));

        Comparator<Product> chainedComparator = new CategoryComparator().
            thenComparing(new PriceComparator());

        Collections.sort(products, chainedComparator);

        for (Product product : products) {
```

```
            System.out.println(product);
        }
    }
}
```

```
Product{category='Electronics', price=199.99}
Product{category='Electronics', price=999.99}
Product{category='Groceries', price=1.99}
Product{category='Groceries', price=2.99}
```

Custom sorting also plays an important role in enhancing data retrieval and display operations in user interfaces. For instance, a contact management application may need to sort contacts by last name or by the date of the last interaction. Here, lambda expressions and method references can simplify the comparator implementation.

To sort contacts by the date of the last interaction using a LocalDate attribute lastInteraction:

```
import java.time.LocalDate;

class Contact {
    String lastName;
    LocalDate lastInteraction;

    Contact(String lastName, LocalDate lastInteraction) {
        this.lastName = lastName;
        this.lastInteraction = lastInteraction;
    }

    // Getters and toString method omitted for brevity
}

public class CustomSortingLambda {
    public static void main(String[] args) {
        List<Contact> contacts = new ArrayList<>();
        contacts.add(new Contact("Smith", LocalDate.of(2023, 1, 1)));
        contacts.add(new Contact("Doe", LocalDate.of(2022, 6, 15)));
        contacts.add(new Contact("Brown", LocalDate.of(2023, 3, 10)));

        contacts.sort(Comparator.comparing(Contact::getLastInteraction));

        for (Contact contact : contacts) {
            System.out.println(contact);
        }
    }
}
```

```
Contact{lastName='Doe', lastInteraction=2022-06-15}
Contact{lastName='Smith', lastInteraction=2023-01-01}
Contact{lastName='Brown', lastInteraction=2023-03-10}
```

Using method references ensures that custom sorting logic remains concise and readable.

Furthermore, there may be scenarios requiring reverse ordering. For instance, sorting students by their grades in descending order can be implemented using the Comparator.reverseOrder method.

```
class Student {
    String name;
    double grade;

    Student(String name, double grade) {
        this.name = name;
        this.grade = grade;
    }

    // Getters and toString method omitted for brevity
}

public class CustomReverseOrder {
    public static void main(String[] args) {
        List<Student> students = new ArrayList<>();
        students.add(new Student("Alice", 85.0));
        students.add(new Student("Bob", 92.5));
        students.add(new Student("Charlie", 78.0));

        students.sort(Comparator.comparing(Student::getGrade).reversed());

        for (Student student : students) {
            System.out.println(student);
        }
    }
}
```

```
Student{name='Bob', grade=92.5}
Student{name='Alice', grade=85.0}
Student{name='Charlie', grade=78.0}
```

Custom sorting with comparators, method references, and chaining techniques provides developers with powerful tools for manipulating and organizing collections. These tools are indispensable for solving diverse problems efficiently and effectively in real-world applications.

Chapter 9

Concurrent Collections: Thread-Safe Data Structures

This chapter examines thread-safe data structures within the Java Collections Framework known as concurrent collections. It discusses their importance in multi-threaded environments and explores key implementations such as ConcurrentHashMap, CopyOnWriteArrayList, CopyOnWriteArraySet, and various BlockingQueue types. The chapter also covers non-blocking alternatives like ConcurrentLinkedQueue and thread-safe sorted collections like ConcurrentSkipListSet and ConcurrentSkipListMap. Performance considerations and practical use cases are addressed, providing a thorough understanding of utilizing concurrent collections effectively in Java applications.

9.1 Introduction to Concurrent Collections

Concurrent collections in Java provide a set of thread-safe data structures meant for use in multi-threaded environments. Achieving thread safety for collections in concurrent programs is essential to prevent concurrent modification exceptions, race conditions, and memory consistency errors. The standard implementations in the java.util.concurrent package are specifically designed to handle synchronization internally, allowing multiple threads to operate on collections concurrently without corrupting the data.

The historical approach to synchronizing collections involved manually wrapping standard collections with synchronization using the synchronized keyword or employing Collections.synchronizedMap() and Collections.synchronizedList(). This method often led to performance bottlenecks due to high contention and limited concurrent scalability. The concurrent collections address these issues by using advanced synchronization patterns, lock-free algorithms, and fine-grained locking mechanisms.

To illustrate the advantages of concurrent collections, consider the task of updating a shared map. Using a regular HashMap in a multi-threaded context would necessitate manual synchronization as shown below:

```
Map<String, Integer> map = Collections.synchronizedMap(new HashMap<>());

synchronized (map) {
    map.put("key", 1);
    // Additional operations
}
```

While this approach ensures thread safety, it serializes access to the entire map, resulting in poorer performance under high contention. In contrast, ConcurrentHashMap improves performance by allowing concurrent reads and fine-grained locking for writes.

```
ConcurrentHashMap<String, Integer> concurrentMap = new ConcurrentHashMap
    <>();

concurrentMap.put("key", 1);
// Additional operations without external synchronization
```

Various implementations of concurrent collections provided in the java.util.concurrent package are optimized for different use cases. Some of the notable implementations include:

- ConcurrentHashMap
- CopyOnWriteArrayList
- CopyOnWriteArraySet
- BlockingQueue implementations like LinkedBlockingQueue, ArrayBlockingQueue, and PriorityBlockingQueue
- ConcurrentLinkedQueue

- ConcurrentSkipListSet
- ConcurrentSkipListMap

Each of these data structures employs different strategies to ensure thread safety and performance. For instance, ConcurrentHashMap uses a segmented locking mechanism, whereas CopyOnWriteArrayList and CopyOnWriteArraySet use a copy-on-write strategy to handle concurrency.

It is essential to understand the behavior and internal working of these collections to use them effectively. For example, CopyOnWriteArrayList is optimal for scenarios where read operations are vastly more frequent than modifications, as modifications involve creating a copy of the underlying array. This results in considerable memory overhead but provides a lock-free read operation.

```
CopyOnWriteArrayList<String> cowList = new CopyOnWriteArrayList<>();
cowList.add("element");
// Read operations are lock-free
for (String element : cowList) {
    System.out.println(element);
}
```

On the other hand, BlockingQueue implementations like LinkedBlockingQueue and ArrayBlockingQueue are crucial for producer-consumer scenarios, providing convenient blocking operations such as put() and take().

```
BlockingQueue<String> queue = new LinkedBlockingQueue<>();

// Producer
new Thread(() -> {
    try {
        queue.put("element");
    } catch (InterruptedException e) {
        Thread.currentThread().interrupt();
    }
}).start();

// Consumer
new Thread(() -> {
    try {
        String element = queue.take();
        System.out.println(element);
    } catch (InterruptedException e) {
        Thread.currentThread().interrupt();
    }
}).start();
```

Non-blocking data structures like ConcurrentLinkedQueue allow for highly efficient and scalable queues but do not support blocking operations, making them suitable for different use cases.

```
ConcurrentLinkedQueue<String> nonBlockingQueue = new ConcurrentLinkedQueue
    <>();
nonBlockingQueue.offer("element");
String element = nonBlockingQueue.poll();
```

Understanding when and how to use each concurrent collection type is pivotal for creating performant and correct multi-threaded applications. The subsequent sections will delve into each of these implementations, discussing their specific mechanisms, use cases, and performance characteristics.

9.2 Understanding Thread Safety

Thread safety is a crucial concept in concurrent programming, ensuring that shared resources are accessed and modified by multiple threads in a controlled and predictable manner. In Java, thread safety is vital when dealing with collections in multi-threaded contexts. A thread-safe collection guarantees that no corrupted data states arise when multiple threads concurrently access or mutate the collection.

In the Java Collections Framework, thread-safe collections are designed to handle concurrent access by internal synchronization mechanisms. This section aims to clarify the concept of thread safety, present the challenges involved in achieving it, and illustrate the techniques used in Java to ensure that collections operate correctly in a multi-threaded environment.

Thread safety can generally be achieved by synchronization, which entails controlling the access to shared resources so that only one thread can access a resource at a time. Here are some fundamental strategies and mechanisms used in Java for thread safety:

- **Mutual Exclusion:** This ensures that when one thread accesses a resource, other threads are blocked from doing so until the first thread finishes. Java provides this through the synchronized keyword and Lock classes.
- **Atomic Operations:** These operations execute completely without any possibility of interruption. In Java, this is ensured for basic data types using classes from the java.util.concurrent.atomic package, such as AtomicInteger and AtomicReference.
- **Thread Coordination:** This involves techniques such as wait-

notify mechanisms provided by the Object class methods wait() and notify().

- **Volatile Variables:** The volatile keyword in Java ensures that the value of a variable is always read from the main memory and not from a thread's local cache, thus maintaining visibility across threads.

Consider the following example of a thread-safe increment operation using synchronization:

```
class Counter {
    private int count = 0;

    public synchronized void increment() {
        count++;
    }

    public synchronized int getCount() {
        return count;
    }
}
```

In the above example, the Counter class uses the synchronized keyword to ensure that the increment() and getCount() methods can be accessed by only one thread at a time. This prevents race conditions where multiple threads might attempt to update the count simultaneously, leading to an inconsistent state.

However, using synchronized blocks or methods can induce performance bottlenecks because they force threads to execute critical sections one at a time. To alleviate these limitations, Java's java.util.concurrent package offers more sophisticated constructs like Reentrant Locks and concurrent collections.

For instance, the ReentrantLock provides more flexible thread synchronization compared to the synchronized keyword:

```
import java.util.concurrent.locks.ReentrantLock;

class Counter {
    private int count = 0;
    private final ReentrantLock lock = new ReentrantLock();

    public void increment() {
        lock.lock();
        try {
            count++;
        } finally {
            lock.unlock();
        }
    }
```

```
    public int getCount() {
        lock.lock();
        try {
            return count;
        } finally {
            lock.unlock();
        }
    }
}
```

In the above example, the ReentrantLock is explicitly locked and unlocked to increment and retrieve the count. The use of try-finally ensures that the lock is released even if an exception occurs within the critical section.

Beyond locks, Java offers atomic variables to perform lock-free thread-safe operations. Atomic variables leverage low-level atomic CPU instructions, providing very fine-grained "compare-and-swap" (CAS) operations that are faster and less blocking than traditional locks.

The example below demonstrates thread-safe increment using an AtomicInteger:

```
import java.util.concurrent.atomic.AtomicInteger;

class Counter {
    private final AtomicInteger count = new AtomicInteger(0);

    public void increment() {
        count.incrementAndGet();
    }

    public int getCount() {
        return count.get();
    }
}
```

Here, the incrementAndGet() and get() methods are atomic, ensuring thread safety without explicit synchronization. AtomicInteger internally uses CAS to achieve high-performance concurrent updates.

Java's concurrent collections like ConcurrentHashMap, CopyOnWriteArrayList, and BlockingQueue combine these synchronization and atomicity principles to allow safe modification and iteration in a multithreaded environment.

The ConcurrentHashMap:

- Uses segment locks to divide the map into regions, allowing multiple threads to read/write without full map locking.
- Offers methods like computeIfAbsent and forEach that operate

atomically.

The CopyOnWriteArrayList and CopyOnWriteArraySet:

- Create a fresh copy of the underlying array upon each modification, ensuring that reads are never blocked.
- Are suited for scenarios with more read than write operations, given the cost of copying.

Thread-safe queue implementations like ArrayBlockingQueue and LinkedBlockingQueue:

- Provide blocking operations put and take which wait for the queue to be in a state where the operation can proceed.
- Use internal condition variables to manage blocking behavior, ensuring efficient thread coordination.

Understanding these mechanisms and correctly applying them is pivotal to mastering the concurrency capabilities of Java's collections. Through employing proper thread-safety techniques, developers can avert concurrency issues and maintain robust, performant applications even under the complexity of multi-threaded operations.

9.3 ConcurrentHashMap: Thread-Safe Maps

The ConcurrentHashMap is a highly efficient implementation of a thread-safe map data structure, introduced in the java.util.concurrent package. It is specifically designed to handle concurrent access by multiple threads and provide a high level of thread safety without the significant performance hit encountered with traditional synchronization techniques.

Internal Structure and Concurrency Control:

The ConcurrentHashMap is designed to partition its data across several segments, which allows distinct threads to operate on different segments concurrently. Each segment is essentially a mini-hashmap, and the segment locks itself when performing updates. By reducing the contention for a single lock that is common in Hashtable and synchronized HashMap, ConcurrentHashMap achieves greater concurrency.

```
import java.util.concurrent.ConcurrentHashMap;

ConcurrentHashMap<String, Integer> map = new ConcurrentHashMap<>();
map.put("key1", 1);
map.put("key2", 2);
```

In the example above, an instance of ConcurrentHashMap is created, and two key-value pairs are inserted. Multiple threads can safely perform put, get, remove, and other operations on the map without explicit synchronization.

Specialized Methods for Atomic Operations:

Unlike other implementations of map, the ConcurrentHashMap provides methods designed to handle special-case atomic operations. These include, but are not limited to, putIfAbsent, remove, replace.

```
map.putIfAbsent("key3", 3);
Integer val = map.get("key3");
if (val != null) {
    System.out.println("Value for key3: " + val);
}

map.replace("key3", 3, 4);
System.out.println("Updated value for key3: " + map.get("key3"));

map.remove("key3", 4);
System.out.println("Removed key3 successfully.");
```

In the above code: - putIfAbsent method adds the key-value pair only if the key is not already present. - replace method replaces the value for a key only if it is currently mapped to a specified value. - remove method removes the entry only if the key is currently mapped to a specified value.

Such methods make ConcurrentHashMap extremely useful for performing complex operations atomically, without the need for additional synchronization.

Iterators and Bulk Operations:

The ConcurrentHashMap supports high-performance iterators and bulk operations such as forEach, search, and reduce. These operations are designed to be used in concurrent programming environments and are free from the ConcurrentModificationException.

```
map.forEach(1, (k, v) -> {
    System.out.println(k + " : " + v);
});
Integer result = map.search(1, (k, v) -> {
    if ("someKey".equals(k)) {
        return v;
```

```
    }
    return null;
});
Integer sum = map.reduce(1, (k, v) -> v, Integer::sum);
System.out.println("Sum of values: " + sum);
```

Here, the forEach method allows parallel processing over the entries, search method can perform a concurrent search, and reduce method enables parallel reduction, which is very efficient for large-scale data processing.

Dynamic Resizing and Space Efficiency:

The ConcurrentHashMap employs a sophisticated resizing mechanism that allows it to dynamically adjust its size to maintain an optimal load factor. This resizing process is handled in a lock-free manner, ensuring that concurrent operations are minimally affected. The map also ensures space efficiency, eliminating the need for a fixed size, which is a limitation in many synchronized map implementations.

```
map.put("key4", 4);
map.put("key5", 5);
map.put("key6", 6);

System.out.println("Size of map: " + map.size());
```

This dynamic growth ensures that the map maintains efficiency both in terms of space and access time, even as it scales to accommodate a large number of entries.

Performance Considerations:

The performance of the ConcurrentHashMap is generally superior to other synchronized map implementations due to its lock stripping mechanism, which minimizes contention. Performance scales well with the number of threads due to its granular locking strategy.

Several performance benchmarks and studies highlight that while the ConcurrentHashMap incurs some overhead compared to non-thread-safe HashMaps, this overhead is significantly lower than what is observed in Hashtable or synchronized HashMap due to contention. It is recommended to use ConcurrentHashMap in multi-threaded environments to vastly improve throughput and reduce latency associated with map operations.

These design considerations make ConcurrentHashMap a centerpiece in concurrent programming, providing a robust, scalable, and efficient thread-safe map that excels under high contention scenarios.

9.4 CopyOnWriteArrayList: Thread-Safe Lists

The CopyOnWriteArrayList is an implementation of the List interface that provides thread-safe operations through a copy-on-write mechanism. This unique design ensures that modifications such as add, remove, or set result in creating a new copy of the underlying array. As a result, any read operations occurring concurrently with the write operations will not interfere, thereby achieving thread safety without extensive synchronization.

Instantiation

To instantiate a CopyOnWriteArrayList, you can use its default constructor or initialize it with a specified collection:

```
CopyOnWriteArrayList<E> list = new CopyOnWriteArrayList<>();
CopyOnWriteArrayList<E> listFromCollection = new CopyOnWriteArrayList<>(
    existingCollection);
```

Behavior and Characteristics

The CopyOnWriteArrayList excels in scenarios where reads are significantly more frequent than writes. This is because the read operations have minimal overhead—they merely access the array, which is immutable during these operations. However, the trade-off is that each write operation (insert, delete, update) incurs the cost of creating a new array and copying the elements of the existing array.

Thread Safety

The thread safety of CopyOnWriteArrayList relies on its immutable snapshot during read operations. Each read operation works on a consistent and unchanging state of the array, thus eliminating the possibility of seeing a partially updated state, a common problem in traditional synchronized lists.

Consider the following example where multiple threads read from and write to a CopyOnWriteArrayList:

```
// Create a CopyOnWriteArrayList of Integers
CopyOnWriteArrayList<Integer> cowList = new CopyOnWriteArrayList<>();

// Thread to add elements
Runnable writer = () -> {
    for (int i = 0; i < 10; i++) {
        cowList.add(i);
        try {
            Thread.sleep(50); // Simulate some delay
```

```
        } catch (InterruptedException e) {
            Thread.currentThread().interrupt();
        }
    }
};

// Thread to read elements
Runnable reader = () -> {
    for (int i = 0; i < 10; i++) {
        System.out.println(cowList);
        try {
            Thread.sleep(100); // Simulate some delay
        } catch (InterruptedException e) {
            Thread.currentThread().interrupt();
        }
    }
};

// Start threads
new Thread(writer).start();
new Thread(reader).start();
```

The read operation in this example will always see a consistent view of the list as it was at the moment the read began. Although the list is updated by the writer thread, the reader threads' views remain unaffected until they perform a new read.

Performance Considerations

While CopyOnWriteArrayList is beneficial for high-read-low-write scenarios, its performance deteriorates with frequent write operations due to the cost of copying the array. It is essential to evaluate the read-/write ratio of your application to determine if CopyOnWriteArrayList is suitable.

The following benchmark code compares the performance of CopyOnWriteArrayList against a synchronized ArrayList:

```
import java.util.ArrayList;
import java.util.Collections;
import java.util.List;
import java.util.concurrent.CopyOnWriteArrayList;

public class CopyOnWriteArrayListBenchmark {

    public static void main(String[] args) {
        int size = 1000;
        int iterations = 100000;

        List<Integer> syncList = Collections.synchronizedList(new ArrayList<>());
        CopyOnWriteArrayList<Integer> cowList = new CopyOnWriteArrayList<>();

        // Fill both lists with initial values
        for (int i = 0; i < size; i++) {
            syncList.add(i);
            cowList.add(i);
        }
```

```
        // Benchmark synchronizedList
        long start = System.nanoTime();
        for (int i = 0; i < iterations; i++) {
            synchronized (syncList) {
                syncList.add(i);
                syncList.remove(0);
            }
        }
        long end = System.nanoTime();
        System.out.println("SynchronizedList time: " + (end - start) + " ns");

        // Benchmark CopyOnWriteArrayList
        start = System.nanoTime();
        for (int i = 0; i < iterations; i++) {
            cowList.add(i);
            cowList.remove(0);
        }
        end = System.nanoTime();
        System.out.println("CopyOnWriteArrayList time: " + (end - start) + " ns");
    }
}
```

```
SynchronizedList time: 345678910 ns
CopyOnWriteArrayList time: 567890123 ns
```

This benchmark illustrates the potential performance cost of CopyOnWriteArrayList due to array copying on each write.

Use Cases

Given its characteristics, the CopyOnWriteArrayList is suitable for applications where:

- The list is primarily read and infrequently modified.
- Iterators are required to be fail-safe, meaning they operate on a snapshot of the collection at the time of their creation and do not throw ConcurrentModificationException.
- The overhead of synchronized methods is undesirable, yet thread safety must be guaranteed.

Examples include:

- Managing a list of listeners or observers where updates are less frequent than notifications.
- Caching frequently accessed, immutable sets of data updated periodically.
- Use cases involving read-mostly scenarios where stale data during iteration is acceptable.

By carefully considering the trade-offs, CopyOnWriteArrayList provides a robust solution for specific concurrency requirements within Java applications. Its immutable snapshot approach affords thread safety, albeit with a performance cost for write-heavy tasks.

9.5 CopyOnWriteArraySet: Thread-Safe Sets

The CopyOnWriteArraySet is a member of the Java Collections Framework, specifically designed to provide thread-safe set operations. Unlike traditional sets that may require external synchronization to be safely used in concurrent contexts, CopyOnWriteArraySet handles synchronization internally, thus relieving the programmer from managing it explicitly. This section delves into its internal working mechanism, use cases, and performance implications to offer a comprehensive understanding.

CopyOnWriteArraySet is backed by a CopyOnWriteArrayList, which means that all its set operations are implemented on top of a list. Consequently, the properties and behaviors of CopyOnWriteArrayList are inherited by CopyOnWriteArraySet. The foundational principle behind this collection is the idea of copy-on-write, where any modifying operation (e.g., add, remove, clear) results in creating a new copy of the underlying array. Here is an example to illustrate setting up and using CopyOnWriteArraySet:

```
import java.util.concurrent.CopyOnWriteArraySet;

public class CopyOnWriteArraySetExample {
    public static void main(String[] args) {
        CopyOnWriteArraySet<String> set = new CopyOnWriteArraySet<>();

        set.add("Element1");
        set.add("Element2");
        set.add("Element3");

        // Iterating through the CopyOnWriteArraySet
        for (String element : set) {
            System.out.println(element);
        }

        // Removing an element
        set.remove("Element2");

        // Checking if the set contains a specific element
        boolean containsElement3 = set.contains("Element3");
        System.out.println("Set contains 'Element3': " + containsElement3);
    }
}
```

The output of this code will be:

```
Element1
Element2
Element3
Set contains 'Element3': true
```

The CopyOnWriteArraySet provides an iterator that does not throw ConcurrentModificationException, making it robust in the face of concurrent modifications. The iterator operates on a snapshot of the set at the time the iteration was initiated, ensuring that the iteration remains consistent and free from side effects due to concurrent changes.

Key characteristics of CopyOnWriteArraySet:

- **Thread-Safety**: All operations are thread-safe, providing safe concurrent access without requiring external synchronization.
- **Snapshot Isolation**: Iterators and other read-only operations work on a stable snapshot of the data, ensuring consistency.
- **Iteration Performance**: Since operations are based on snapshot arrays, read operations can achieve high performance, especially iteration, which is faster compared to other thread-safe collections that may require locks.
- **Memory Overhead**: Copying the entire array on write operations introduces extra memory overhead, particularly for large sets.
- **Immutability of Elements**: As the set internally uses equals and hashCode methods to ensure uniqueness, the immutability of elements and maintaining their consistent state is crucial for correctness.

Performance considerations must be taken into account when choosing to use CopyOnWriteArraySet. The creation of new arrays on every write operation potentially leads to significant overhead, especially in write-heavy workloads. Conversely, it excels in read-heavy scenarios where iterations and fetch operations outperform other thread-safe alternatives due to the absence of lock contention.

Here is a deeper look into the implementation of the add method provided by CopyOnWriteArraySet:

```
public boolean add(E e) {
    return al.addIfAbsent(e);
}
```

The add method delegates to the addIfAbsent method of the underlying CopyOnWriteArrayList, ensuring that duplicate elements are not added:

```
public boolean addIfAbsent(E e) {
    final ReentrantLock lock = this.lock;
    lock.lock();
    try {
        Object[] elements = getArray();
        int len = elements.length;
        for (int i = 0; i < len; i++) {
            if (eq(e, elements[i])) {
                return false;
            }
        }
        Object[] newElements = Arrays.copyOf(elements, len + 1);
        newElements[len] = e;
        setArray(newElements);
        return true;
    } finally {
        lock.unlock();
    }
}
```

In this implementation, the ReentrantLock is employed to ensure atomicity of the add operation. The getArray() method retrieves the current array, iterates through it to check for existing elements, and creates a new array incorporating the new element if it is not already present. This modified array then becomes the current array for subsequent operations.

The non-blocking nature of read operations and the managed synchronization ensures CopyOnWriteArraySet remains a viable option for concurrent applications, particularly in scenarios where the frequency of read operations significantly outweighs that of write operations. The immutable snapshot during iteration remains critical for ensuring view consistency without the need for explicit external locks or additional synchronization mechanisms.

9.6 BlockingQueue: Thread-Safe Queues

The BlockingQueue interface in the Java Collections Framework represents a type of queue that supports operations that wait for the queue to become non-empty when retrieving an element, and wait for space to become available in the queue when storing an element. This makes BlockingQueue implementations particularly useful in producer-consumer scenarios where one set of threads (producers) adds to the queue and another set of threads (consumers) removes from it.

BlockingQueue extends the Queue interface and adds methods that handle thread safety and blocking behavior, such as put() and take(). These methods enable thread coordination and avoid concurrency issues by either waiting or timing out when the queue is full or empty. BlockingQueue does not accept null elements, and the methods generally throw a NullPointerException if a null is provided.

Common implementations of BlockingQueue include:

- ArrayBlockingQueue
- LinkedBlockingQueue
- PriorityBlockingQueue
- DelayQueue

ArrayBlockingQueue is a bounded BlockingQueue implementation backed by an array. This means the queue has a fixed capacity which must be specified at the time of its creation. Internally, ArrayBlockingQueue uses a single lock to prevent multiple threads from entering the put() or take() method simultaneously.

```
import java.util.concurrent.ArrayBlockingQueue;

public class ArrayBlockingQueueExample {
    public static void main(String[] args) {
        ArrayBlockingQueue<Integer> queue = new ArrayBlockingQueue<>(10);

        try {
            queue.put(1);
            queue.put(2);

            System.out.println(queue.take());
            System.out.println(queue.take());
        } catch (InterruptedException e) {
            e.printStackTrace();
        }
    }
}
```

In this example, queue.put(1) adds an element to the queue, waiting if the queue is full. Similarly, queue.take() retrieves and removes an element from the head of the queue, waiting if no elements are present.

LinkedBlockingQueue can be bounded or unbounded and is backed by linked nodes. It typically has a higher throughput than ArrayBlockingQueue due to its ability to handle concurrent producers and consumers separately using distinct locks, unlike ArrayBlockingQueue which uses a single lock.

```
import java.util.concurrent.LinkedBlockingQueue;

public class LinkedBlockingQueueExample {
    public static void main(String[] args) {
        LinkedBlockingQueue<Integer> queue = new LinkedBlockingQueue<>(10);

        try {
            queue.put(1);
            queue.put(2);

            System.out.println(queue.take());
            System.out.println(queue.take());
        } catch (InterruptedException e) {
            e.printStackTrace();
        }
    }
}
```

PriorityBlockingQueue is an unbounded blocking queue that uses the same ordering rules as PriorityQueue. This implies that elements are ordered according to their natural ordering or by a Comparator provided at queue construction time. However, PriorityBlockingQueue does not allow null elements.

```
import java.util.concurrent.PriorityBlockingQueue;

public class PriorityBlockingQueueExample {
    public static void main(String[] args) {
        PriorityBlockingQueue<Integer> queue = new PriorityBlockingQueue<>();

        queue.offer(3);
        queue.offer(1);
        queue.offer(2);

        System.out.println(queue.poll());
        System.out.println(queue.poll());
        System.out.println(queue.poll());
    }
}
```

PriorityBlockingQueueExample demonstrates that elements are retrieved in their sorted order, even if they are inserted in a different order, with the smallest element first.

DelayQueue is a specialized implementation of the BlockingQueue where elements can only be retrieved after a certain delay has passed. This queue is typically used in scenarios where tasks or messages need to be scheduled for future execution or processing.

```
import java.util.concurrent.DelayQueue;
import java.util.concurrent.Delayed;
import java.util.concurrent.TimeUnit;

class DelayedElement implements Delayed {
    private final long delay;
```

```
    private final long expire;
    private final String data;

    public DelayedElement(long delay, String data) {
        this.delay = delay;
        this.data = data;
        this.expire = System.currentTimeMillis() + delay;
    }

    @Override
    public long getDelay(TimeUnit unit) {
        long diff = expire - System.currentTimeMillis();
        return unit.convert(diff, TimeUnit.MILLISECONDS);
    }

    @Override
    public int compareTo(Delayed o) {
        if (this.expire < ((DelayedElement) o).expire) {
            return -1;
        }
        if (this.expire > ((DelayedElement) o).expire) {
            return 1;
        }
        return 0;
    }

    public String getData() {
        return data;
    }
}

public class DelayQueueExample {
    public static void main(String[] args) {
        DelayQueue<DelayedElement> queue = new DelayQueue<>();

        queue.offer(new DelayedElement(5000, "Delayed element 1"));
        queue.offer(new DelayedElement(10000, "Delayed element 2"));

        try {
            System.out.println(queue.take().getData());
            System.out.println(queue.take().getData());
        } catch (InterruptedException e) {
            e.printStackTrace();
        }
    }
}
```

In the given example, DelayedElement is an implementation of the Delayed interface, and elements placed in the DelayQueue will only be available for retrieval after their stipulated delay period.

BlockingQueue implementations cater to diverse needs, from bounded array-backed queues to unbounded, delay-supporting structures. By understanding the specific advantages and uses of each, developers can effectively employ BlockingQueue in concurrent applications, optimizing for throughput, ordering, and delay-based execution.

9.7 ConcurrentLinkedQueue: Non-Blocking Queues

The ConcurrentLinkedQueue class is an implementation of a non-blocking queue based on the principles of non-blocking algorithms, specifically utilizing the compare-and-swap (CAS) mechanism. As such, it forms a part of the java.util.concurrent package, catering to scenarios requiring high-throughput, thread-safe insertion and removal operations without the overhead of locking mechanisms.

ConcurrentLinkedQueue internally employs a linked-node structure where each node holds a reference to the subsequent node, ensuring operations achieve $O(1)$ time complexity. The fundamental operations supported by the queue include offer, poll, and peek. Each of these operations takes advantage of the atomic nature of the CAS operations to maintain thread safety.

Below is an illustration of a simple ConcurrentLinkedQueue instantiation and usage example:

```
import java.util.concurrent.ConcurrentLinkedQueue;

public class ConcurrentLinkedQueueExample {
    public static void main(String[] args) {
        ConcurrentLinkedQueue<Integer> queue = new ConcurrentLinkedQueue<>();

        // Adding elements to the queue
        queue.offer(1);
        queue.offer(2);
        queue.offer(3);

        // Accessing elements in the queue
        System.out.println("Queue elements: " + queue);
        System.out.println("Head of the queue: " + queue.peek());

        // Removing elements from the queue
        int removed = queue.poll();
        System.out.println("Removed element: " + removed);
        System.out.println("Queue after removal: " + queue);
    }
}
```

Executing the above code results in the following output:

```
Queue elements: [1, 2, 3]
Head of the queue: 1
Removed element: 1
Queue after removal: [2, 3]
```

The offer method is used to insert elements into the queue. It places the new element at the tail of the queue, returns true upon successful insertion. This method does not block, ensuring that the queue remains non-blocking even under high contention.

The poll method removes and returns the head of the queue or returns null if the queue is empty. This operation modifies the queue's state, updating the head reference atomically using CAS, ensuring thread safety without locking.

The peek method provides a non-modifying means to access the head of the queue, returning the head element or null if the queue is empty. It is a constant-time operation that preserves the invariant of the queue.

An algorithmic perspective on the operation updates in ConcurrentLinkedQueue can be summarized as follows:

Algorithm 5: Offer Operation in ConcurrentLinkedQueue

Input: Element e

Result: Boolean value indicating the success of the operation

```
node ← new Node(e);
tail ← tailNode.get();
while true do
    next ← tail.next;
    if next == null then
        if CAS(tail.next, next, node) then
            CAS(tail, tail, node);
            return true;
    else
        CAS(tail, tail, next);
```

This algorithm captures the essence of non-blocking insertion where CAS operations are employed to ensure atomicity. If contention is detected (where another thread has modified the state), the algorithm retries until a successful insertion is achieved.

Similarly, the poll operation can be described:

Again, the operation utilizes CAS to maintain atomicity. It is designed to handle contention through retries, ensuring the correct node is removed.

The ConcurrentLinkedQueue is particularly advantageous in scenarios involving multiple producer and consumer threads due to:

- **Lock-free Design:** Maximizes throughput by avoiding locks, re-

Algorithm 6: Poll Operation in ConcurrentLinkedQueue

```
Result: The head element or null if the queue is empty
while true do
    head ← headNode.get();
    first ← head.next;
    if first == null then
        return null;
    if CAS(head, head, first) then
        value ← first.value;
        return value;
```

ducing contention, and exploiting hardware-level atomic operations.

- **Thread Safety:** Ensures thread-safe modifications without the necessity for synchronized blocks.

- **Scalability:** Suitable for high-concurrency environments, offering better performance under load compared to traditional synchronized collections.

For instance, the non-blocking nature of ConcurrentLinkedQueue makes it ideal for implementing task scheduling systems where multiple threads may concurrently enqueue and dequeue tasks. This ensures swift task assignment and execution without bottleneck delays.

9.8 ConcurrentSkipListSet: Thread-Safe Sorted Sets

The ConcurrentSkipListSet<E> class in Java provides a scalable and thread-safe implementation of a navigable set based on a concurrent skip-list data structure. It ensures that the set maintains its elements in ascending order, allowing for concurrent access and modifications by multiple threads without compromising thread safety.

ConcurrentSkipListSet is part of the java.util.concurrent package and is ideal for applications requiring highly concurrent and quick read and write access while preserving a sorted order. Similar to other concurrent collections, it is designed to optimize performance in multi-threaded environments.

```
import java.util.concurrent.ConcurrentSkipListSet;
import java.util.Iterator;

// Create a ConcurrentSkipListSet instance
ConcurrentSkipListSet<Integer> skipListSet = new ConcurrentSkipListSet<>();

// Add elements to the set
skipListSet.add(5);
skipListSet.add(1);
skipListSet.add(3);

// Iterate over the elements
Iterator<Integer> iterator = skipListSet.iterator();
while (iterator.hasNext()) {
    System.out.println(iterator.next());
}
```

In the above example, we create a new instance of ConcurrentSkipListSet and populate it with integers. The elements will be sorted in ascending order, and as per the characteristics of skip lists, both insertion and traversal operations are efficient.

ConcurrentSkipListSet inherits from AbstractSet and implements NavigableSet<E>, meaning it provides functionalities for traversing the set in a navigable fashion. The primary operations supported include:

- add(E e): Inserts the specified element if it is not already present.
- remove(Object o): Removes the specified element from the set if present.
- contains(Object o): Checks if the set contains the specified element.
- iterator(): Returns an iterator over the elements in ascending order.
- pollFirst(): Retrieves and removes the first (lowest) element, or returns null if the set is empty.
- pollLast(): Retrieves and removes the last (highest) element, or returns null if the set is empty.

These operations are designed to be thread-safe, relying on the underlying skip list structure to allow for concurrent modifications by multiple threads without requiring explicit synchronization.

Concurrency and Performance:

The ConcurrentSkipListSet employs non-blocking algorithms to manage concurrency. This is primarily achieved through the skip list data structure, which allows for multiple threads to simultaneously read and modify the list with minimal contention. In particular, its operations do not generally block, which makes ConcurrentSkipListSet suitable for highly concurrent applications.

Performance characteristics of ConcurrentSkipListSet are similar to those of skip lists:

- $O(\log n)$ time complexity for most basic operations (add, remove, and contains).
- The skip list's probabilistic balancing ensures that the operations perform efficiently on average, even though the worst-case time complexity can degrade to $O(n)$. However, this scenario is highly unlikely.

Practical Applications:

ConcurrentSkipListSet can be used in various scenarios:

- Real-time monitoring systems: Where concurrent insertion and removal of timestamps or events must be handled in a sorted order efficiently.
- Financial systems: To maintain ordered records such as stock prices or transaction histories accessible by multiple threads.
- Multi-threaded sorting: As a concurrent alternative to other sorted collections like TreeSet but with added thread safety.

Example: Thread-Safe Access

To demonstrate thread-safe access, consider the following example where multiple threads modify a shared ConcurrentSkipListSet:

```
import java.util.concurrent.ConcurrentSkipListSet;

public class ConcurrentSkipListSetExample {
    public static void main(String[] args) {
        ConcurrentSkipListSet<Integer> skipListSet = new ConcurrentSkipListSet<>()
            ;

        // Thread 1 adds elements
        Thread thread1 = new Thread(() -> {
            for (int i = 0; i < 100; i++) {
```

```
                skipListSet.add(i);
            }
        });

        // Thread 2 removes some elements
        Thread thread2 = new Thread(() -> {
            for (int i = 50; i < 100; i++) {
                skipListSet.remove(i);
            }
        });

        thread1.start();
        thread2.start();

        try {
            thread1.join();
            thread2.join();
        } catch (InterruptedException e) {
            Thread.currentThread().interrupt();
        }

        // Print remaining elements
        skipListSet.forEach(System.out::println);
    }
}
```

In this example, two threads interact with the ConcurrentSkipListSet instance. Thread 1 sequentially adds integers from 0 to 99, while Thread 2 concurrently removes integers from 50 to 99. The example showcases how ConcurrentSkipListSet manages concurrent access without any explicit synchronization.

The ConcurrentSkipListSet is a robust option for achieving thread-safe operations on sorted sets. By leveraging a concurrent skip list for its internal representation, it efficiently supports simultaneous read and write operations by multiple threads. This combination of thread safety, performance, and ease of use makes ConcurrentSkipListSet a valuable tool in the Java concurrency toolkit.

9.9 ConcurrentSkipListMap: Thread-Safe Sorted Maps

The ConcurrentSkipListMap is a member of the Java Collections Framework, specifically within the java.util.concurrent package. It provides a thread-safe, scalable, and efficient concurrent map that maintains its entries in a sorted order, according to their natural ordering or by a specified comparator. This makes it an ideal choice for applications requiring concurrent access to a sorted map.

ConcurrentSkipListMap is a non-blocking alternative to other sorted map implementations such as TreeMap. It employs a skip list data structure, which allows it to achieve an average-case time complexity of $O(\log n)$ for most common operations like insertion, deletion, and access. This is comparable to the performance characteristics of balanced binary search trees, such as those used in TreeMap, but ConcurrentSkipListMap adds the advantage of being inherently thread-safe.

Here is a simple example of using the ConcurrentSkipListMap:

```
import java.util.concurrent.ConcurrentSkipListMap;

public class SkipListMapExample {
    public static void main(String[] args) {
        ConcurrentSkipListMap<String, Integer> map = new ConcurrentSkipListMap
            <>();

        // Adding elements to the map
        map.put("one", 1);
        map.put("two", 2);
        map.put("three", 3);

        // Accessing elements
        System.out.println("Value for key 'one': " + map.get("one"));

        // Iterating over the map
        for (String key : map.keySet()) {
            System.out.println(key + " => " + map.get(key));
        }
    }
}
```

ConcurrentSkipListMap's concurrency properties facilitate multiple threads to perform operations such as reads, updates, and iterates without needing explicit synchronization, thus enhancing performance on multi-core systems.

The skipping nature of the skip list used by ConcurrentSkipListMap plays a key role in its efficiency. It maintains multiple layers of linked lists, each allowing faster traversal by skipping over some nodes, reducing the levels of traversal required. This architecture assures the logarithmic complexity for typical operations. Below is a depiction of the skip list structure:

```
Level 3:  -Inf -> ----- -> ----- -> ---*   -> +Inf
Level 2:  -Inf -> ----- -> ---*    -> +Inf
Level 1:  -Inf -> ---*  -> ---*    -> +Inf
Level 0:  -Inf -> --*-> --*-> --* -> +Inf
```

The star (*) represents the actual entries within the map. The higher levels contain fewer entries, allowing faster traversal through skip levels.

Consider an implementation of skip list insertion within ConcurrentSkipListMap:

Algorithm 7: Insertion Procedure in a ConcurrentSkipListMap

```
Data: ConcurrentSkipListMap map, key k, value v
Result: Insertion of key k and value v in map
initial level ← map current highest level;
update← array of size (level + 1);
node ← map's header node;
for level from highest to lowest do
    while node.next[level] ≠ null and node.next[level].key <
     key do
        node ← node.next[level];
    end
    update[level] ← node;
end
level ← random level;
if level > map's current highest level then
    for i from (map's current highest level + 1) to level do
        update[i] ← map's header node;
    end
    map's current highest level ← level;
end
node ← new node with key k and value v;
for i from 0 to level do
    node.next[i] ← update[i].next[i];
    update[i].next[i] ← node;
end
```

It is imperative to comprehend how ConcurrentSkipListMap maintains thread safety. It avoids locks in many operations using techniques such as *compare-and-swap* (CAS). These operations employ the Unsafe class internally, manipulating low-level memory operations to ensure atomicity without blocking the threads.

ConcurrentSkipListMap also supports advanced functionalities such as:

- Submaps with the methods subMap, headMap, and tailMap, allowing users to work with portions of the map in a thread-safe manner.
- Navigable methods, including ceilingEntry, floorEntry, higherEn-

try, and lowerEntry, providing navigation capabilities through the map's entries.

- Concurrent iteration where iterators are weakly consistent, meaning they reflect the state of the map at the time they were created and can proceed concurrently with updates to the map.

Additionally, implementing atomic variables in conjunction with ConcurrentSkipListMap can enhance specific use cases. For example:

```
import java.util.concurrent.ConcurrentSkipListMap;
import java.util.concurrent.atomic.AtomicInteger;

public class AtomicSkipListMapExample {
    public static void main(String[] args) {
        ConcurrentSkipListMap<String, AtomicInteger> atomicMap = new
              ConcurrentSkipListMap<>();

        atomicMap.put("one", new AtomicInteger(1));
        atomicMap.put("two", new AtomicInteger(2));

        atomicMap.get("one").incrementAndGet();

        System.out.println("Updated value for key 'one': " + atomicMap.get("one"));
    }
}
```

This example demonstrates how ConcurrentSkipListMap can store and manipulate AtomicInteger objects, allowing for thread-safe updates to numeric values without additional locking.

Understanding and leveraging the ConcurrentSkipListMap provides a robust means to handle sorted maps in concurrent environments, ensuring both performance and thread safety.

9.10 Atomic Variables with Concurrent Collections

Atomic variables are a critical component when working with concurrent collections in Java. They provide a means of performing atomic operations, avoiding the pitfalls of race conditions without the overhead of synchronization. The java.util.concurrent.atomic package includes several classes that support lock-free, thread-safe programming on single variables.

AtomicInteger, **AtomicLong**, **AtomicBoolean**, and **AtomicReference** are some of the essential classes provided by this package.

These classes extend the notion of volatile variables, providing critical operations like compareAndSet, getAndIncrement, getAndSet, and others that are executed atomically.

AtomicInteger is a versatile class that supports atomic operations on integer values:

```
AtomicInteger atomicInt = new AtomicInteger(0);

// Increment and get the new value
int newValue = atomicInt.incrementAndGet();
System.out.println("New Value: " + newValue);
```

```
New Value: 1
```

The above code snippet demonstrates the use of the incrementAndGet method, which atomically increments the current value by 1 and returns the new value.

Similarly, AtomicLong for long values and AtomicBoolean for boolean values offer straightforward yet powerful atomic operations. These classes ensure that all updates are visible across threads instantaneously, leveraging a combination of hardware-level support and low-level primitives.

AtomicReference allows for atomic updates to an object reference. This is particularly useful in concurrent algorithms where multiple threads need to update shared objects safely.

```
AtomicReference<String> atomicString = new AtomicReference<>("initial");

boolean updated = atomicString.compareAndSet("initial", "updated");
System.out.println("Updated: " + updated + ", Current Value: " + atomicString.get())
    ;
```

```
Updated: true, Current Value: updated
```

In the above example, compareAndSet atomically sets the value to "updated" only if the current value equals "initial", illustrating a typical compare-and-swap pattern.

Integrating atomic variables within concurrent collections can enhance their functionality and efficiency. For instance, combining an AtomicInteger with a ConcurrentHashMap to maintain thread-safe counters is a common use case.

```
ConcurrentHashMap<String, AtomicInteger> map = new ConcurrentHashMap<>();

// Initialize the counter for a key
map.putIfAbsent("key1", new AtomicInteger(0));

// Increment the counter atomically
```

```
map.get("key1").incrementAndGet();
```

In this scenario, inserting an AtomicInteger into the ConcurrentHashMap enables atomic increment operations on a per-key basis, ensuring thread safety without explicit synchronization.

When considering atomic variables, it is important to note their coordination with volatile fields. Typically, atomic variables are built on top of volatile semantics but offer extended functionalities via atomic methods, thereby ensuring visibility and ordering guarantees.

Additionally, atomic variables are a building block in advanced concurrent algorithms like non-blocking data structures. They play a pivotal role in creating lock-free algorithms that can significantly enhance system throughput and reduce latency. These implementations often use atomic variables for maintaining state, such as the head and tail pointers in a ConcurrentLinkedQueue.

AtomicStampedReference and AtomicMarkableReference are two specialized classes that address the ABA problem with reference updates. They not only update the reference atomically but also maintain a version or mark to detect changes.

```
AtomicStampedReference<Integer> stampedRef = new AtomicStampedReference<>(1,
        0);
int[] stamp = new int[1];
Integer currentValue = stampedRef.get(stamp);

// Attempt an atomic update
boolean success = stampedRef.compareAndSet(currentValue, 2, stamp[0], stamp[0] + 1)
        ;
System.out.println("Updated successfully: " + success);
```

```
Updated successfully: true
```

Here, AtomicStampedReference updates the integer reference and its stamp atomically, providing a robust mechanism against concurrent modifications.

Understanding and correctly utilizing atomic variables are fundamental when developing efficient and thread-safe operations in concurrent collections. Proper implementation allows for minimal synchronization overhead while safely coordinating shared state modifications across multiple threads.

9.11 Performance Considerations for Concurrent Collections

Evaluating the performance of concurrent collections is critical for developing efficient multi-threaded applications. When selecting a particular concurrent collection, considerations need to encompass both the underlying implementation and the expected workload. This section elucidates key factors influencing the performance of concurrent collections and provides guidelines for optimal utilization.

1. Contention

Contention occurs when multiple threads attempt to access the same resource simultaneously, which can degrade performance. Lock-based collections, like those using synchronized blocks, often suffer from high contention. Concurrent collections, designed with efficient synchronization mechanisms, reduce contention through techniques such as lock striping and non-blocking algorithms.

```
ConcurrentHashMap<Integer, String> map = new ConcurrentHashMap<>();
IntStream.range(0, 1000).parallel().forEach(i -> map.put(i, "Value " + i));
```

Lock striping in ConcurrentHashMap enhances concurrent access by distributing locks across multiple segments.

2. Throughput

Throughput refers to the number of operations a concurrent collection can handle per unit of time. While lock-based collections can serialize access, concurrent collections employ finer-grained locking or lock-free techniques to improve throughput.

```
ConcurrentLinkedQueue<Integer> queue = new ConcurrentLinkedQueue<>();
IntStream.range(0, 1000).parallel().forEach(queue::offer);
```

In the example above, ConcurrentLinkedQueue uses a lock-free algorithm to maintain high throughput while offering elements concurrently.

3. Latency

Latency measures the time taken to complete a single operation. In concurrent collections, latency can be affected by the chosen synchronization mechanism. Non-blocking collections typically offer lower latency compared to lock-based collections.

```
ConcurrentSkipListSet<Integer> skipListSet = new ConcurrentSkipListSet<>();
IntStream.range(0, 1000).parallel().forEach(skipListSet::add);
```

ConcurrentSkipListSet utilizes a skip list data structure, allowing fast insertions and lookups, thereby minimizing latency.

4. Scalability

Scalability refers to the ability of a concurrent collection to maintain performance as the number of threads increases. Many concurrent collections are designed to scale effectively by minimizing contention and employing efficient algorithms.

```
CopyOnWriteArrayList<Integer> copyOnWriteArrayList = new CopyOnWriteArrayList
    <>();
IntStream.range(0, 1000).parallel().forEach(copyOnWriteArrayList::add);
```

While CopyOnWriteArrayList works well for read-heavy workloads due to its efficient snapshot-based strategy, it may not scale linearly for write-intensive applications.

5. Memory Overhead

Concurrency mechanisms can introduce memory overhead. For instance, ConcurrentHashMap requires additional memory for segment locks, whereas CopyOnWriteArrayList will incur overhead due to copying the entire list on modifications.

6. Algorithms and Data Structures

The choice of underlying algorithms and data structures plays a significant role in performance. Concurrent collections utilize advanced algorithms — such as non-blocking CAS (Compare and Swap), lock-free and wait-free techniques, and fine-grained locking.

```
ConcurrentLinkedQueue<Integer> concurrentLinkedQueue = new
    ConcurrentLinkedQueue<>();
IntStream.range(0, 1000).parallel().forEach(concurrentLinkedQueue::offer);
```

ConcurrentLinkedQueue's non-blocking operations are built on non-blocking algorithms like Michael-Scott queues, minimizing waiting times and enhancing performance under high concurrency.

7. Practical Example: Benchmarking Concurrent Collections

Consider benchmarking different concurrent collections to compare their performance characteristics under various workloads. Employing frameworks such as JMH (Java Microbenchmark Harness) can provide empirical data.

```
@State(Scope.Benchmark)
public class ConcurrentCollectionBenchmark {
    private ConcurrentHashMap<Integer, String> concurrentHashMap;
    private ConcurrentLinkedQueue<Integer> concurrentLinkedQueue;
```

```
    @Setup
    public void setUp() {
        concurrentHashMap = new ConcurrentHashMap<>();
        concurrentLinkedQueue = new ConcurrentLinkedQueue<>();
    }

    @Benchmark
    public void testConcurrentHashMap() {
        IntStream.range(0, 1000).parallel().forEach(i -> concurrentHashMap.put(i, "
             Value " + i));
    }

    @Benchmark
    public void testConcurrentLinkedQueue() {
        IntStream.range(0, 1000).parallel().forEach(concurrentLinkedQueue::offer);
    }
}
```

This JMH benchmark measures and compares the insertion operations for ConcurrentHashMap and ConcurrentLinkedQueue, providing insights into their performance under concurrent access.

By evaluating these performance considerations comprehensively, developers can make informed decisions when selecting and utilizing concurrent collections in Java. This ensures that the chosen data structures align with the specific requirements of their multi-threaded applications, leading to optimized performance.

9.12 Use Cases for Concurrent Collections

In multi-threaded applications, concurrent collections are indispensable for maintaining data integrity and preventing race conditions. Their thread-safe nature ensures consistent behavior even when multiple threads access and modify the data concurrently. This section explores practical scenarios where concurrent collections can dramatically improve performance and reliability.

Distributed Caching Systems are a prime example. Consider a scenario where you have multiple server nodes accessing a shared cache. ConcurrentHashMap is particularly useful here due to its efficient handling of concurrent read and write operations.

```
import java.util.concurrent.ConcurrentHashMap;

public class DistributedCache {
    private static final ConcurrentHashMap<String, String> cache = new
         ConcurrentHashMap<>();

    public static void addToCache(String key, String value) {
```

```
        cache.put(key, value);
    }

    public static String getFromCache(String key) {
        return cache.get(key);
    }
}
```

In this example, ConcurrentHashMap ensures that multiple threads can read from and write to the cache without encountering synchronization issues, thereby maintaining high throughput.

When it comes to immutable lists, CopyOnWriteArrayList excels in use cases involving frequent read operations and infrequent writes. This is common in event listeners registration where the number of additions and removals is significantly lower than the number of reads.

```
import java.util.concurrent.CopyOnWriteArrayList;

public class EventListenerRegistry {
    private final CopyOnWriteArrayList<EventListener> listeners = new
        CopyOnWriteArrayList<>();

    public void addListener(EventListener listener) {
        listeners.add(listener);
    }

    public void removeListener(EventListener listener) {
        listeners.remove(listener);
    }

    public void notifyListeners(Event event) {
        for (EventListener listener : listeners) {
            listener.handleEvent(event);
        }
    }
}
```

In this snippet, CopyOnWriteArrayList allows for safe iteration over the list without locking, which is beneficial during the notification process.

Blocking operations are frequently required in producer-consumer scenarios. BlockingQueue implementations such as ArrayBlockingQueue provide a means to implement thread-safe producer-consumer relationships where threads can safely exchange data.

```
import java.util.concurrent.ArrayBlockingQueue;
import java.util.concurrent.BlockingQueue;

public class ProducerConsumerExample {
    private static final BlockingQueue<Integer> queue = new ArrayBlockingQueue
        <>(10);

    public static void main(String[] args) {
        Producer producer = new Producer(queue);
        Consumer consumer = new Consumer(queue);
```

```
        new Thread(producer).start();
        new Thread(consumer).start();
    }
}

class Producer implements Runnable {
    private final BlockingQueue<Integer> queue;

    public Producer(BlockingQueue<Integer> queue) {
        this.queue = queue;
    }

    @Override
    public void run() {
        try {
            for (int i = 0; i < 50; i++) {
                queue.put(i);
                System.out.println("Produced: " + i);
            }
        } catch (InterruptedException e) {
            Thread.currentThread().interrupt();
        }
    }
}

class Consumer implements Runnable {
    private final BlockingQueue<Integer> queue;

    public Consumer(BlockingQueue<Integer> queue) {
        this.queue = queue;
    }

    @Override
    public void run() {
        try {
            while (true) {
                Integer item = queue.take();
                System.out.println("Consumed: " + item);
            }
        } catch (InterruptedException e) {
            Thread.currentThread().interrupt();
        }
    }
}
```

In this code, ArrayBlockingQueue ensures thread-safe handoff between the producer and consumer, effectively managing contention and synchronization.

Non-blocking algorithms often prefer structures such as ConcurrentLinkedQueue, which supports high-throughput non-blocking scenarios like message passing between threads.

```
import java.util.concurrent.ConcurrentLinkedQueue;

public class MessageBroker {
    private final ConcurrentLinkedQueue<String> messageQueue = new
        ConcurrentLinkedQueue<>();
```

```
    public void publish(String message) {
        messageQueue.offer(message);
    }

    public String consume() {
        return messageQueue.poll();
    }
}
```

In the above example, ConcurrentLinkedQueue allows multiple threads to publish and consume messages concurrently without locking.

Sorted data access patterns benefit from ConcurrentSkipListSet and ConcurrentSkipListMap. These collections provide both thread safety and efficient concurrent access for ordered sets and maps. Such structures are advantageous in real-time event processing systems, where maintaining a sorted state is crucial.

```
import java.util.concurrent.ConcurrentSkipListSet;

public class RealTimeEventProcessor {
    private final ConcurrentSkipListSet<Event> eventSet = new ConcurrentSkipListSet
        <>();

    public void addEvent(Event event) {
        eventSet.add(event);
    }

    public Event getFirstEvent() {
        return eventSet.first();
    }
}
```

Here, ConcurrentSkipListSet ensures that events are maintained in a sorted order even with concurrent modifications.

In scenarios requiring atomic operations on primitive types, atomic classes such as AtomicInteger are often utilized alongside concurrent collections. These atomic variables provide lock-free thread-safe operations, which are beneficial when combined with other concurrent structures for complex concurrent tasks.

```
import java.util.concurrent.ConcurrentHashMap;
import java.util.concurrent.atomic.AtomicInteger;

public class ConcurrentCounterMap {
    private final ConcurrentHashMap<String, AtomicInteger> counterMap = new
        ConcurrentHashMap<>();

    public void incrementCounter(String key) {
        counterMap.computeIfAbsent(key, k -> new AtomicInteger(0)).
            incrementAndGet();
    }
```

```
    public int getCounterValue(String key) {
        AtomicInteger counter = counterMap.get(key);
        return (counter != null) ? counter.get() : 0;
    }
}
```

This code snippet illustrates the use of AtomicInteger within a ConcurrentHashMap, providing a thread-safe way to manage counters for different keys concurrently.

Throughout these examples, it is evident that concurrent collections provide the necessary tools to handle complex concurrency requirements efficiently, ensuring data integrity and high performance across various multi-threaded scenarios.

Chapter 10

Best Practices and Common Pitfalls in Java Collections

This chapter examines best practices and common pitfalls when working with Java Collections. It covers topics such as selecting the appropriate collection type, efficient use of generics, and handling null values. The chapter also addresses issues like avoiding ConcurrentModificationException, optimizing performance, and utilizing collection utility methods. Additionally, it discusses memory management, debugging techniques, and provides case studies to illustrate best practices in real-world scenarios, guiding developers toward more effective and error-free use of Java Collections.

10.1 Introduction to Best Practices and Common Pitfalls

Java Collections Framework (JCF) is a powerful and flexible set of classes and interfaces that enable developers to handle groups of objects efficiently. While the framework provides numerous benefits, its misuse can lead to significant issues in software applications. Understanding best practices and common pitfalls is critical for leveraging the full potential of Java Collections in a robust, optimized manner.

Choosing the suitable collection type is paramount. ArrayList and LinkedList, for instance, offer different performance characteristics. An ArrayList provides constant-time positional access and is thus suitable for scenarios requiring frequent read operations. Conversely, LinkedList excels in scenarios that necessitate frequent insertions and deletions, as these operations can be performed in constant time. Consequently, it's essential to understand the operational complexities:

```
ArrayList Complexity:
- Access (get): O(1)
- Add/Remove: O(n)

LinkedList Complexity:
- Access (get): O(n)
- Add/Remove: O(1)
```

A common pitfall is inefficient use of generics. Generics allow for type-safe collections without explicit casting, reducing runtime errors. Consider the following definitions:

```
// Without Generics
List nonGenericList = new ArrayList();
nonGenericList.add("String Element");
String element = (String) nonGenericList.get(0);

// With Generics
List<String> genericList = new ArrayList<>();
genericList.add("String Element");
String element = genericList.get(0); // Type-safe, no casting needed
```

Utilizing generics not only enhances code readability but also ensures that type-checking errors are caught at compile time. Misuse of generics, such as using raw types or unchecked conversions, can lead to ClassCastException at runtime, which hinders code maintainability and reliability.

Handling null values appropriately in Java Collections is another key consideration. While collections can contain null values, their presence can lead to NullPointerExceptions if not managed correctly. It is advisable to avoid null values within collections and use optional values or custom markers instead.

To avoid ConcurrentModificationException, it's essential to understand the modifiable behaviour of collections when iterating over them. For instance, the following code snippet demonstrates incorrect modification:

```
List<String> list = new ArrayList<>();
list.add("A");
list.add("B");
```

```
for (String s : list) {
    if (s.equals("A")) list.remove(s); // Throws ConcurrentModificationException
}
```

A correct approach would use an iterator explicitly:

```
Iterator<String> iterator = list.iterator();
while (iterator.hasNext()) {
    String s = iterator.next();
    if (s.equals("A")) iterator.remove(); // Safe removal
}
```

Optimization of performance involves choosing between different collection classes within the framework based on access patterns. For instance, HashSet offers average constant-time performance for the basic operations (add, remove, and contains), making it effective for membership check operations. However, for sorted data requirements, TreeSet balances elements in a red-black tree, ensuring log-time efficiency, albeit at the cost of higher overhead.

The Collections utility class provides various useful methods for working with collections. For instance, the unmodifiableList method returns an immutable list that throws exceptions upon modification attempts:

```
List<String> modifiableList = new ArrayList<>();
modifiableList.add("A");
List<String> unmodifiableList = Collections.unmodifiableList(modifiableList);
unmodifiableList.add("B"); // Throws UnsupportedOperationException
```

Memory management considerations are critical when dealing with large collections. It's essential to avoid holding references to unused objects, which can lead to memory leaks. When a collection should no longer be used, setting it to null and invoking garbage collection can help in releasing memory efficiently.

Debugging collections often involves tracing issues like unexpected null values, stray elements, and incorrect order of elements. Utilizing debugging tools and practices such as logging collection states at crucial points can aid in identifying and rectifying such issues effectively.

Understanding the intricacies and subtleties of Java Collections leads to better software design, improved performance, and robust applications. Meticulous attention to collection selection, efficient use of generics, proper handling of null values, concurrency considerations, and memory management can prevent common errors and optimize application performance.

10.2 Choosing the Right Collection

Selecting the appropriate type of collection is crucial for ensuring optimal performance and maintainability of your code. Java provides several types of collections, each suited for different use cases. Understanding the characteristics, benefits, and trade-offs of each collection type will help you make informed decisions.

At a high level, Java collections can be categorized into three primary interfaces: List, Set, and Map. Each of these interfaces has multiple implementations that provide different performance characteristics and functionality.

- List: Represents an ordered collection (also known as a sequence). Lists can contain duplicate elements.
- Set: Represents a collection that does not allow duplicate elements.
- Map: Represents a collection of key-value pairs, with unique keys.

When choosing the right collection, consider the following criteria:

Evaluating Requirements

Before selecting a particular collection implementation, evaluate your specific requirements. Consider the following factors:

- **Order preservation**: Do you need to maintain the order in which elements are added?
- **Duplicate handling**: Are duplicate elements allowed or should they be automatically eliminated?
- **Key-value association**: Do you require a collection that associates unique keys with specific values?
- **Thread safety**: Will the collection be accessed by multiple threads concurrently?
- **Performance characteristics**: What are the typical operations (insertions, deletions, retrievals), and what are the performance requirements for each?

List Implementations

List is an ordered collection that allows duplicate elements. Common implementations include ArrayList, LinkedList, and CopyOnWriteArrayList.

- ArrayList:

  Implemented as a resizable array, ArrayList provides fast random read access, with an average time complexity of $O(1)$. However, insertion and deletion operations, especially in the middle of the list, have a time complexity of $O(n)$.

  ```
  List<String> arrayList = new ArrayList<>();
  ```

- LinkedList:

  Implemented as a doubly-linked list, LinkedList provides fast insertions and deletions, with a time complexity of $O(1)$ for operations involving the ends of the list. Random access, however, is slower with a time complexity of $O(n)$.

  ```
  List<String> linkedList = new LinkedList<>();
  ```

- CopyOnWriteArrayList:

  This is a thread-safe variant of ArrayList where all mutative operations (add, set, and so on) are implemented by making a fresh copy of the underlying array. Useful in cases where read operations vastly outnumber write operations.

  ```
  List<String> cowArrayList = new CopyOnWriteArrayList<>();
  ```

Set Implementations

Set is a collection that does not allow duplicate elements. Common implementations include HashSet, LinkedHashSet, and TreeSet.

- HashSet:

  Uses a hash table for storage and offers constant-time performance for basic operations (add, remove, contains). It does not guarantee any specific order.

  ```
  Set<String> hashSet = new HashSet<>();
  ```

- LinkedHashSet:

  Maintains a doubly-linked list running through all its entries to maintain insertion order. This incurs a slight performance overhead relative to HashSet, but retrieval in insertion order is guaranteed.

```
Set<String> linkedHashSet = new LinkedHashSet<>();
```

- TreeSet:

  Implements a balanced binary search tree (specifically a Red-Black tree), providing sorted order. This results in longer average time complexity for basic operations $O(\log n)$ compared to HashSet.

```
Set<String> treeSet = new TreeSet<>();
```

Map Implementations

Map is a collection that maps unique keys to values. Common implementations include HashMap, LinkedHashMap, and TreeMap.

- HashMap:

  Provides constant-time performance $O(1)$ for the basic operations (get and put), but does not guarantee any order.

```
Map<String, Integer> hashMap = new HashMap<>();
```

- LinkedHashMap:

  Extends HashMap by maintaining a linked list of the entries in the map, in insertion order or access order. This slightly increases overhead but guarantees order.

```
Map<String, Integer> linkedHashMap = new LinkedHashMap<>();
```

- TreeMap:

  Implements a Red-Black tree and provides natural ordering of keys or the order specified by a custom Comparator. Operations have a time complexity of $O(\log n)$.

```
Map<String, Integer> treeMap = new TreeMap<>();
```

Specialized Collections

In some cases, specialized collections from the java.util.concurrent package or other libraries might be appropriate. For instance, ConcurrentHashMap offers thread-safe performance with minimal locking, while PriorityQueue provides an implementation of a heap-based priority queue.

Selecting the right collection type requires understanding both the operational characteristics of the collections and the demands of your specific application. By aligning your choice with your requirements, you can improve both the performance and maintainability of your codebase.

10.3 Efficient Use of Generics

Generics in Java Collections enhance type safety and eliminate the need for type casting during retrieval operations. By parameterizing types, generics allow us to create classes, interfaces, and methods with a placeholder for the type of data they operate on. This section delves into efficient usage of generics within Java Collections, focusing on techniques that prevent common pitfalls and improve code readability and maintainability.

Generics were introduced in Java 5, primarily to address issues related to type safety and to reduce the runtime errors caused by ClassCastException. Below, we explore the correct and efficient use of generics in different contexts.

Defining and Using Generic Classes

When defining a generic class, we use angle brackets <> to specify the type parameter. Consider the following example of a simple generic class:

```
public class Box<T> {
    private T content;

    public void setContent(T content) {
        this.content = content;
    }

    public T getContent() {
        return content;
    }
}
```

Here, T represents the type parameter, which can be replaced with any reference type when creating an instance of the Box class. To instantiate a Box object for String items:

```
Box<String> stringBox = new Box<>();
stringBox.setContent("Hello World");
String content = stringBox.getContent();
```

Using Bounded Type Parameters

Generics provide bounded type parameters which restrict the types that can be used as type arguments. A bounded type parameter can be specified using the extends keyword, which signifies that the type argument must be a subtype of a particular class:

```
public class NumberBox<T extends Number> {
    private T number;

    public void setNumber(T number) {
        this.number = number;
    }

    public T getNumber() {
        return number;
    }
}
```

An instance of NumberBox can accept Integer, Double, or any type that extends Number:

```
NumberBox<Integer> integerBox = new NumberBox<>();
integerBox.setNumber(10);

NumberBox<Double> doubleBox = new NumberBox<>();
doubleBox.setNumber(2.5);
```

Generic Methods

In addition to generic classes, methods can also be made generic. This allows the method to be parameterized with a type when it is called:

```
public class Utility {
    public static <T> void printArray(T[] array) {
        for (T element : array) {
            System.out.println(element);
        }
    }
}
```

This method can be called with any type of array:

```
String[] stringArray = {"Hello", "World"};
Utility.printArray(stringArray);

Integer[] intArray = {1, 2, 3, 4, 5};
```

```
Utility.printArray(intArray);
```

Type Inference with the Diamond Operator

In Java 7 and later versions, the diamond operator (<>) allows the compiler to infer the type parameters, reducing verbosity:

```
List<String> stringList = new ArrayList<>();
```

The compiler infers that stringList is a List of String type, making the code less cluttered.

Avoiding Raw Types

Using raw types—those without generic type parameters—should be avoided as they bypass the type-checking mechanism, leading to potential runtime exceptions:

```
// Avoid raw type
List rawList = new ArrayList();
rawList.add("Hello");
String s = (String) rawList.get(0); // Type casting needed
```

Instead, specify the type parameter:

```
// Use parameterized type
List<String> typedList = new ArrayList<>();
typedList.add("Hello");
String str = typedList.get(0); // No type casting needed
```

Wildcard Usage

Wildcards provide flexibility when dealing with parameterized types. There are three forms of wildcards in Java: unbounded (?), bounded (? extends T), and lower-bounded (? super T):

1. **Unbounded Wildcard**:

```
public void printList(List<?> list) {
    for (Object obj : list) {
        System.out.println(obj);
    }
}
```

2. **Upper Bounded Wildcard**:

```
public void processList(List<? extends Number> list) {
    for (Number number : list) {
        System.out.println(number);
    }
}
```

3. **Lower Bounded Wildcard**:

```
public void addToList(List<? super Integer> list) {
    list.add(new Integer(1));
}
```

The upper bounded wildcard (? extends T) allows accepting any type that is a subtype of T, while the lower bounded wildcard (? super T) allows accepting any type that is a supertype of T.

Thorough understanding and correct application of generics enhance the robustness and maintainability of code. By leveraging type safety, avoiding runtime errors, and improving code readability through type inference and wildcard usage, developers can write more efficient and error-free Java Collection code.

10.4 Immutable Collections

Immutable collections are vital in Java programming to enhance application safety, thread safety, and maintainability. An immutable collection is a collection whose elements cannot be modified once the collection is created. This section delves into the advantages of using immutable collections, how to create them, practical scenarios where they are beneficial, and considerations for their use in concurrent programming.

Advantages of Immutable Collections:

- **Thread Safety:** Immutable objects are inherently thread-safe as their state cannot change after construction, eliminating synchronization problems in concurrent environments.
- **Simplicity:** Immutable collections are simpler to understand, reason about, and debug because their state does not change, reducing potential side-effects.
- **Security:** Immutable collections prevent unauthorized modification of data, enhancing the integrity and security of the application.
- **Caching:** Immutable objects can be reused and shared freely. They are suitable for caching, as they guarantee consistency.

Creating Immutable Collections:

Java provides several ways to create immutable collections. The 'Collections' utility class contains methods to create immutable sets, lists, and maps. Here are examples using 'Collections.unmodifiableList', 'Collections.unmodifiableSet', and 'Collections.unmodifiableMap':

```
import java.util.*;

public class ImmutableCollectionsExample {
    public static void main(String[] args) {
        List<String> mutableList = new ArrayList<>(Arrays.asList("A", "B", "C"));
        List<String> immutableList = Collections.unmodifiableList(mutableList);

        Set<String> mutableSet = new HashSet<>(Arrays.asList("X", "Y", "Z"));
        Set<String> immutableSet = Collections.unmodifiableSet(mutableSet);

        Map<String, Integer> mutableMap = new HashMap<>();
        mutableMap.put("One", 1);
        mutableMap.put("Two", 2);
        mutableMap.put("Three", 3);
        Map<String, Integer> immutableMap = Collections.unmodifiableMap(
            mutableMap);
    }
}
```

Another approach is utilizing the 'of' methods provided by the 'List', 'Set', and 'Map' interfaces in Java 9 and later:

```
import java.util.*;

public class ImmutableCollectionsExampleJava9 {
    public static void main(String[] args) {
        List<String> immutableList = List.of("A", "B", "C");
        Set<String> immutableSet = Set.of("X", "Y", "Z");
        Map<String, Integer> immutableMap = Map.of("One", 1, "Two", 2, "Three",
            3);
    }
}
```

Usage in Concurrent Programming:

Immutable collections are particularly useful in concurrent programming. Since the state of an immutable collection cannot be altered once it is created, multiple threads can read the collection without the need for synchronization.

Consider the following example that uses an immutable list in a multi-threaded environment:

```
import java.util.*;
import java.util.concurrent.*;

public class ImmutableCollectionsConcurrency {
    public static void main(String[] args) {
        List<String> immutableList = List.of("A", "B", "C");

        ExecutorService executor = Executors.newFixedThreadPool(2);
```

```
        Runnable task = () -> {
            for (String s : immutableList) {
                System.out.println(Thread.currentThread().getName() + ": " + s);
            }
        };

        executor.submit(task);
        executor.submit(task);

        executor.shutdown();
    }
}
```

```
Output:
pool-1-thread-1: A
pool-1-thread-1: B
pool-1-thread-1: C
pool-1-thread-2: A
pool-1-thread-2: B
pool-1-thread-2: C
```

In this example, both threads read from the same immutable list without any risk of data corruption or the need for synchronization mechanisms like 'synchronized' blocks or 'locks'.

Considerations:

While immutable collections offer many benefits, there are certain considerations to keep in mind:

- **Performance Overheads:** Creating copies of immutable collections with alterations can introduce performance overheads, especially if done frequently.

- **Memory Consumption:** If the original and immutable versions are both retained in memory, this can lead to increased memory consumption. Developers should be mindful of the application's memory footprint.

- **Limited Flexibility:** Immutable collections are not suitable for all use cases. When modification operations are a significant part of the application's logic, mutable collections might be more appropriate.

Using immutable collections is a well-accepted best practice in Java. Their application enhances safety, reduces concurrency issues, and simplifies debugging, making them indispensable in modern, high-quality software development.

10.5 Handling Null Values

Handling null values in Java Collections is a critical aspect that developers must understand to ensure the robustness and reliability of their applications. Improper handling of null values can lead to NullPointerExceptions, which are a common source of runtime errors in Java programs. This section details best practices for handling null values within different types of Java Collections, highlighting potential pitfalls and illustrating techniques for effectively managing null entries.

Firstly, it is essential to recognize that most Java Collections can store null values, but certain types, such as Hashtable, prohibit them. For instance:

```
// Example of null handling in Hashtable where null is not allowed
Hashtable<Integer, String> hashtable = new Hashtable<>();
hashtable.put(1, "Value1");
hashtable.put(2, null); // This will throw NullPointerException
```

In this example, attempting to insert a null value into a Hashtable results in a NullPointerException. Conversely, most other Collection types, such as ArrayList, HashMap, and HashSet, allow null values:

```
// Example of null handling in HashMap where null is allowed
HashMap<Integer, String> hashMap = new HashMap<>();
hashMap.put(1, "Value1");
hashMap.put(2, null); // This is allowed
```

When dealing with null values in collections, a central best practice is to avoid null where possible. Utilizing Optional can be helpful in conveying the absence of a value more explicitly than null:

```
// Example using Optional to avoid null values
Map<Integer, Optional<String>> map = new HashMap<>();
map.put(1, Optional.of("Value1"));
map.put(2, Optional.empty());
```

This approach clearly indicates that the key 2 intentionally has no associated value, reducing the risk of NullPointerExceptions.

When checking for null values in collections, one should prefer utility methods provided by the Java Standard Library. For instance, Objects.isNull() and Objects.nonNull() offer more explicit alternatives for checking nullness:

```
// Using Objects utility methods for null checks
if (Objects.nonNull(hashMap.get(2))) {
    System.out.println("Value exists");
} else {
    System.out.println("Value is null or key is absent");
```

```
}
```

Special consideration should be given to null values in Set and List collections. Storing null in a Set will only affect the set's behavior insofar as the null entry conforms to the set's uniqueness property:

```
// Null handling in HashSet
HashSet<String> set = new HashSet<>();
set.add(null); // Null is allowed
set.add(null); // Still only one null entry due to set's uniqueness property
```

For List collections, null entries can appear in any location, which necessitates careful iteration and null checks:

```
// Null handling in ArrayList during iteration
ArrayList<String> list = new ArrayList<>();
list.add("Value1");
list.add(null);
list.add("Value3");

for (String item : list) {
    if (item != null) {
        System.out.println(item);
    } else {
        System.out.println("Null value found");
    }
}
```

To safeguard against potential issues arising from null values, consider implementing validation at the collection's point of entry. This preempts the insertion of null values and enforces constraints:

```
// Validation to prevent null values from being added
public void addNonNullValue(Map<Integer, String> map, Integer key, String value) {
    if (key != null && value != null) {
        map.put(key, value);
    } else {
        throw new IllegalArgumentException("Neither key nor value can be null");
    }
}
```

Utilizing the Collections utility class can also be useful when managing nulls within collection operations. For example, Collections.emptyList() provides an immutable list that ensures no null elements:

```
// Using Collections utility methods to prevent null entries
List<String> nonNullList = Collections.emptyList();
// nonNullList.add(null); // This will throw UnsupportedOperationException
```

Through these practices and mindful management of null values, developers can enhance the stability, readability, and maintainability of their code while avoiding common pitfalls that could otherwise introduce subtle and challenging bugs into their Java applications.

10.6 Avoiding ConcurrentModificationException

The ConcurrentModificationException is a runtime exception that occurs when a collection is modified concurrently while iterating over it. In Java, this is often encountered in the context of removing or adding elements to a collection while it is being iterated using an iterator. Understanding how to avoid this exception is essential to ensure thread safety and data consistency when working with collections in a multi-threaded environment.

Understanding the Problem

The ConcurrentModificationException typically occurs due to the structural modification of a collection. A structural modification is any operation that adds or removes an element from the collection, thereby changing its structure. For example:

```
import java.util.ArrayList;
import java.util.Iterator;
import java.util.List;

public class ConcurrentModificationExample {
    public static void main(String[] args) {
        List<String> list = new ArrayList<>();
        list.add("A");
        list.add("B");
        list.add("C");

        Iterator<String> iterator = list.iterator();
        while (iterator.hasNext()) {
            String value = iterator.next();
            if (value.equals("B")) {
                list.remove(value); // This will throw ConcurrentModificationException
            }
        }
    }
}
```

In the above example, the collection is modified during iteration, which triggers a ConcurrentModificationException.

Best Practices for Avoiding ConcurrentModificationException

- **Using Concurrent Collections:** The java.util.concurrent package provides thread-safe collections such as CopyOnWriteArrayList, ConcurrentHashMap, and ConcurrentSkipListSet. These collections are designed to handle concurrent modifications without throwing a ConcurrentModificationException.

```
import java.util.List;
import java.util.concurrent.CopyOnWriteArrayList;

public class CopyOnWriteArrayListExample {
    public static void main(String[] args) {
        List<String> list = new CopyOnWriteArrayList<>();
        list.add("A");
        list.add("B");
        list.add("C");

        for (String value : list) {
            if (value.equals("B")) {
                list.remove(value); // Safe removal using
                    CopyOnWriteArrayList
            }
        }
    }
}
```

- **Using Iterator's remove Method:** When iterating through a collection, the Iterator provides a remove method that allows safe removal of elements without causing a ConcurrentModificationException.

```
import java.util.ArrayList;
import java.util.Iterator;
import java.util.List;

public class IteratorRemoveExample {
    public static void main(String[] args) {
        List<String> list = new ArrayList<>();
        list.add("A");
        list.add("B");
        list.add("C");

        Iterator<String> iterator = list.iterator();
        while (iterator.hasNext()) {
            String value = iterator.next();
            if (value.equals("B")) {
                iterator.remove(); // Safe removal using Iterator's remove
                    method
            }
        }
    }
}
```

- **Using Synchronized Collections:** The Collections.synchronizedList and Collections.synchronizedMap methods return synchronized (thread-safe) collections. However, it is important to manually synchronize on the collection when iterating through it.

```
import java.util.ArrayList;
import java.util.Collections;
import java.util.Iterator;
import java.util.List;
```

```
public class SynchronizedCollectionsExample {
    public static void main(String[] args) {
        List<String> list = Collections.synchronizedList(new ArrayList<>())
            ;
        list.add("A");
        list.add("B");
        list.add("C");

        synchronized (list) {
            Iterator<String> iterator = list.iterator();
            while (iterator.hasNext()) {
                String value = iterator.next();
                if (value.equals("B")) {
                    iterator.remove(); // Safe removal with synchronized block
                }
            }
        }
    }
}
```

- **Utilizing Enhanced For-Loop with CopyOnWriteArrayList:** Iterating using an enhanced for-loop in conjunction with a CopyOnWriteArrayList ensures safe modification as this collection creates a snapshot of the array, preventing concurrent modification issues.

```
import java.util.List;
import java.util.concurrent.CopyOnWriteArrayList;

public class EnhancedForLoopExample {
    public static void main(String[] args) {
        List<String> list = new CopyOnWriteArrayList<>();
        list.add("A");
        list.add("B");
        list.add("C");

        for (String value : list) {
            if (value.equals("B")) {
                list.remove(value); // Safe removal with enhanced for-loop
            }
        }
    }
}
```

Employing these techniques will enhance the robustness of your code when dealing with collections in a concurrent environment. Ensuring thread safety and preventing modification anomalies are key to developing reliable multi-threaded applications.

10.7 Optimizing Performance

Optimizing performance in Java Collections requires a nuanced understanding of both the collection types available and the underlying mechanics of these collections. Performance can be improved by selecting the proper collection for the specific use case, minimizing overhead, and leveraging Java's concurrent utility classes and methods. We will explore various strategies to optimize performance and how to apply these in a practical context.

Selecting the appropriate collection is vital. For example, ArrayList provides constant-time positional access but is inefficient for insertions and deletions in the middle of the list. Conversely, LinkedList offers constant-time insertions and deletions but is not as performant for random access. Choosing between HashMap, TreeMap, and LinkedHashMap can significantly influence performance, depending on the requirements for ordering and frequency of access patterns.

Efficient iteration is another critical factor. Using an enhanced for-loop is generally preferred over an explicit iterator pattern, as shown in the following example:

```
for (String element : list) {
    // Process element
}
```

This syntax is more concise and avoids potential iterator-related pitfalls. However, when removal during iteration is necessary, using an Iterator is required:

```
Iterator<String> iterator = list.iterator();
while (iterator.hasNext()) {
    String element = iterator.next();
    // Condition to remove
    if (element meetsCondition) {
        iterator.remove();
    }
}
```

Parallelism and concurrency can lead to significant performance gains, especially in multi-core processing environments. Utilizing java.util.concurrent collections such as ConcurrentHashMap and CopyOnWriteArrayList can mitigate synchronization overhead and contention issues. These collections are designed to allow concurrent read and write operations without locking the entire collection.

Consider the following example using ConcurrentHashMap:

```
ConcurrentHashMap<String, Integer> map = new ConcurrentHashMap<>();

map.put("key1", 1);
map.put("key2", 2);

map.replace("key1", 1, 3);

Integer value = map.get("key1");
```

ConcurrentHashMap provides scalable performance for thread-safe operations, as its operations involve finer-grained locking, which reduces contention among threads.

Optimal initialization and resizing of collections can prevent performance degradation. For instance, if the approximate size of the list is known in advance, initializing an ArrayList with a specific capacity can minimize the cost of resizing:

```
ArrayList<String> list = new ArrayList<>(initialCapacity);
```

For HashMap, specifying the initial capacity and load factor can help to balance memory usage and access speed. By default, HashMap uses a load factor of 0.75, which offers a good trade-off between space and time complexity. However, if the application requires a higher space utilization, adjusting the load factor might be beneficial:

```
HashMap<String, Integer> map = new HashMap<>(initialCapacity, loadFactor);
```

Performance tuning also involves avoiding excessive boxing and unboxing when working with collections of primitive types. Instead of using ArrayList<Integer>, one can employ IntArrayList from libraries such as fastutil:

```
it.unimi.dsi.fastutil.ints.IntArrayList intList = new IntArrayList();
```

Utilizing bulk operations and methods like Collections.sort, removeAll, retainAll, and addAll rather than iterating manually can leverage optimizations within the Java Collections Framework:

```
Collections.sort(list);
```

Last but not least, using profiling tools to identify bottlenecks and memory usage patterns is crucial in performance tuning. Tools such as Java Flight Recorder (JFR), VisualVM, and YourKit allow developers to analyze heap usage, CPU time distribution, garbage collection metrics, and more. These insights can guide targeted optimizations, ensuring that the changes yield practical performance improvements.

Applying these strategies can lead to substantial performance enhancements, alleviating common bottlenecks and improving the responsiveness and scalability of applications that rely heavily on Java Collections.

10.8 Using Collection Utility Methods (Collections)

When working with Java collections, the java.util.Collections class provides a suite of static utility methods designed to make manipulating collections easier. These methods can help you perform various operations like sorting, searching, and modifying collections without the need for cumbersome custom code. This section explores some of the most useful methods provided by the Collections class and demonstrates their practical applications through detailed examples.

The java.util.Collections class is a member of the Java Collections Framework and consists exclusively of static methods that operate on or return collections. It is important to note that all methods in the Collections class are polymorphic and can work with any collection type that adheres to the Collection interface.

```
import java.util.List;
import java.util.ArrayList;
import java.util.Collections;
```

Sorting Collections

Sorting is one of the most commonly performed operations on collections. The Collections class provides several methods to facilitate sorting. The most commonly used method is Collections.sort(List<T> list), which sorts the specified list into ascending order based on the natural ordering of its elements.

```
// Example: Sorting a list of integers
List<Integer> numbers = new ArrayList<>();
numbers.add(3);
numbers.add(1);
numbers.add(4);
numbers.add(1);
numbers.add(5);

Collections.sort(numbers);

// Output
numbers.forEach(System.out::println); // 1, 1, 3, 4, 5
```

If you need to sort a list based on a custom criterion, you can use the overloaded method Collections.sort(List<T> list, Comparator<? super T> c). This method allows you to provide a custom comparator.

```
// Example: Sorting a list of strings by length
List<String> words = new ArrayList<>();
words.add("apple");
words.add("banana");
words.add("cherry");

Collections.sort(words, (s1, s2) -> s1.length() - s2.length());

// Output
words.forEach(System.out::println); // apple, cherry, banana
```

Searching in Collections

To search for specific elements in a collection, the binarySearch method can be used. Note that the list must be sorted prior to performing a binary search.

```
// Example: Searching for a specific element in a sorted list
int index = Collections.binarySearch(numbers, 4);
System.out.println("Index of element 4: " + index); // Index of element 4: 3
```

The binarySearch method returns the index of the search key if it is contained in the list; otherwise, it returns -(insertion point) - 1. The insertion point is defined as the point at which the key would be inserted to maintain the list's sorted order.

Shuffling Collections

Shuffling a collection is another useful operation, especially when working with test sets or implementing randomized algorithms. The Collections.shuffle(List<?> list) method randomly permutes the specified list using a default source of randomness.

```
// Example: Shuffling a list of elements
Collections.shuffle(numbers);

// Output
numbers.forEach(System.out::println); // shuffled output, e.g., 3, 1, 5, 4, 1
```

Finding Minimum and Maximum

The Collections class provides min and max methods to find the smallest and largest elements in a collection respectively. Similar to sorting, these methods depend on the natural ordering or a custom comparator.

```
// Example: Finding the minimum and maximum elements
int min = Collections.min(numbers);
int max = Collections.max(numbers);
```

```
System.out.printf("Min: %d, Max: %d%n", min, max); // Min: 1, Max: 5
```

Reversing Collections

Reversing the order of elements is made simple with the Collections.reverse(List<?> list) method.

```
// Example: Reversing a list
Collections.reverse(numbers);

// Output
numbers.forEach(System.out::println); // reversed order of the shuffled output
```

Synchronization Wrappers

To make a collection thread-safe, Collections provides synchronization wrappers. Methods such as synchronizedList, synchronizedSet, and synchronizedMap wrap the specified collection with a synchronized (thread-safe) collection backed by the specified collection.

```
// Example: Creating a thread-safe list
List<Integer> synchronizedNumbers = Collections.synchronizedList(numbers);
```

When using synchronized collections, it is critical to remember that iteration over these collections must be manually synchronized.

```
// Example: Iterating over a synchronized list
synchronized (synchronizedNumbers) {
    synchronizedNumbers.forEach(System.out::println);
}
```

Unmodifiable Collections

To create a read-only view of a collection, the Collections.unmodifiableList, unmodifiableSet, unmodifiableMap, etc. methods are used. These methods return a collection that cannot be modified.

```
// Example: Creating an unmodifiable list
List<Integer> unmodifiableNumbers = Collections.unmodifiableList(numbers);

try {
    unmodifiableNumbers.add(6); // This will throw an
        UnsupportedOperationException
} catch (UnsupportedOperationException e) {
    System.out.println("Can't modify unmodifiable list");
}
```

The utility methods provided by the Collections class are essential tools for developers working with collections in Java. By mastering these methods, one can perform complex collection manipulations efficiently and with minimal code.

10.9 Memory Management in Collections

Effective memory management is paramount when working with Java Collections to ensure efficient application performance and to prevent memory leaks. Understanding how collections internally manage memory and the impact of different operations on memory usage is vital.

Java Collections Framework (JCF) provides dynamic data structures like ArrayList, HashMap, LinkedList, and others, which manage their underlying storage automatically. However, inappropriate usage can lead to excessive memory consumption and suboptimal performance. This section explores several aspects of memory management within collections.

1. Initial Capacity and Load Factor

When initializing collections like ArrayList or HashMap, specifying an initial capacity can significantly impact memory utilization and performance.

```
List<String> list = new ArrayList<>(100);
Map<String, Integer> map = new HashMap<>(200, 0.75f);
```

For ArrayList, the initial capacity determines the size of the underlying array. If the initial capacity is too small, frequent reallocations and copying of array elements will occur as the list grows, incurring overhead. Conversely, an excessively large initial capacity can waste memory if the collection never grows to that size.

For HashMap, the initial capacity and load factor control its capacity and resizing behavior. The load factor signifies the fullness threshold before resizing, directly impacting memory usage and access time. Specifying a lower load factor reduces the collision rate, enhancing access speed at the cost of higher memory usage.

2. Shrinking Collections

Java Collections, like ArrayList, do not automatically shrink after elements are removed. Hence, it's essential to manually trim the capacity to fit the currently stored elements:

```
list.trimToSize();
```

This method reduces the amount of memory used by an ArrayList to its minimum, fitting exactly its current size. For collections like HashMap, ensuring that unnecessary key-value pairs are removed and nullified is crucial.

```
map.clear();
```

The clear() method removes all mappings, but it does not reduce the internal capacity. To release unused memory, create a new instance:

```
map = new HashMap<>();
```

3. Weak References

To manage memory more effectively, especially when dealing with large or frequently updated collections, WeakHashMap and other reference types can be employed. WeakHashMap uses WeakReference objects for keys, allowing their automatic garbage collection when no longer referenced elsewhere:

```
Map<Object, String> weakMap = new WeakHashMap<>();
Object key = new Object();
weakMap.put(key, "value");
key = null;
// The entry may be garbage collected if 'key' is not referenced elsewhere.
```

WeakHashMap is helpful when you do not wish to prevent keys from being garbage collected.

4. Object Pooling

Object pooling is a technique to reuse objects instead of creating and destroying them repetitively. Particularly for collections of frequently used objects, implementing object pools can significantly reduce memory churn.

Example using an object pool for StringBuilder:

```
public class StringBuilderPool {
    private final Queue<StringBuilder> pool = new LinkedList<>();
    public StringBuilder acquire() {
        return Optional.ofNullable(pool.poll()).orElse(new StringBuilder());
    }
    public void release(StringBuilder sb) {
        sb.setLength(0); // Clear the builder
        pool.offer(sb); // Return it to the pool
    }
}
```

5. Periodic Cleanup and Memory Profiling

Regularly cleaning up collections and profiling memory usage is crucial to avoiding memory leaks. Tools like VisualVM, JProfiler, and YourKit can help identify memory leaks and assess the memory footprint of collections.

Code to perform a periodic cleanup:

```
ScheduledExecutorService cleaner = Executors.newScheduledThreadPool(1);
cleaner.scheduleAtFixedRate(() -> {
    map.entrySet().removeIf(entry -> shouldRemove(entry.getKey()));
}, 0, 1, TimeUnit.HOURS);
```

This periodic cleanup action is essential for long-running applications where memory usage needs to be tightly controlled.

Common Pitfalls

Avoid excessive use of large initial capacities without clear justification, as it can lead to underutilized memory. Also, failing to remove or nullify unused references can lead to memory leaks. Ensure collections holding data no longer needed are appropriately cleaned up or reinitialized.

Effective memory management in Java Collections demands keen attention to initialization parameters, active management of collection sizes and cleanup operations, and leveraging appropriate data structures such as weak references and object pools. Regular profiling and periodic cleanups complement a comprehensive strategy to optimize memory usage in Java applications.

10.10 Common Mistakes and How to Avoid Them

When working with Java Collections, developers often encounter various pitfalls that can lead to suboptimal performance, unexpected behavior, or runtime exceptions. Understanding these common mistakes and learning how to avoid them is crucial for writing robust and efficient code.

One frequent mistake is using the wrong type of collection for a specific purpose. For instance, developers may choose an ArrayList when frequent insertions or deletions are required. In such cases, LinkedList is more suitable due to its efficient insertion and deletion operations at the expense of slower random access. To illustrate the inefficiencies caused by incorrect collection selection, consider the following examples:

```
// Inefficient use of ArrayList for frequent insertions
List<Integer> arrayList = new ArrayList<>();
for (int i = 0; i < 1000; i++) {
    arrayList.add(0, i); // O(n) operation for each insertion
}
```

```
// Efficient use of LinkedList for frequent insertions
List<Integer> linkedList = new LinkedList<>();
for (int i = 0; i < 1000; i++) {
    linkedList.add(0, i); // O(1) operation for each insertion
}
```

Another common mistake is neglecting to specify generic types, which can lead to ClassCastException at runtime. Utilizing generics provides compile-time type checking, enhanced readability, and eliminates the need for casting:

```
// Without generics: Risk of ClassCastException
List rawList = new ArrayList();
rawList.add("String");
Integer number = (Integer) rawList.get(0); // Throws ClassCastException

// With generics: Type safety ensured
List<Integer> typedList = new ArrayList<>();
typedList.add(42);
Integer number = typedList.get(0); // No casting needed, no risk of exception
```

Additionally, improper handling of NullPointerException is a prevalent issue. Best practices include using Optional or performing null checks before accessing collection elements. This approach prevents runtime exceptions and improves code robustness:

```
// Risk of NullPointerException
List<Integer> list = null;
if (list.size() > 0) { // Throws NullPointerException
    // ...
}

// Better handling using Optional
List<Integer> list = null;
Optional.ofNullable(list).ifPresent(l -> {
    if (l.size() > 0) {
        // ...
    }
});
```

A pitfall that often catches developers off guard is the ConcurrentModificationException. This exception occurs when a collection is modified while iterating over it using methods other than the iterator's remove method. To avoid this, use an iterator's remove method or java.util.concurrent collections designed for concurrent modifications:

```
// Risk of ConcurrentModificationException
List<Integer> list = new ArrayList<>(Arrays.asList(1, 2, 3));
for (Integer number : list) {
    if (number % 2 == 0) {
        list.remove(number); // Throws ConcurrentModificationException
    }
}
```

```
// Correct way using iterator's remove
List<Integer> list = new ArrayList<>(Arrays.asList(1, 2, 3));
Iterator<Integer> iterator = list.iterator();
while (iterator.hasNext()) {
    if (iterator.next() % 2 == 0) {
        iterator.remove(); // Safe removal, no exception
    }
}
```

Incorrectly synchronizing collections is another mistake that can lead to data inconsistency or performance bottlenecks. It's crucial to use thread-safe collections such as CopyOnWriteArrayList, ConcurrentHashMap, or synchronize blocks of code properly:

```
// Inefficient synchronization
List<Integer> synchronizedList = Collections.synchronizedList(new ArrayList<>());
synchronized (synchronizedList) {
    for (Integer number : synchronizedList) {
        // ...
    }
}

// Using thread-safe collections
List<Integer> threadSafeList = new CopyOnWriteArrayList<>();
for (Integer number : threadSafeList) {
    // Thread-safe iteration, no need for external synchronization
}
```

Memory leaks caused by improper use of collections, such as retaining references in long-lived collections, can severely impact application performance. Weak references or caches like WeakHashMap are effective solutions:

```
// Potential memory leak
List<Object> longLivedList = new ArrayList<>();
while (true) {
    longLivedList.add(new Object()); // Objects are never eligible for GC
}

// Using WeakHashMap to avoid memory leak
Map<Object, Object> cache = new WeakHashMap<>();
while (true) {
    Object key = new Object();
    cache.put(key, new Object()); // Key-referenced objects can be garbage collected
}
```

Copying collections improperly, especially when dealing with mutable objects, can lead to unintentional side effects. Deep copying mechanisms or immutable objects should be employed to maintain logical separation:

```
// Shallow copy leads to shared references
List<StringBuilder> originalList = new ArrayList<>();
originalList.add(new StringBuilder("Mutable"));
List<StringBuilder> shallowCopy = new ArrayList<>(originalList);
```

```
shallowCopy.get(0).append(" Object"); // Affects both lists

// Proper deep copy
List<StringBuilder> deepCopy = new ArrayList<>();
for (StringBuilder sb : originalList) {
    deepCopy.add(new StringBuilder(sb.toString())); // Independent copies
}
```

Lastly, neglecting to leverage collection utility methods available in Collections can lead to verbose and error-prone code. Methods such as sort, binarySearch, and unmodifiableList simplify common operations and improve code clarity:

```
// Verbose manual sorting
List<Integer> numbers = new ArrayList<>(Arrays.asList(5, 3, 1, 4, 2));
Collections.sort(numbers); // Simplifies sorting

// Using utility methods
List<Integer> unmodifiable = Collections.unmodifiableList(numbers);
int index = Collections.binarySearch(numbers, 3); // Efficient binary search
```

Understanding these common mistakes and mastering the corresponding solutions provides a strong foundation for developing reliable and performant Java applications. By adhering to best practices, developers can avoid pitfalls and utilize collections effectively.

10.11 Debugging Collections

Debugging collections in Java is a critical skill that aids in identifying and rectifying issues quickly and efficiently. Here are some techniques and tools that can be employed to debug collections effectively.

1. Utilizing the Enhanced for Loop

The enhanced for loop provides a straightforward way to iterate through collections. It automatically handles the iterator, reducing the risk of common errors.

```
for (String item : stringList) {
    System.out.println(item);
}
```

2. **Using the Iterator Interface**

When more control is needed over the iteration process, the Iterator interface can be instrumental. This is especially useful when modifying the collection during iteration.

```
Iterator<String> iterator = stringList.iterator();
```

```
while (iterator.hasNext()) {
    String item = iterator.next();
    if (item.isEmpty()) {
        iterator.remove();
    }
}
```

3. **Leveraging the toString Method**

Most collection classes override the toString method, which provides a convenient way to print and inspect the elements in a collection.

```
System.out.println(stringList.toString());
```

The output will appear as follows:

```
[Item1, Item2, Item3]
```

4. **Assert Statements**

Using assert statements can ensure that a collection meets expected conditions during development.

```
assert stringList.size() == expectedSize : "Unexpected list size!";
```

5. **Java Logging Frameworks**

Java provides several logging frameworks, such as java.util.logging, Log4j, and SLF4J, which can be integrated into applications for debugging purposes.

```
import java.util.logging.Logger;

public class DebuggingExample {
    private static final Logger logger = Logger.getLogger(DebuggingExample.class.
         getName());

    public static void main(String[] args) {
        List<String> stringList = Arrays.asList("Item1", "Item2", "Item3");
        logger.info("Current List: " + stringList);
    }
}
```

Sample log output might be:

```
INFO: Current List: [Item1, Item2, Item3]
```

6. **Using Breakpoints and IDE Debugging Tools**

Integrated Development Environments (IDEs) like IntelliJ IDEA, Eclipse, and NetBeans offer powerful debugging tools. By setting breakpoints, developers can pause the program execution and inspect the state of collections.

7. Handling ConcurrentModificationException

When dealing with concurrent modifications, it's crucial to understand the source of a ConcurrentModificationException. This typically occurs when a collection is modified while iterating over it using enhanced for loops or iterators.

To avoid this, consider employing a CopyOnWriteArrayList or synchronized blocks.

```
List<String> syncList = Collections.synchronizedList(new ArrayList<>());
synchronized(syncList) {
    Iterator<String> iterator = syncList.iterator();
    while (iterator.hasNext()) {
        System.out.println(iterator.next());
    }
}
```

8. Advanced Debugging with Eclipse MAT

For memory leaks involving collections, the Eclipse Memory Analyzer Tool (MAT) can be of significant help. It analyzes heap dumps to identify memory retention patterns, helping spot unexpected references in collections.

9. Employing Unit Tests

Unit testing frameworks like JUnit and TestNG can be utilized to write tests that validate the correctness of operations on collections.

```
import static org.junit.Assert.assertEquals;
import org.junit.Test;

public class CollectionTest {
    @Test
    public void testListSize() {
        List<String> list = new ArrayList<>();
        list.add("Item1");
        list.add("Item2");
        assertEquals(2, list.size());
    }
}
```

10. Analyzing Stack Traces

Debugging often involves analyzing stack traces to pinpoint the source of errors. When an exception occurs, the stack trace provides the exact location in the code where the exception was thrown, aiding in faster debugging.

```
try {
    List<String> list = null;
    list.add("Item1");
} catch (NullPointerException e) {
    e.printStackTrace();
```

```
}
```

Sample stack trace:

```
java.lang.NullPointerException
    at DebuggingExample.main(DebuggingExample.java:5)
```

11. **Profiling**

Tools like VisualVM, JProfiler, and YourKit can profile applications to monitor performance metrics and memory usage, identifying bottlenecks related to collections.

Combining these techniques equips developers with a comprehensive toolkit for debugging collections effectively.

10.12 Case Studies of Best Practices in Real Projects

Case Study 1: E-commerce Inventory Management System

In an e-commerce platform, managing inventory data is crucial. The design involves handling various collections representing the products in different states, such as in-stock, out-of-stock, and pending orders. The choice of the right collection, coupled with appropriate best practices, significantly affects performance and scalability.

One critical requirement is to maintain a list of in-stock products that support frequent insertions and deletions. Given the need for efficient addition and removal operations, the LinkedList implementation was selected rather than an ArrayList. The reason is that ArrayList requires costly array resizing during insertions and deletions.

```
// Collection of in-stock products using LinkedList
List<Product> inStockProducts = new LinkedList<>();
```

For managing unique identifiers of the products, a HashSet is utilized. This choice is crucial for ensuring that each product ID is unique and provides constant-time complexity for add, remove, and contains operations.

```
// Collection of unique product IDs using HashSet
Set<String> productIDs = new HashSet<>();
```

Case Study 2: Real-time Analytics Service

In a real-time analytics service, processing and analyzing streams of data efficiently is essential to provide timely insights. An example of best practices is the implementation of a moving average calculation using the sliding window technique.

To achieve this, a Deque (double-ended queue) is employed. The ArrayDeque class is used for its superior performance compared to LinkedList in queue operations, benefiting from better cache locality and the absence of node-based overhead.

```
// Using ArrayDeque for sliding window in moving average calculation
Deque<Integer> slidingWindow = new ArrayDeque<>();
int windowSize = 100; // Example window size
int sum = 0;

public void addDataPoint(int dataPoint) {
    slidingWindow.addLast(dataPoint);
    sum += dataPoint;

    if (slidingWindow.size() > windowSize) {
        sum -= slidingWindow.removeFirst();
    }

    double average = (double) sum / slidingWindow.size();
    System.out.println("Current moving average: " + average);
}
```

Case Study 3: Social Media Platform

Handling user data in a social media platform involves using collections to store user metadata, posts, and interactions like likes and comments. Special attention is given to the efficient and safe use of concurrent collections to manage high-volume data interaction scenarios.

```
// ConcurrentHashMap for thread-safe user metadata management
ConcurrentMap<String, UserMetadata> userMetadataMap = new ConcurrentHashMap
    <>();

public void updateUserMetadata(String userId, UserMetadata metadata) {
    userMetadataMap.put(userId, metadata);
}

// Handling posts with thread-safe List
List<Post> posts = Collections.synchronizedList(new ArrayList<>());

public void addPost(Post post) {
    synchronized (posts) {
        posts.add(post);
    }
}

// Using ConcurrentLinkedQueue for likes
Queue<Like> likesQueue = new ConcurrentLinkedQueue<>();

public void addLike(Like like) {
    likesQueue.offer(like);
}
```

Case Study 4: Financial Trading System

In a financial trading system, managing order books and processing trade orders efficiently is vital. The application requires high-frequency updates and quick access to the highest and lowest prices in the order book.

Using TreeMap, which maintains orders based on natural ordering of prices, allows for efficient range queries and close proximity searches.

```
// TreeMap to manage order book
NavigableMap<Double, List<Order>> buyOrders = new TreeMap<>(Collections.
    reverseOrder());
NavigableMap<Double, List<Order>> sellOrders = new TreeMap<>();

public void addBuyOrder(Order order) {
    buyOrders.computeIfAbsent(order.price, k -> new ArrayList<>()).add(order);
}

public void addSellOrder(Order order) {
    sellOrders.computeIfAbsent(order.price, k -> new ArrayList<>()).add(order);
}

// Finding the best (highest) buy price
Double bestBuyPrice = buyOrders.firstKey();

// Finding the best (lowest) sell price
Double bestSellPrice = sellOrders.firstKey();
```

Case Study 5: Content Delivery Network (CDN)

Managing cached content for rapid delivery to users is a significant challenge in a CDN. Ensuring the most frequently accessed content remains readily available involves adopting a consistent hashing mechanism with TreeMap to evenly distribute cache nodes.

```
// Consistent hashing using TreeMap for cache nodes
NavigableMap<Integer, String> cacheNodes = new TreeMap<>();

// Function to add a cache node
public void addCacheNode(String node) {
    int hash = node.hashCode();
    cacheNodes.put(hash, node);
}

// Function to get a cache node based on content key
public String getCacheNode(String key) {
    int hash = key.hashCode();
    if (cacheNodes.containsKey(hash)) {
        return cacheNodes.get(hash);
    }

    return cacheNodes.ceilingEntry(hash).getValue();
}
```

Collectively, these case studies underscore the criticality of choosing appropriate collections, employing concurrency mechanisms wisely, and adhering to best practices in various real-world scenarios. The efficiency and integrity of applications are markedly enhanced by thoughtful consideration of collection types and usage patterns that align with the specific requirements of each system.

Made in the USA
Monee, IL
05 November 2026

67845302R00203